P9-DKD-440

335.43W515a 1980
The aging of

2 1765 0004 3297 4

*Published in cooperation with
the Hoover Institution,
Stanford University,
Stanford, California*

DATE DUE

MAR 15 1996		
DEC 8 1996		

THE
AGING
OF
COMMUNISM

THE
AGING
of
COMMUNISM

Robert Wesson

PRAEGER

PRAEGER SPECIAL STUDIES • PRAEGER SCIENTIFIC

Library of Congress Cataloging in Publication Data

Wesson, Robert G
  The aging of communism.

  Includes bibliographical references and index.
  1. Communism--1945-   I. Title.
HX44.W42   335.43   80-16000
ISBN 0-03-057053-0

Published in 1980 by Praeger Publishers
CBS Educational and Professional Publishing
A Division of CBS, Inc.
521 Fifth Avenue, New York, New York 10017 U.S.A.

© 1980 by Praeger Publishers

All rights reserved

0123456789   038   987654321

Printed in the United States of America

PREFACE

Americans speak of the Soviet Union taking military superiority. If this is realistic, it is the climax of a grand success story. From November 7, 1917, when Lenin's ragtag band scattered the nearest thing Russia has ever had to a democratic government, the Leninist or Communist movement has passed through fearful struggles from victory to victory. It won control of the empire of the tsars, built a new kind of society, and industrialized old Russia faster than we supposed possible. Western intellectuals looked up to it as the model of the future, even while Stalin was ravaging his people in the purges. World War II and its aftermath brought more states, including China and most of Eastern Europe, into the Communist sphere. The Sino-Soviet bloc, dynamic, monolithic, and purposeful, seemed to many to be driving like an avalanche toward universal victory.

But the Soviet space exploits of 1957 and the next few years probably represented the high point of Lenin's dream. In 1961 there still was sufficient elan for Khrushchev to proclaim, and many to believe, that by 1970 or thereabouts the Soviet Union would far surpass the United States economically, and that political would inevitably follow economic dominion. Yet Communisim already had suffered a major blow in 1948 when Tito's Yugoslavia rebelled against Stalin. By 1961 the Sino-Soviet split was coming into the open, and it was soon to turn into bitter enmity. By this time, too, the Chinese would-be economic miracle, the Great Leap Forward, had fallen very flat; and Soviet economic growth evidently had begun to lose its irresistible impetus. Since then, while Communist triumphs have continued in less developed nations, such as Vietnam, Angola, and Afghanistan, troubles have piled up and inspiration has been washed away.

Nonetheless, a decade ago the idea that Communist systems were necessarily decaying was heretical. Many claimed that Communist states were evil, oppressive, and wasteful, but that they were not viable was hardly to be considered. By now, the manifold troubles of Communist states are common knowledge: shortages of goods, need to import technology, dissidents, refugees, underground literature, preference for rock music and chewing gum over Leninist virtues, and so forth. They plainly suffer many ills from which they had claimed immunity, such as corruption, high crime rates, alcoholism, and black markets. Communist states have become stiff and bureaucratic under aging, lackluster leaders. Unless they can find some magic to turn the trend around, they seemed doomed to decadence—and the word is appropriate because the Communist states not only fall short of

Western values, but also evolve in ways opposite to the ideals of their founders.

It would be easy now to write a book detailing the running down of the once inspirational and revolutionary Communist system, but it is no longer necessary. It would be useful, however to delineate the directions of evolution of the Communist world. Much of what may be learned of the oldest, the Soviet Union, is valid for all that have basically the same Marxist-Leninist pattern of government, because the chief factor in the development of all is the same, namely, the effort of the governing party to maintain a complete monopoly of power.

Observation of the direction of development implies projection of a vague picture into the future. So far as this projection resembles a prediction, however, it must be strongly qualified. For one thing, it does not take into account international affairs, foreign pressures, and possible conflicts. It is assumed that Communist societies will march on much as they have over recent decades, within their present boundaries and in relations to the non-Communist world much like those that have existed since World War II. A major victorious war presumably would reinvigorate any Communist state involved, just as World War II reinvigorated Stalinist Russia; and any large expansion of Communist power would affirm the system. On the other hand, if Communist states should become markedly weaker vis-à-vis Western powers, the penetration of foreign ideas would be multiplied, the Communist ethos would be undermined, and the dilapidation of the state would be hastened.

A second reservation is that developments may be rapid or slow. The next decade may see marked change as has the last decade, and it is not impossible that change may accelerate as disillusionment feeds cynicism, which contributes to the weakening of economic control, causing declining material standards and deeper disillusionment. On the other hand, if one senses a declining intellectual level because of the politicization of education, this will be decisive only over a generation. Political decay is more rapid now than in the past, but Chinese dynasties weakened for centuries before they finally collapsed.

With these qualifications, the temptation to guess about the future of Communist states is strong. Practically from their birth or since emergence from the energizing and purifying bath of war, they have been evolving rather clearly in a single direction. There have been only minor remissions, such as the temporary and partial rejuvenation of the Polish state after riots in 1970 forced the replacement of Gomulka by Gierek. Seldom are political trends so unidirectional and clear-cut. The future of the Communist system is probably as predictable as anything in this chaotic political universe.

CONTENTS

THE
AGING
of
COMMUNISM

INTRODUCTION:
CHANGE IN COMMUNIST SYSTEMS

Outwardly, the Soviet Union and the Communist states (except China) are remarkable for fixity and stability. Since Stalin completed Lenin's revolution by collectivizing the peasants, pushing industrialization of a bureaucratically planned economy, and crushing independent thought by terror in the 1930s, changes have been secondary. *Pravda* reads much as it did 40 years ago, and the slogans glorifying the leader and urging more production are perennial. Although the standard of living has improved and Stalin's massive terrorism has been replaced by limited and orderly repression, the reality of arbitrary rule by the leadership of the Communist Party remains untouched. There have been disorders, as in Poland and Hungary in 1956 and the attempt to democratize Communism in Czechoslovakia in 1968, but the overall picture is of stability to the point of rigidity. No Communist country has permanently set aside or deeply modified its basic institutions of party rule. Even Mao's Cultural Revolution of 1966–69 led ultimately to no new departure; old ways of party domination were restored after the hubbub quieted down.

Yet much of the content of Communism has changed. The state that once could drive forward at breakneck speed to industrialization now has to be content with very modest economic growth or none at all. In Stalin's day, high party position was as insecure as it was rewarding; now the insecurity is gone, and Communist oligarchies, especially the Soviet, are the oldest in the world. Most important, the idealism of the revolutionary movement has been worn out, and ideology has become a dead doctrinal exercise. Such changes are, of course, only natural. Revolutions of the past have always run down or have been reversed, usually after a lifetime much shorter than those that many Marxist-Leninist states already boast. But in fascination with the most dynamic political movement of modern times, it often is forgotten that a revolution is an event, not a permanent condition.

There have been innumerable interpretations of change in Communist systems, depending mostly on the political outlook of the interpreter. The most common view, however, has been the basically sensible one that they tend to become more like the West. This is the theme of disillusioned leftists, including some Communists, who for decades have accused the Soviet leadership, and recently the Chinese, of being reactionary or revisionist, forgetting about social goals and backsliding to something like capitalism. To save China from this, Mao in 1966 undertook his Cultural Revolution against "capitalist roaders" in the party and the government. Toward the end of his life, Lenin himself was trying to find ways of saving the revolutionary character of his state.

Western observers from the day after Lenin's revolution have nourished the expectation or hope that Bolshevism or Communism was only a temporary aberration, an abnormality that could not endure in a civilized world. It began to look more permanent when the Leninists won the civil war, but almost immediately thereafter Lenin permitted a partial return of capitalism to rebuild the devastated country. It was logically believed (by many in Soviet Russia as well as abroad) that this was a repudiation of extremism and a turn to rationality that could only continue. This seemed confirmed as the semimarket economy prospered; surely any government would keep a successful system. But once Stalin had rid himself of rivals toward the end of the 1920s, he plunged his country into a frenzied industrialization at a cost no Western government could contemplate. The nightmarish purges, climaxing in 1936–38, completed the impression that the Soviet state was a new species, which some hoped would bring utopia, but that others saw as a despotic perversion of civilization called totalitarianism. Even at this time, however, there was a promise of movement toward Western ways, as the 1936 constitution set up the framework of a potentially democratic state.

In World War II the Soviet Union again seemed to be reverting to normalcy. Stalin's earlier excesses, from frantic building of heavy industry to the purges, were attributed to farsighted defense policies, the necessity for the construction of a munitions industry, and the liquidation of potentially treasonable elements. To win the war, Stalin somewhat relaxed his despotism, dropped Marxist ideology in favor of nationalism, came to an accommodation with the Orthodox church, and dissolved the Communist International. The victorious Soviet Union, secure and respected, surely would relax and normalize. Instead, Stalin brought back ideology and repression in the cold war against his country's recent allies.

When Stalin died in 1953 it was believed that the unnatural tyranny would cease without the tyrant. During a decade there were many moves toward easing the Soviet system, including increasing foreign trade and other contacts, relaxing control of the economy, the end of murder as policy (the last acknowledged political executions were in 1956), emphasis on "socialist legality," and some slackening of censorship. There were some contrary moves, such as closing many of the remaining churches and applying capital punishment to economic crimes, but there was an unmistakable amelioration of the atmosphere, which, it was assumed, would continue to improve.

Consequently, in the 1960s, the theory of convergence became popular.[1] Assuming a kind of economic determinism, this postulated that urbanized industrial societies, particularly the United States and the Soviet Union, have fundamental similarities and problems, and hence in the long run tend toward broadly similar economic, social and political systems. On the one hand, government in the United States and other Western countries was controlling ever more of the economy, assuming more and more responsibilities, and channeling a growing portion of the national product through bureaucratic ("socialized") channels. On the other hand, the Communists were shedding much of their stiffness and dogmatism as they matured and became better educated. Facing a range of problems for which Marxism-Leninism had no answer, from innovation in the economy to environmental pollution, the industrialized Communist society could only continue to move, it seemed, toward rationality and democratization,[2] with growing pluralism, articulation of group interests, bargaining replacing command, decision making in cooperation with those affected, growing legality of rule, and all that these changes imply.

This optimistic view reached its apogee in the first months of the post-Khrushchev regime, when it seemed that managers and technocrats were taking over from party bosses and ideologues. Ideology was evidently giving way to pragmatism.[3] By 1966 it was often said that "schism is over" between Eastern and Western Europe.[4] Undeniably, the Soviet Union had become less unlike Western societies since the zenith of Stalinism in 1949, with the continued erosion of vestiges of revolutionism, apparent decline of ideological commitment, growth of foreign trade and cultural exchanges, and moderation of coercion. By the early 1970s it was believed that "needs of modernization" or "requirements of industrial development" would lead to systematic change if the system came to be a barrier to economic growth. As Fainsod put it, in order to minister to the needs of a highly industrialized country, "the Soviet leadership must perforce accord greater weight and authority within the party to those who possess the knowledge and technical skills to make an industrialized society work," and maintain an atmosphere conducive to innovation and scientific creativity.[5]

But these were not the priorities of the Communist leadership, for whom convergence is anathema because it denies the specialness of Communist society and threatens the legitimacy of their rule. Around 1966 the trend to relaxation in the Soviet Union was reversed by a turn toward more militancy and insistence on the role of the party. This trend was accentuated after the crushing of the Czech reform movement in August 1968. In the latter 1970s the Soviet Union was hardly more liberal than 20 years earlier, in some respects less so.

One can no longer be confident that economic growth necessarily propels the Communist state toward what is usually considered political modernization, that is, an open, legalistic, responsible system similar to those that have achieved high productivity in the West. Various other predictions have been made. Apter, for example, foresaw that the "mobilization system" probably would grow in "strength until the point of high industrialization is reached, at which time it will begin to decline as a result of its great need for information. With a decline in coercion and the widening of accountability through decentralization, the system will change to another type."[6] A generation ago Barrington Moore postulated such a turn toward traditional Russian patterns; much of what he envisioned has been realized.[7] Most writers foresee a pacific evolution. Some, such as Lyons, have argued that a new revolution is probable sooner or later because of the rigidity of the Soviet system and its inability to adapt to new demands.[8] Amalrik, asking *Will the Soviet Union Survive Until 1984?* forecast a breakdown triggered by war, perhaps suggested by the war-provoked collapse of the tsarist regime that opened the way to Bolshevik power.[9] Reshetar considered such alternatives as restoration of totalitarianism, subsidence into something like traditional authoritarianism, bureaucratic rule, oligarchic leadership, more widespread modernization, and an imperial role—overlapping categories.[10] Scholars differ in their estimates of the willingness or ability of the Communist leadership to broaden its popular base, the priority of economic versus political needs, the strength of divisive forces, the role of the military, and the capacity of the regime to stifle dissent.[11] Scenarios vary from rosy pictures of the promised land of social democracy to visions of permanent despotism softened by inefficiency and corruption.

DIRECTIONS OF CHANGE

The state established by a Communist revolution changes in two fundamental ways. One is the establishment of new institutions, the realization of the program, and the carrying out of the ideas of the revolution in ways the revolutionaries could only partially foresee. The other kind of change is the burning out of the revolutionary fire, erosion of the exceptional that was achieved by violence, and return to more normal or traditional ways.

In the first aspect, the revolution is a birth, generating a new system that will grow, affirm itself, and produce new contours. In the other, it is more like a fever from which the society may be expected to recuperate, a disturbance that naturally subsides to a more normal state. In terms of the ideals of the revolution and the early Communist state, the one represents construction, the other decadence. The two aspects do not necessarily conflict; in some ways the settling down of the state is almost equivalent to its deradicalization. When institutions have been put in place, they are to be upheld. When ideology becomes a school subject, it is drained of emotion.

A writer for the first decade or two after the revolution would properly devote most attention to the constructive aspect, the formation of the communist state. Now, however, the achievements have been amply described for many years both by the regimes themselves and by foreign observers, and there are few important new achievements to record, nor is there any need to dwell further upon the slow upbuilding of the "developed socialist society." Purposeful development toward the utopia of socialism obviously has run down, and senescence is the significant fact.

As the revolution recedes into the past, its achievements come to be taken for granted, and its limitations become evident, People tire of repetitious rhetoric, and no heroes replace the shining images of yesteryear. New generations arriving without the experience and direct inspiration of the revolution are educated in the ideas and ways of the new system, purposefully in the schools and unintentionally by observing the new order in action. They are different people from those who made the revolution, although their lips may be trained to form the same words. The leaders, too, change in character; they not only belong to a new generation but also are chosen very differently from their predecessors in the revolutionary turmoil. Revolution and rulership are antithetical. The outlook and values of the aging revolutionary state are antithetical to those that gave it birth.

Principal directions of long-term change may be summarized as follows:[12]

From	To
utopianism	complacency
radicalism	conservatism
dedication	apathy and self-seeking
creativity	aridity
egalitarianism	stratification
autarky	dependence on foreign trade
xenophobia	normal foreign relations
charismatic leadership	institutionalized leadership
youthful leadership	aged leadership
party as engine of change	party as bar to change
insecurity of cadres	security of cadres
effective centralization	limited de facto pluralism
terrorism	security of cadres
disciples	bureaucrats

Fundamental is the reversal of roles. The makers of the revolution are outsiders, fighters against odds, zealots for the overthrow of the established order. They become masters but continue for a time to drive to annihilate the old system and forge the new. In time their dynamism wears out and they become upholders of status, like those against whom they once conspired. The party founded to attack the old regime becomes the builder of a new order and then the bulwark of the new-old system of privilege. Idealists go over to opposition to the mighty bureaucratic state. Success sets revolution on the way to eventual winding down. The order born of combat, stress and emergency wears out in peace and tranquility. The Communist state, which was historically novel, becomes ordinary. Like other forms of government, Communism is subject to the perversity of human nature that makes history depressing, interesting, and repetitive.

REVERSION

If the new state loses the drives and emotions of the revolution, which above all made its special character, it necessarily reverts to something more like the state it replaced, or what one might suppose the old regime to have become if there had been no revolution. Old habits and attitudes return once the excitement has worn off. Russia and China were accustomed to imperial-bureaucratic government since far beyond memory, and it was inevitable for new rulers to govern more or less in the mode they know. Moreover, the fundamental conditions and needs of the country remain through the revolutionary upheavals. Prior to 1917, for example, the tsarist autotocracy held itself up as the only way to preserve the unity of the empire; after 1917, Lenin's party performed the same function.

From the revolution on, the Soviet bureaucracy has looked a good deal like tsarist bureaucracy, but the differences introduced by revolutionary spirit at first were striking. Now these obviously have much receded. The Russian and the Soviet state was/is governed by a conservative, largely self-perpetuating apparatus, in which the military had/has much influence. Soviet censorship has become leaky, although it is still far more effective than its tsarist counterpart. The Soviet Union has its alienated intellectuals and a growing private economy. Nationalism has become more effective than Marxism-Leninism, and religion has regained some of its hold on popular feelings. The number of political prisoners in the Soviet Union now is closer to the number in tsarist than in Stalinist times. Stalin recognized a certain kinship with the sixteenth-century Ivan the Terrible, and he made a multitude of such reactionary changes as restoring epaulets in the army and renaming "commissars" (a title Lenin liked because it "smelled of revolution") into conventional "ministers." The People's Republic of China, too, seems increasingly to resemble politically the China of the great dynasties, with its exclusive mandarinate. The egalitarianism, the mass mobilizations, and the frantic campaigns seem to have passed with Mao.

With due accounting for vast material changes, the picture of Communist states using up the impetus of revolution and returning politically to somewhere near the starting point is useful for understanding. It does not adequately answer questions, however, about where they are going. The old regimes, after all, are long defunct; one can only guess where they might be if there had never been a revolution. It is not very helpful to consider a state converging toward an extinct form. The old regimes, moreover, were traditional and had institutions that the Communist states lack and cannot replace. For example, hereditary monarchy provided a means of structuring power and changing ministers in a way that the basically more anarchic Communist states cannot follow.

Moreover, the future of a Communist state is not necessarily reversion toward the pre-Communist condition. It is not certain that Czechoslovakia in the next decade or so will become more democratic. Conceivably, authoritarian patterns will become more deeply imprinted. If Czechoslovakia should experience reversion, it might not be toward the democratic state of the interwar period but toward the dependent condition in the Austrian empire. The latter seems more probable if Czechoslovakia continues to be subject to external power in the future as it was before 1918. But the past is not a magnet, and Communist rule has made profound changes in Czech life and society; the new order is the starting point for a destiny that may be closer to the Soviet Union than Western Europe.

It is more enlightening to view Communist states as gradually losing much or most of the specialness that sets them off from non-Western authoritarian regimes. The effect of the Communist transformation has been to modernize economies (to varying degrees) while making political power more arbitrary and absolute. The essence of Leninism-Stalinism in its various versions is to Westernize materially while de-Westernizing politically. If material change carried political change in tow, the pleasant theory of the convergence of East and West would be true, and liberalization of Communist states would be a reasonable expectation. It seems, however, that the political side of Communism increasingly works against its material advancement. If so, it is possible that the Communist states of the future will increasingly resemble authoritarian Third World states that have never had a comparable revolution under a Marxist-Leninist party.

There is no clear-cut common pattern among the approximately one hundred Third World states, but most of them have much in common. Leaders are chosen irregularly and hold office indefinitely. There are usually elections, but governments cannot be changed by the electoral process. The military authorities control the government or are in a position to do so whenever they should desire. The bureaucracy is the other major governing power, and official service is usually the chief employment of the educated.

Ideology is usually unimportant, although semi-Marxist slogans and vocabulary are much used in many countries. Corruption is a common scourge. The distribution of wealth and power is grossly unequal, far more so than in the West. Press and radio are censored, but no great efforts are made to indoctrinate the people. The state interferes extensively in the economy but usually does not try to manage much of it. The citizens enjoy a fair degree of freedom as long as they stay out of politics, and the state does not demand much of them.

Only a handful of non-Western countries (excluding small islands) are democratic, chiefly Japan, perhaps India, Sri Lanka (Ceylon), Costa Rica, and three or four others. Their number has shown no long-term tendency to grow. It is true that the most productive countries are democratic, and there is some correlation between human rights and prosperity. But there is no evidence that industrialization of itself leads to democracy and political freedom. The political effects of technological progress are ambiguous. There are Third World authoritarian regimes at extremely varying levels of technology; and some, such as Singapore, have per capita GNP comparable to that of the most highly industrialized Communist countries.

The Communist states are rather farther from Western patterns than ordinary Third World dictatorships, at least the more enlightened and less arbitrary of them. But in respect to all of the characteristics enumerated above, Communist countries are becoming politically more like Third World authoritarianisms and less like the state envisioned by Lenin.

NOTES

1. Discussed by Alfred G. Meyer, "Theories of Convergence," in *Change in Communist Systems*, ed. Chalmers A. Johnson (Stanford: Stanford University Press, 1970), pp. 313–42.

2. Andrew C. Janos, "Systemic Models," in *Authoritarian Politics in Communist Europe: Uniformity and Diversity in One-Party States*, ed. Andrew C. Janos (Berkeley: Institute of International Studies, 1976), p. 25.

3. As deduced by Peter C. Ludz, *The Changing Party Elite in East Germany* (Cambridge: MIT Press, 1972), p. 11.

4. Arrigo Levi, "The Evolution of the Soviet System," in *Dilemmas of Change in Soviet Politics*, ed. Zbigniew Brzezinski (New York: Columbia University Press, 1969), p. 137.

5. Merle Fainsod, "Roads to the Future," in *Dilemmas of Change in Soviet Politics*, p. 133.

6. David E. Apter, *The Politics of Modernization* (Chicago: University of Chicago Press, 1965), p. 390.

7. Barrington Moore, Jr., *Terror and Progress, USSR: Some Sources of Change and Stability in the Soviet Dictatorship* (Cambridge: Harvard University Press, 1954), p. 226.

8. Eugene Lyons, "The Realities of a Vision," in *Dilemmas of Change in Soviet Politics*, pp. 49–55.

9. Andrei Amalrik, *Will the Soviet Union Survive until 1984?* (New York: Harper & Row, 1970).

10. John S. Reshetar, Jr., *The Soviet Polity* (New York: Harper & Row, 1978), pp. 336–61.

11. Several are discussed by George A. Breslauer, *Five Images of the Soviet Future: A Critical Review and Synthesis* (Berkeley: Institute of International Studies, 1978).

12. Several of these are mentioned by Samuel P. Huntington, "Social and Institutional Dynamics of One-Party Systems," in *Authoritarian Politics in Modern Society*, ed. Samuel P. Huntington and Clement H. Moore (New York: Basic Books, 1970), p. 230.

1

THE COMMUNIST STATE

ORIGINS OF COMMUNISM

The special character of Communist governments can be understood in terms of their origin as a blend of old and new elements. They have an old inspiration, the sharing of property in brotherhood, the dream of utopian philosophers and a perennial demand of rebels against injustice. This idea is combined with principles of authoritarian empire, centralized authority, an elitehood of service, and the duty of obedience to the rulership, such as prevailed in Russia, China, and most of the non-Western world for centuries. These principles provide the framework of the new order despite popular anger at injustices of the bureaucratic order of imperial despotism. To the amalgam of these elements, the Leninists added a modern rationale and purpose. Marxism, as modified and adapted by Lenin, was applied to the non-Western society and used as defense and counterattack against the Western onslaught. Energized by anger and given political form by remaking the autocratic state with a Western facade, Marxism-Leninism was incarnated in the Communist state.

This system was never conceived whole but took shape gradually in response to conditions and events in Russia in the first quarter of this century. The seminal idea was Lenin's. Caught up in the Marxist fashion of the Russian intelligentsia of the 1890s, Lenin resolved to turn talk to action through a new political party that incorporated something of the Marxist social democracy of Western Europe, but more of the traditional Russian conspiratorial tradition. Offering a plan of action with a Marxist intellectual framework, he pulled together discontented intellectuals, workers, peasants, and minority nationalities to make his party an instrument of power. Lenin's genius to the contrary, it was a feeble instrument in normal times. But when the old regime collapsed under the blows of war and the Western-oriented Provisional Government defaulted, Lenin grasped the levers of state and used them to make his and his party's power absolute. The civil war that followed ground out the moderates, eliminated the middle classes, hardened the new Soviet state in militaristic shape, and made possible ruthless control of society.

From the historical point of view, Leninism amounted to a restoration of Russian authoritarianism, embellished with a mission borrowed from Western socialism.[1] Communism probably could have been generated only in Russia. Russia was basically autocratic and elitist, yet given to egalitarian pretenses; it was anti-Western, antiliberal, and anti-individualist, yet receptive to Western ideas, and long accustomed to borrowing Western technology and modes to reinforce its imperial power. That Russia was a multinational empire made it possible for Lenin (who tended to be anti-Russian) to secure power. Only a multinational state could be receptive to a creed that would serve as the basis for an international Communist movement. No less important, huge Russia, master of a hundred lesser nations, was grandiose and pretentious, yet disproportionately poor and ignorant. Russian pride was exacerbated by a sense of inferiority. Necessarily messianic in its mission of rulership over a land mass far greater than all of Europe, Russia built up a grandiose self-image that clashed with reality as contacts with the West increased in the nineteenth century. Russia's unhappy Western-educated intelligentsia felt it should have been far richer and stronger than it was; imperial ruler in Asia, it was a poor cousin in Europe. This dissonance engendered extremism and a willingness to embrace theories or movements, such as Bolshevism, that promisd a new destiny. Communism as developed by Lenin and his successors was thus a system for using Western political ideas and institutions, or part of them, to assist the restoration of native values and authority in non-Western countries threatened politically, economically, and culturally by the industrialized West. Communism borrowed from the liberal societies the better to reject them.

For these reasons, Russia stumbled into the Communist mold when fighting the Western power with which it had most contact, Germany, and even more so during the following civil war, which the Leninists envisaged as a contest against world capitalism.[2] For much-abused China, Communism meant a restoration of national greatness after years of humiliation. As Mao said upon proclaiming the Chinese People's Republic on October 1, 1949, "The Chinese people has stood up!" Jiang Qing, Mao's wife, saw the respect China had gained in the world as the greatest achievement of the revolution.[3]

For Albanians, Vietnamese, and Cubans, Communism represented the cause of national independence won from what were seen as capitalist-imperialist powers. African states that have more or less adopted Marxist-Leninist patterns, such as Mozambique, Angola, Ethiopia, Guinea, Equatorial Guinea, and the Congo, are among the poorest and most aggrieved states of the Third World.

War brought Communism to Russia, China, Eastern Europe (both where Communist forces triumphed on their own, in Yugoslavia and Albania, and where the Soviet military presence was decisive), North Korea, Vietnam, Laos, and Cambodia. Castro turned to Communism in a confrontation with the United States. As the Jefe Supremo put it immediately after the defeat of the landing at the Bay of Pigs (Playa Girón):

> Because our Marxist-Leninst Party was really born at Girón; (applause) membership in our Party is recognized from that date on; from that date on, socialism was cemented forever with the blood of our workers, peasants and students; from that date on, a new and completely different destiny opened up before the people of this continent because of the liberty and dignity that one of them had conquered in the face of aggression from the powerful empire that subjected all.[4]

In consequence, Communism has been in large part a movement of military mobilization. On the one hand, war, at least an unsuccessful war, breaks down resistance to radicalism and raises demands for deep change; on the other hand, in a time of dire need the Communist party steps in as the most effective reorganizer. Lenin in 1906 and again in 1917 wanted an armed people to enter the fight; he even proposed that the people's army, mobilizing women as well as men, distribute food and housing and educate the masses.[5] The Soviet state took shape during the desperate civil war, when party members were equivalent to soldiers; it retained much of its military outlook in peacetime. Thus in 1925 the commissar of war, M. V. Frunze, made "militarization of the entire population" his slogan.[6] The Stalinist priority for heavy industry (which continues to this day) was for strength over welfare, and the military remains a chief pillar of Soviet society.

In the Chinese revolution, army and party were almost indistinguishable; in the first years after victory in 1949, the army was the state. In the Cultural Revolution, Chairman Mao called upon all to "learn from the PLA," which became the mainstay of Communist purity and the Mao cult when the party itself was found "revisionist." Maoism can be interpreted as an endeavor to perpetuate the glorious time of hardship and heroism. In North Korea the entire adult population is supposed to belong to the militia, and there is endless drilling and war play. Castro's chief contribution to Marxist-Leninist theory has been to equate guerrilla warfare with class conflict. Cuban songs and textbooks are filled with the symbolism of struggle,[7] and "Patria o Muerte," is printed all over banknotes. Fidel is "Commandante en jefe." In 1962 two-thirds of the Central Committee members were military.[8] Almost every worker was in the militia and no one was supposed to complain of hardships, for "we are at war, you know."[9]

Communism often has been treated as basically a program of modernization for preindustrial societies. Its spokesmen contend that their ultimate concern is for welfare; heavy industry is to make machines to make consumption goods. But the basic passion of Communism is rejection of the Western type of commercialized, pluralistic society. Its chief virtues are loyalty and discipline, and its greatest excellence is in combat.

COMMUNISM AS STALINISM

The Communist states exalt Lenin as prophet and founder, while Stalin has been generally relegated to obscurity. Only China and Albania continue to revere the former long-term idol of world Communism. Stalin, however, was the second founder of the Soviet state and the fulfiller of Lenin's beginnings. Communism expanded under the patronage of Stalinist power and the guidance of the parties of the Communist International as remade by Stalin.

In Leninism, the transformation of Marxism from the ideology of European social democracy to that of anti-Western autocracy was incomplete. Lenin's state was hardly Communist in the sense that that term acquired after 1930, since it permitted much private trade and industry and an almost entirely private agricultural sector and made little effort to direct art and literature. Lenin's revolution still looked to the West for succor; it was made mostly by pacifist idealists carrying some of the spirit of the coffeehouses of Paris and Geneva where Lenin and fellow exiles spent many years discussing Marx and Hegel, materialism, the dialectics of history, and party squabbles. Stalin got rid of such people, replacing them with native bosses unsoftened by Westernization and unconcerned with the fine points of philosophy. Stalin's great deeds—collectivization of agriculture, forced development of industry under successive plans, and the purges—all had precedents in Lenin's policies. But Stalin pushed far beyond what Lenin seemingly desired. He made Communism equivalent to power, and ideology was reduced to the rationalization of rulership. Stalin, who had little interest in theories and scant respect for Marx or the Social Democratic movement in the West, erased the remnants of libertarianism in Bolshevism, emphasized force and command, and brought nativism and xenophobia to the fore. Virtue was loyalty to the party and Stalin. The cause of socialism became equivalent to the greatness of the Soviet state and its leader.

Leaving Marxist theory behind, maturing Communism also shifted emphasis away from the proletariat, although the word remained sacred. Thus, the Chinese Communists, defeated in the cities in the latter 1920s, raised a peasant revolution against both the Japanese invaders and the old order, speaking all the while of the proletariat (a "class" that became virtually equivalent to the poor). Tito recruited peasants (called "proletariat brigades") into his partisan forces to fight for national liberation and the power of the party. In Cuba, Che Guevara found that those who joined his revolution became ipso facto "proletarians." Communism thus became a nationalist movement appropriate for the Third World with a verbal kinship to Marxism as originally understood. The party harnessed whatever discontents and social forces it could (mostly anti-Western nationalism and the peasantry in predominantly peasant countries) to lift a small minority (nearly all of middle-class origins) to absolute rulership.

CHARACTERISTICS OF COMMUNISM

The Communist states, as ordinarily understood, are 16,* territorially contiguous except for Cuba. They are extremely diverse in culture, historical background, and economic level, but they have been brought by political action (that is, organized violence) into the pattern set by Lenin's revolution. They are the best demonstration of the power of political structures managed by strong-willed and self-righteous individuals to override varying antecedents.

The general characteristics of Communist states are understandable in terms of the Communist revolution as an assertion of the total right to govern a society in the name of raising it and making it truly modern rapidly and independently. Because of this claim and corresponding organization, the Communist are the most highly guided and mobilized societies, with maximum political control of the economy, information, and the lives of citizens, a control made possible by the Leninist-style political party rationalized by Marxism-Leninism. So far as possible, all aspects of social existence, from organized sports to the social security system, are under direction of the party. The degree of control has varied from Yugoslavia, with "market socialism" and some latitude for divergent (although not basically critical) opinions, to China in 1976, where, in the words of a visitor, "there is no forbidden list at all. Instead, all activity is forbidden except for that which is specially permitted and promoted by the party, certain bodily functions aside."[10] No large society is simple, and Communist society has developed an overly complex network of institutions, but the Communist state imposes, at least superficially, a grand simplification through an obligatory philosophy and a single center of important decision making.

Causes and results of this political and ideological monopoly include the

---

*Albania, Bulgaria, China, Cuba, Czechoslovakia, German Democratic Republic, Hungary, Kampuchea (Cambodia), Laos, Mongolia, North Korea, Poland, Romania, Soviet Union, Vietnam, and Yugoslavia.

preeminence of political concerns, a tightly organized elite acting as repository of right and wrong, most often a single strong leader, advancement dependent on favor of superiors, lack of organized political groups within the party as well as outside it, and a utopian vision of the future. Communist states seek systematically to eliminate not only visible but also potential opposition. With complete control of education, they seek to reshape the personality of their citizens through intensive indoctrination to make the "New Man." A mandatory approach to art and literature, Socialist Realism, is similarly applied in many Communist countries. Cuba and several East European states are somewhat more relaxed, but the canons of edification, character building, collectivist morality, and support for the social order through the arts are alike in China and the Soviet Union. All Communists states, and no others, are officially antireligious, although policies vary; Polish Communists solicit the cooperation of the church, while Albania proclaims itself churchless. Scientists suffer similar restrictions in all Communist countries, enjoying most freedom in divergent Yugoslavia. Secrecy is everywhere a fetish. Even in Yugoslavia political decision making is shrouded, and in the smaller Asian Communist states even the existence of leading party bodies may be blanketed.

Much of the similarity of various Communist countries is due to straightforward copying of the Soviet model, a procedure that is easier and safer than experimentation. After the Communist victory in 1949, China set about installing a political system on the lines of the Soviet "Big Brother"; East European countries under Soviet occupation did so less voluntarily. Fidel Castro tried to devise a superior brand of Communism for a decade, but after many failures he accepted Soviet advice and implanted a full set of Soviet-style institutions. In Vietnam, a land halfway around the world from Moscow, political methods, doctrine, police, and the bureaucratic apparatus were reported to be "entirely Russian."[11] With rather minor exceptions, one Communist ruling party looks much like another, with a central committee, overlapping politburo and secretariat, congresses and conferences, bureaus, secretaries, and departments at various territorial levels.

Despite a certain artificiality, the Communist political structure has proved more or less successful in maintaining order, managing the economy, building up military strength, and reshaping the mentalities of diverse peoples. However, Communist regimes, so far as is known, never have been really popular except when submerged in a national cause, as in Vietnam under bombing, the Soviet union in World War II, Yugoslavia in the contest with Stalin, or Czechoslovakia when trying to break away from the Soviet grip in 1968. The Communist system is imposed by a small minority and presumably operates to the benefit of that minority (without necessarily implying absence of idealism); hence a *pays légal* stands above the *pays réel*. This is justified in the name of history and the supreme happiness of the people. In other words, Communism is idealized—perhaps idealistic—despotism. Communist states are much alike throughout history because the maximization of powers generally follows certain useful modes. They also resemble one another because most of them are mutually supportive against what they regard as hostile ("imperialist") forces. The weaker are inclined to follow their leader-protector; and the strong, that is, the Soviet Union and to a much less extent China, endeavor to convert the others to their ways.

The Communist states, however, cannot control their own revolution. Having been erected by extraordinary political will, they are subject to unavoidable change. Ideological drive and dedication ebb. Political problems mount. Mobilization of the economy slackens, and control over society becomes less effective. Foreign, primarily Western, influences increasingly creep in to erode the pillars of the order. So far as such changes proceed, the work of the founders of the Communist state is undone.

NOTES

1. As detailed by Robert G. Wesson, *The Russian Dilemma* (New Brunswick: Rutgers University Press, 1974), chap. 4.

2. As seen by Carr, the Russian revolution represented a reaction of Russian national tradition against Western encroachments. Edward H. Carr, *Socialism in One Country 1924–1926* (New York: Macmillan, 1958), p. 8.

3. Roxane Witke, *Comrade Chiang Ch'ing* (Boston: Little, Brown, 1977), p. 441.

4. *Granma* (weekly edition), May 2, 1976, p. 2.

5. N. K. Krupskaya, *Reminiscences of Lenin* (New York: International Publishers, 1960), p. 339.

6. William E. Odom, "The Militarization of Soviet Society," *Problems of Communism* 25 (September–October 1976): 34.

7. Cf. R. Fagen, "Mass Mobilization in Cuba: The Symbolism of Struggle," in *Cuba in Revolution*, ed. Rolando E. Bonachea and Nelson R. Valdes (Garden City, N.Y.: Anchor, 1972), especially pp. 201–2.

8. Carmelo Mesa-Lago, *Cuba in the 1970s: Pragmatism and Institutionalism* (Albuquerque: University of New Mexico Press, 1974), p. 66.

9. Mohamed A. Rauf, Jr., *Cuban Journal* (New York: Crowell, 1964), p. 65.

10. Edward N. Luttwak, "Seeing China Plain," *Commentary* 62 (December 1976): 31.

11. *New York Times*, March 21, 1977, p. 26.

2

EROSION OF BELIEF

USES OF IDEOLOGY

The Communist state is inconceivable without its edifice of beliefs and the values based upon them, the utopian vision and the prescription for its realization.[1] Leaders are not mere agents of the people but exponents of a cause, and political power is exercised not by "rules of the game" but in the name of a higher purpose best known to the authorities. The party is not accountable to the nation but to history.[2] If faith and dedication are strong, problems can be solved; if faith fails, the whole must crumble. The more arbitrary and autocratic the state, the greater its need for a rationale whereby the rulership becomes part of a grand scheme of things and its demands are related to higher needs.

Ideology corresponds to the nature of the political society. (Reference is made here to ideologies of rule, not of dissent; antiregime ideologies also reflect the prevalent political universe, although more subtly.) The monopolistic, purposefully refined ideology of the Soviet Union corresponds to the rule of the tight knit Communist party and its monopoly of organization and public communications. Maoist ideology was more loosely woven, less consistent, and more changeable. The Maoist state was less fully centralized, more given to factionalism, and more subject to radical swings of policy than the Soviet. In contrast, the relatively relaxed Communist government of Yugoslavia cultivates an undogmatic Marxism. Less fully fashioned authoritarianisms, such as Peron's Argentina or Nkrumah's Ghana, had only feebly developed ideologies, *justicialismo* and *consciencism*.

Ideological doctrines remained remarkably constant in most Communist countries over many years. The message in the Soviet Union, in particular, has hardly changed since the 1920s. Capitalism is innately evil, unreformable, and doomed. Communism is correspondingly good, has won innumerable victories, and must one day triumph worldwide.[3] The party is completely wise and never errs; the leader is infallible as long as he is leader. The rights of the working class, exercised for it by the party, are supreme; any opposition ipso facto is class inspired, and subject to repression in the name of class struggle. From this flows the endlessly repeated denial of the possibility of ideological coexistence.

Communist ideology is a mixture of idealism and obfuscation. Like any other ideology, it appeals both to noble and base purposes. It provides at once a formalized language of politics and a standard of virtue by which to decry individualism. It is a means of setting workers against intellectuals. It lumps peoples and generations together as "workers" in opposition to the "bourgeoisie." In it, "freedom and "democracy" signify the opposite of the originals, especially when prefixed by "class" or "proletarian." "Needs of the workers" and "betrayal of the proletariat" are euphemisms for "needs of the party" and "opposition to the party." A "class" approach to a problem is one that gives priority to party interests. The Berlin Wall becomes an "antifascist bastion," while countries placed under Soviet rule celebrate the anniversary of "liberation."

Ideology makes it possible to use labels for arguments. Such phrases as "struggle with international imperialism," "antisocialist forces," "Soviet patriotism," and the like serve not to convey ideas but to stimulate conditioned reflexes.[4] Anything contrary to the official ideology is by definition false. As a Russian put it, "The truth may also be a class enemy."[5] Marxist ideology denies the legitimacy of political conquest except on behalf of the party, hence the legitimacy of questioning authority or calling for freedom.[6]

The heart of Leninism, long before it became a governing power, was the superiority of "consciousness" to "spontaneity," that is, the need for guidance by the enlightened few. "Consciousness" requires a doctrine that commits the few to organized rulership and calls for the obedience of the unorganized many. The authority to exercise power ruthlessly is explained in terms of the role of the Marx-annointed working class incarnated in the party. The victories of the party in revolution, war, and economic construction are proof that it is on the way to utopia. Hence the party, in the official rendering, always marches from triumph to triumph. Coercion gains effect as leaders are liberated from traditional inhibitions and victims see the hopelessness of protest. To produce paralysis and awe instead of anger and resistance, terror invokes a high ideal.

The Communist party's claim to the right to rule is based not only on Marxism but also on the idea of progress and modernization. For Lenin, even before victory in the civil war, electrification became (along with Soviet power) equivalent to Communism. For Stalin, industrialization practically meant socialism; and collectivization of agriculture was rationalized both as a means to mechanization (before any significant amount of farm machinery was on hand) and as fulfillment of Marxism.

At the same time, Marxism-Leninism consecrates the thesis of ever-lasting conflict with capitalism, that is, the pluralistic Western society. The idea of threat from an evil external universe sustains militancy, control of the economy, priority for heavy industry, the obligation of all to work and sacrifice for the cause, secrecy, and coercion or terrorism. Although Lenin's theory of inevitable military conflict was laid aside by Khrushchev, there always has been a ruthless and implacable capitalist-imperialist enemy. Even in times of relative detente, the world scene is depicted as an arena of relentless combat between dark and light, and hundreds of thousands of lecturers warn against subversive Western ideas.

"Class enemy" is perhaps the most useful idea in the armory of Marxism-Leninism. The winning of the contest as well as the promise of the future Eden serve as stimuli to production and the basis for "moral incentives" beyond material ones. Marxism-Leninism is triply useful in the factory: it gives a cause for effort and discipline, it assures the workers that they are working in their own plants and for themselves, and it explains the party's role in guiding the workers because it represents all workers and knows their true needs.

No less significantly, ideology gives shape and will to the elite. The striving for utopia is a promise of total power, while hostility to the hateful outside world is the basis of party solidarity.[7] Marxism-Leninism sanctions for the party cohorts their power not only as a political usufruct but also as mastery of minds; it saves them from guilt feelings such as those that weakened the tsarist elite. Its nominal egalitarianism increases the satisfaction of privileges presumably based only on merit. It enables Eastern European leaders to accept subordination to Soviet power as the incorporation of international socialism, whereas they would be ashamed to see themselves as Soviet puppets.

The propagation of the official view is the part- or full-time occupation of a large fraction of Communist party members and activist adherents. Ideology is a major component of everyone's education, and candidates for high political ranks spend extra years absorbing Marxism-Leninism at party schools. Where Communist discipline is strong, ordinary citizens are expected to spend much time on their political education: under Mao, for example, peasants and workers sat through endless meetings. Citizens of North Korea are supposed to spend several hours daily imbibing Kimism, the wisdom of the near-divine leader.

This does not imply that actions are necessarily much guided by ideology; the contrary has usually seemed the case. The party has acted in the interests of its power, and Marxism-Leninism has been called upon to support its action; if necessary, the doctrine is modified to suit the policies. Newer Communisms are more possessed by ideology than older ones. It is difficult to account for the seeming absurdity of nationalizing Cuban street vendors, individual artisans, shoeshine boys, and the like (in 1968), without invoking ideological fixation. The Castroite predilection for free services in a condition of general shortages and for moral over monetary incentives for work must be at least in part ideological. Ideological fixations apparently impelled Che Guevara to abandon his comfortable and powerful position at Castro's right hand in 1965 in order to undertake to kindle revolution in Bolivian jungles.

In China it has seemed at times more important to be Red than expert. The organization of hundreds of millions of peasants in people's communes in 1958 (they already had been collectivized Soviet style) was a triumph of faith over reason; by correct thinking, will and organization, China would leapfrog poverty and construct the perfect order, which the Soviets postponed to a distant future. The Great Leap Forward, complementing the establishment of communes, was likewise to demonstrate the power of mind over matter, the ability of the masses mobilized in revolutionary enthusiasm to achieve miracles of production.

The Chinese were summoned regularly to campaigns of rectification or improvement, from exposing sinners to catching sparrows. Ideological mobilization came to its height in the Great Proletarian Cultural Revolution, beginning in the summer of 1966 and subsiding only from 1969 on. Mao Thoughts then filled the land, perhaps more completely than any other country has ever been filled by the ideas of a single person. Material production (at least in the cities) was neglected, as progress was seen to consist primarily of improved human relations or spiritual transformation achieved by the study of Mao Thought, which made crops grow and healed the sick.[8]

China has been exceptional in the attention given to correct thinking and the willingness to sacrifice economic growth to political ideals, an anomalous reversal of Marxist materialist philosophy. But the conceptual universe has been of inordinate importance for all Communist societies. It seems necessary to affirm and reaffirm the basic commitment, and leaders again and again restate the theses of their political world: proletarian right, party authority, class struggle, and future destiny; and people should believe what they have heard thousands of times.

EVOLUTION OF IDEOLOGY

When the party attains its supreme goal and secures control of the state, outsiders become insiders, rebels make themselves rulers, revolution becomes orthodoxy, and the movement is converted into bureaucracy. A second turning point, less clearly marked, comes when the new order has been established, the program has been put into effect about as far as possible, and the impetus of basic ideas is exhausted. The revolutionaries, who rule in the name of change, become (or are replaced by) a possessing elite, which governs in the name of its achievements.

One spectacular event, the overthrow of the old regime, marks the dawn of the new day. But as it recedes into the misty past, the colors fade. The ecstasy of revolutionary renewal becomes a tepid old story of the propagandists; words remain but feelings dry up. The rhetoric and heroics wear out, and there are no real new heroes. The revolutionaries become proprietors, feel entitled to enjoy peacefully the power that they grasped dangerously. Revolutionary camaraderie is dissipated. Fellow-fighters against oppression and for an inspiring vision are brothers; those who are competing for the fruits of power are necessarily somewhat at odds. There is no longer a great common goal; unity can be sustained only by power.

Revolutionaries must be idealists to dedicate their lives for a distant and perhaps improbable reward; they are ipso facto nonconformists of the highest degree. In the new state, advancement is for nonidealists devoted to their own careers and for conformists who ingratiate themselves with the governing powers. As soon as people start to benefit materially, the quality of their dedication changes; idealists are likely to be repelled. It is not difficult for the all-powerful state to mold to conformism, but enthusiasm derives from experience, example, and participation. Ideology changes from a vision into a set of prescribed answers and rules.

Some dedication is retained as long as the new state is visibly building something new, implementing its program, and nourishing hopes for a better order. But as the new institutions are set in place, ideology yields to institutionalization. Society settles down and the party tries in vain to halt the decay of faith by campaigns and propaganda. Eventually people begin to wonder, as a student at Moscow State University asked a propagandist, "What do these phrases mean? If they mean something, please tell us; if they don't mean anything, why do you keep saying them?"[9] He might have reasoned that assiduity of propagation of the faith is proportional to its stultification.

Communists say that the building of socialism is a long process that requires much enthusiasm. But when the revolutionary agenda is accomplished (so far as proves possible), the glory that lay in the promise of tomorrow slips into the traditions of yesterday. The grand design yields to practical detail and grubby work for small improvements. The utopia, riddled by contradictions and enfeebled by failures, loses value as legitimation; the brighter the promises, the heavier the frustration.[10] The party increasingly must rest its claims mundanely on the expansion of the economy. But industrialization ceases to be exciting, rewards are meager, and it cannot be fully hidden that capitalist countries produce more and better goods. Young Communists, unseared by violent struggle, clamor for blue jeans and rock records, while their seniors want Western shirts and tape players.

Violence gives emotional flesh to the bones of ideology, and foreign dangers rationalize mobilization and repression. A vibrant, victorious conflict, such as the Russian civil war or the Chinese Communist fight against the Japanese and the Nationalists, seems to moralize effectively for about fifteen years. As the decadence of Stalinist despotism in the late 1930s was approaching morbidity, the Soviet state was revitalized by its successful confrontation with Nazism and the greatest victory in Russian history. A generation afterward, this spirit seemed largely exhausted, despite a ceaseless torrent of glorifying books and movies, countless monuments, and solemn ceremonies, such as the newlyweds' visit to the eternal flame.

Many faiths have provided a framework for discourse after emotional conviction has subsided, but Marxism is less viable than the reglions it would relegate to the trash pile. It endeavors to motivate idealism through a materialist philosophy. Its rewards and punishments are weak: instead of heaven and love of God, it promises only a better ordered society and material abundance on earth, despite daily evidence that they have not been attained during many years of Communist power. Instead of divine judgment and damnation, its threat is the police. The class struggle, the heart of Marxism, loses in the allegedly classless society whatever relevance it may have had in the prerevolutionary contest. It offers no guide to right and wrong for the conflicts of individual life.

Marxist faith may give some intellectual security, at least as long as critical voices can be shut out. But it gives little psychological security and no answer for questions of purpose. It is more polemical than reassuring. It has no sense of personal relation with anything above humanity, and it conveys no deep understanding of human nature. Its prophets were abrasive and truculent. Lenin is elevated into a spiritual figure in defiance of his materialist creed, but his bilious arguments are little solace for the dying. He did not strive to be a saint or to found a church, but to forge an obedient party, demolish his opponents, and establish a new political-economic dominion. For these reasons, Marxism-Leninism seems destined to run its course from fervor to aridity more rapidly and completely than more sublimated faiths. All mature Communist states show signs of formalism and spiritual vacuity, with traditional tenets of revolutionary Communism replaced to some degree by militaristic-nationalist or pragmatic motifs.

The Soviet Union has most fully traversed the road of Marxism-Leninism in power, through Stalin's transformation and Khrushchev's somewhat hollow call for the resuscitation of Leninism to the apathy of the Brezhnev era. On the morrow of the revolution, life would soon be entirely new; socialism, Lenin repeatedly told Trotsky, would come in six months.[11] As Bertrand Russell saw it in 1919, the Communist "works sixteen hours a day and foregoes his half holiday on Saturday. He volunteers for any difficult or dangerous work which needs to be done... he lives an austere life...." As a new sun lit up the land, the new ruling class was to produce new ideas, incredible inventions, a new proletarian art. However, the struggle to remake the world soon turned into the struggle of the poor for bread and of the fortunate for luxuries. Even before the civil war was over, Bolsheviks were permitting themselves special access to goods denied the public.[12]

Stalin renewed some of the promise and dedication. In the early days of industrialization, each tractor was a blow against capitalism, and each factory brought utopia nearer. Stakhanovites did Herculean deeds, and prisoners of Gulag were supposed to love the work that was killing them.[13] But material hardships—the Stalinist "Second Revolution" radically reduced the standard of living—made the new utopia less convincing. Faith was increasingly replaced by terror, which confused and frightened those whom it did not eliminate. Revolutionary idealists were mostly killed. Stalin harnessed arts, literature, historiography, social science, and philosophy. Since his rise, the land dedicated to Marxism-Leninism has seen no important Marxist thought and very little Marxist scholarship.

A new world war brought back the sense of common purpose; as Khrushchev recalled, "The war united us once and for all."[14] But the war was fought not for the proletariat but for Mother Russia, in alliance with the leading capitalist powers and the Orthodox church. The international Communist movement proved worthless, and many Soviet people after a generation of indoctrination welcomed the Germans as liberators. But the party and people, angered by Nazi villainy and inspired by patriotism, marched to victory.

The end of the conflict should have permitted relaxation. However, Marxism-Leninism was restored to assist in managing and mobilizing the Soviet domain. But reideologization, reaching its climax around 1948, now seemed artificial and required stifling controls and coercion. Marxism-Leninism, moreover, became Stalinism, the cult of the leader attaining outlandish proportions, mixed with Russianism and xenophobia.

Latter-day Stalinist despotism was suffocating. Khrushchev sought from 1955 to 1962 to revive the party, its mission, and its faith. He made several minor moves toward egalitarianism, brought back the idea of world revolution in a feeble version (Soviet economic and cultural superiority converting the rest of the world to socialism), talked of the New Soviet Man, and offered unexciting panaceas, such as planting corn everywhere. His "hare-brained schemes" (as his successors called them) and efforts to shake up the bureaucracy brought his downfall. Since then, there have been no more heroics, no new ideas or new revelations of Soviet or proletarian destiny, as the Brezhnev regime has partly reverted to Stalinism. At best, the party has tried to call its "developed socialism" scientific, thereby risking its claims to being subjected to scientific scrutiny.

Little is said about the society supposedly being built, and the idea of the withering of the state has withered. There is no promise of radical improvement, only a continuation of past achievements and presumably a rise of the standard of living. If anything, such material advances as automobiles detract from social goals.[15] Students are utterly bored by obligatory courses in dialectical materialism.[16] It is increasingly embarrassing that such capitalist evils as crime, alcoholism, and prostitution grow, that inequality becomes not less but greater, and that the advanced "socialist" state still lags behind the backward "capitalist" economies.

As Andrei Amalrik commented in Paris, "The ideology has lost its force. Formerly a living force, it has become a dead ritual. It is replaced by a nationalist ideology which can result in the dismemberment of the Union. The economy calcifies; ossification of management, apathy of workers...."[17] The artless verbiage goes on, but the symbols of the revolution are bygone. No leaders show up ceremoniously to wield a spade, as Lenin did, on "volunteer" labor days. In the 1920s, to wear a necktie was to risk being put down as bourgeois; now Western clothes or hairstyles, or even foreign magazines, have become status symbols.[18] The youth, once the most dedicated, now think of pleasures and material acquisitions.[19] The leadership increasingly resorts to militaristic themes and glories of the great war, to the national past, and to timeless Russian anti-semitism, which connects Zionism with monopoly capitalism and speaks of the "Judeo-Masonic plot for world dominion." So far as there is hope for the future, it lies not in reordering society, but in science and technology, the technical revolution that should make up for political shortfalls—a theme not very convincing in the face of the widely known technological superiority of the West.

In the 1920s and 1930s numerous people, including not a few Americans, were moved to go to the Soviet Union to do their bit for the cause. In the past decade about 250,000 Soviet citizens have managed to secure permission to emigrate, despite great hardships placed upon them, while hardly anyone has chosen to live permanently in the Soviet Union. In the 1930s Stalin was adulated by countless intelligent foreigners as a mighty agent of change; Brezhnev is a nullity, important only because of the military force behind him. The Soviet Union as a superpower is morally less influential than weak revolutionary Russia. In the 1950s, the KGB could recruit foreign agents to a large extent through ideological appeal; recently it has been virtually limited to material lures, pressures, and entrapments.[20] The New Left of the 1960s rejected the Soviet model (and was itself rejected by the Soviets because of its radicalism), finding an oppressive bureaucratic apparatus where earlier radicals had seen a vibrant movement of social renewal.

In 1977, according to a Soviet writer,

> There is a real religious renascence now. A search for an ideal, a search for a sense of life. We have lost our ideals, we have no more ideals of revolution, Marxism, Leninism. They are lost in this system of bureaucracy and falsehood—a crisis of ideology.[21]

The Stalinists thought they were achieving liberation and modernization as they tore down icons and turned churches into stables. The contemporary Soviet state dutifully restores them as monuments. "People have nothing to believe in, nothing to rely upon," said a nonreligious Moscow woman, "and Easter offers something very spiritual and very beautiful. It is interesting, and life is not filled with interesting things."[22]

The causes of declining ideological commitment—weariness, decreased relevance of the revolutionary vision, failed promises, the changing of generations—prevail no less in other Communist countries. Whereas Communism has fairly well coincided with nationalism in Russia, in most of Eastern Europe it has been antinational, and whatever revolutionary fervor may have once warmed the party is now dead or dying. The last of the old Comintern company committed to the Russian Revolution and the Fatherland of Socialism, those who entered with the Soviet armies to do their duty for socialism, are disappearing. There remain only a few high Communists in Europe who were formed in the revolutionary underground, who suffered in jail or war, such as Honecker, Ceausescu, Hoxha, and Tito, and who still appear dedicated to something called "socialism." But Westernization is propelled not only by a desire to modernize more or less in the Western image but also by dislike for Russian domination. To be a nationalist implies rejection of Russian-imposed patterns. A priest said of the new generation of East Germans, "Their thinking has been subtly and thoroughly changed by their Marxist upbringing, but they are lost to the revolution—all they want is to be left alone, to be able to buy blue jeans and enjoy Western rock music."[23] They have learned to doublespeak. In the official context, they call the Berlin Wall the "antifascist barrier," but in Western company, simply "the Wall." In Romania the enthuiasm for industrialization of the 1950s and early 1960s has worn out, and the country suffers anomie and alienation; the people retreat to individualism.[24] In 1974 Romania hampered the entry of writers into the profession because too few were prepared to follow the party line.[25] Meanwhile, nationalism has virtually swamped Marxism-Leninism in the official faith.

Hungary under Kadar has made the playing down of ideology a national policy. His motto, "All who are not against us are with us," is the antithesis of Leninism. The government is popular precisely because of the absence of ideological pressure. Depoliticization is encouraged, as all but the most superficial citizens' activities are frowned upon. The young, so far as they accept the message, feel that "The new world is here, and there is nothing to expect anymore." Hungary is called "one of the most cynical political cultures that has ever existed."[26]

China might have followed a fairly straightforward course away from Revolutionism, but Mao Zedung fought steadily against bureaucratization and political relaxation, and he periodically undertook campaigns to renew his life's work, the moral reshaping of the Chinese people. In the early 1950s, propaganda and reform campaigns (such as "Three Antis" and "Five Antis") came one after the other. But by 1957 the Great Helmsman commented gloomily, "It seems that Marxism, that was once all the rage, is not so much in fashion now."[27] The poor results of these movements reduced his authority for several years. But in 1966–68 Mao called upon the youth to make a new revolution against the "capitalist-roader" elements, which he saw controlling the party. With more human logic than Leninism, he viewed the rulers of society and the ruled as something like capitalists and proletariat; and he put himself at the head of the proletariat against their masters.[28]

The party was unable to oppose its titular and ideological leader. But the ideologically generated storm had few definite positive ideas, and accomplished little. Nearly all living ousted officials returned to power in the following years. As long as Mao lived, his group kept up a fight for revolutionary purity and egalitarianism against those who wished to place production ahead of politics. However, soon after Mao's death, their principal leaders, headed by Mao's widow with the "Gang of Four," were arrested. Mass demonstrations, even in Shanghai, home base of the radicals, seemed to reflect genuine popular joy over the downfall of those who claimed most of all to love the masses.[29]

The leadership turned to nation building instead of character building. Managers were told to restore discipline and look to production and profits. There was a new eagerness for foreign trade and Western technology. The new rulers promised "a new spring in art and literature," released many banned films and other works, and gave a respite from political meetings. The pragmatic Deng Xiaoping was restored to power for the second time. The schools again were expected to teach facts and skills. The party downgraded Mao and called for modernization by science and technology. Officially, the state insisted on the necessity of socialism, but many Chinese were willing to concede a partial or temporary superiority of capitalism and the need for capitalist methods to promote lagging economic development.

Even in relatively new Communist states, ideological commitment, once fortified by war, subsides. Xenophobic North Korea has resorted to large-scale importation of Western equipment, moderated its truculence on the world scene, and indicated a desire to enter diplomatic and commercial relations with its chief enemy, the United States. Cambodia and Vietnam sufficiently forgot their struggle against U.S. capitalism to fight among themselves, and the Vietnamese adopted a strongly racist program against ethnic Chinese. The Cubans, having so furiously damned Yankee imperialism over many years, by 1977 were eager to reopen trade with the United States. They built new hotels to serve the tourism they earlier scorned.[30] However, their revolutionary spirit seemed to revive in military adventures in Africa and sharpened confrontation with the United States. By sending tens of thousands of men to Angola, Ethiopia, and other countries of Africa, the Cubans found a new role, placing their small, poor country in the forefront of international affairs and (as they saw it) world revolution.

FAITH OF THE LEADERS

Ideology is at least as much for the elite in Communist countries as it is for the masses. It gives coherence, will and morale, guides conduct, and provides a basis for understanding that cements the system and makes it viable. As long as the elite cohere and have faith in their mission, it is not necessary that the masses believe much of what they are told. Governments function reasonably well in Poland, Hungary, and Czechoslovakia even though only a small minority of the population in these (and probably other) Communist countries appears to prefer the kind of government they have.

The beneficiaries of a faith easily believe it. The privileged learn that ordinary people are to be guided and controlled, perhaps helped charitably, not to be given dangerous freedom but to be protected from harmful ideas. Party education trains in the political and psychological management of people.[31] This education was so satisfying in the Soviet Union that Communists thrown into labor camps seemed unable to reassess their faith, continued to regard themselves as special people, and reassured themselves that their misfortune could only be an error of individuals, not the fault of the party or of Stalin.[32] The sense of comprising an elect group with special merits and responsibilities is satisfying, and it is an essential element of the Communist system.

The level of belief of the elite declines, however, in the absence of rejuvenating violence. Makers of the revolution must identify passionately with the party's interpretation of history to have confidence in the outcome. Lenin, Stalin, and their fellows knew the injustices of the old society, internalized an explanation, and fulfilled their personalities in acting out ideological mandates. Class conflict was a metaphor of their ambitions. To be Bolshevik before 1917, or a follower of Mao, Tito, or Ho when the movement was taking shape and the future leaders were being formed, meant to shape one's life after an idea.

When the revolutionary movement becomes the establishment, it is no longer necessary to believe deeply; indeed, it may be detrimental. So long as the party is remaking society, a person probably works more efficiently and advances quicker by taking the message seriously. But flexibility becomes an asset in order to follow easily the turns of policy of the party or the leader. Anyone of consistent views was certain to be dangerously in the wrong at some time during Stalin's decade of consolidation of power. So far as advancement depends on the favor of superiors, idealism is a doubtful asset. Those who make waves for the sake of principle, emphasize unpleasant facts, or maintain their own beliefs are troublesome.

Marxism-Leninism, moreover, is a contradictory faith for a possessing elite. Those who enjoy luxuries as the keepers of higher truth can hardly identify with the ordinary workers who once were supposed to be the vehicle of socialism and makers of the future.[33] The stirring call of Marxism for the overthrow of the possessors by the masses is incongruous for the newly ensconced de facto owners. The works of Marx contain many inconvenient ideas, such as the need for democracy and freedom of the press and the theory of the "Asiatic mode of production" (which sounds much like Stalinism). Lenin's works also include some subversive passages, such as:

Without the permission of the officials the people cannot call meetings, they cannot print books or newspapers! Is this not serfdom? If meetings cannot be freely called, or books freely printed, how can one obtain redress against the officials or against the rich? Of course, the officials suppress every book and every utterance that tells the truth about the people's poverty.... And no prisons, no persecutions can stop the fight for the people's liberty![34]

It is necessary to absorb much indoctrination on the road to status, and one must develop proper verbal reflexes to communicate and demonstrate loyalty. But many political careerists, caring nothing for the masses or the workers, find dialectics tedious; hypocrisy is no bar to political advancement. Clearheaded Communist leaders doubtless perceive the utility of the faith for themselves and the remoteness of the egalitarian future.

Cynicism of high leaders is in the Russian tradition. The atheistic Peter the Great did not hesitate to use the Orthodox church as an auxiliary of government. The church itself served the government for centuries with unflinching hypocrisy. Catherine the Great prated of the egalitarian and humane ideals of the French Enlightenment without dreaming of applying them to her serfs. The outstanding ideologues of tsarist autocracy in the nineteenth century, such as Count Sergei Uvarov and Constantine Pobedonostsev, had minds partitioned into official and unofficial compartments. Uvarov propounded the theme of "Autocracy, Orthodoxy, and Nationality," although he was a nonreligious liberal who always wrote in French or German and never read a Russian book.[35] Pobedonostsev admired Western culture and democratic government, but wanted Russia to be protected from them.[36]

Hypocrisy is built into the system, part of the basic Russian dilemma. The Russian state has for centuries been borrowing ideas from the West and applying them under different political conditions, hence using them differently. To call "freedom" something that educated and intelligent Russians know is unfreedom is not an invention of the Leninists. The Russian elite has desired to be modern, to operate with modern ideas, and to have a modern state, while at the same time it has manipulated ideas to hold and govern the autocratic empire. The inevitable result was what an observer from an individualistic culture would call pharisaism.

The Russian leaders obviously admit no sense of guilt. It may be fruitless to try to discern them as either believers or disbelievers. They would not ask themselves this question. The factual truth of ideology is simply unimportant; political "truth," that is, usefulness, is what counts. This is clearly stated by Marxists in the dictum that theory is proved by praxis, that is, the results of its application. Marxist-Leninist doctrines are designed not to make the world intelligible but to confound the foe.

Even Lenin, although doubtless a dedicated revolutionary, was a political opportunist and his beliefs had to be elastic to cover his changing policies.

Stalin in his early days clearly had a genuine conviction for the cause. In his latter days he was cynical as well as paranoid; he sneered privately at Lenin, whose cult he fostered publicly. Khrushchev is generally regarded as the last Soviet leader really to believe in the system.[37] Yet Khruschev indicated repeatedly in his memoirs that his Marxist-Leninist credo was not very consistent. For example, he feared that the system would collapse or be washed away after the death of Stalin, something inconceivable if it really represented the new order and the tide of history.[38] Again and again he expressed admiration for Western achievements, and even confessed, "We sometimes say jokingly that capitalism is rotten to the core. Yet these 'rotten' capitalists keep coming up with things that make our jaws drop in surprise."[39] He could hardly have believed that "capitalism" was totally rotten. As leader of an emphatically atheistic state, Brezhnev told Carter, in connection with the Salt II treaty in June 1979, "God will not forgive us if we fail."

Western observers often have felt that Soviet (and East European) elites, officials, and intellectuals give Marxism only ritual lip service,[40] or operate in a world of Marxist categories without real content.[41] The Hungarian party, for example, is said to contain few believers.[42] Pampered KGB officials are said to take lightly not only Soviet claims of political virtue but the inflation of leaders' merits.[43] Andrei Sakharov saw Soviet society as "being marked by ideological indifference and the cynical use of ideology as a convenient facade."[44] The Chinese radicals (Gang of Four) were accused of all manner of indulgences in total disharmony with their public devotion to austerity and equality; Jiang Qing desisted from using her private Olympic-size swimming pool for fear of being seen.[45] The impression of insincerity seems general and represents a major change; twenty years ago it was universally assumed that Communist leaders were firmly convinced of the doctrines they espoused.

Soviet (and Eastern European) elites frequently act as though they regard Marxism-Leninism as useful only for others. Extreme fondness for travel in the West, use of Western clothes and gadgets as status symbols, and listening to foreign radio are not consonant with a major thesis of ideology, the moral and cultural superiority of the Soviet (or Eastern European) state.[46] the upper classes indulge in many things held to be poisonous for commoners; for example, high KGB officials enjoy reading anti-Soviet satire.[47] For foreigners and Russians with hard currency privileges, Beryozka stores sell literature considered unsuitable for the people.[48] A Soviet survey of trainee propagandists showed a phenomenal degree of skepticism. Volunteers who had completed a course to qualify as propagandists were questioned anonymously regarding their belief in the propaganda they were to spread: 13 percent expressed disbelief and 25 percent declined to answer.[49] It may be surmised that they wished to show themselves intellectually superior to the message they should carry to the masses. Similarly, it may be that the Soviet elites who follow Western broadcasts do so as a demonstration of their superiority. In the same vein, many Communist leaders, such as Lenin, Stalin, Khrushchev,

Mao, and Jiang Qing, have talked far more freely to Western journalists than to their own people, and Communist diplomats often speak privately with their Western counterparts in very different tones from their public expressions.

If the Soviet (and other Communist) elites revert to the condition of tsarist Russia, whose spokesmen took for granted that faith was for the populace, the system cannot fail to suffer. The cynicism of the upper classes seeps down to people who have been to school and wish to consider themselves enlightened like their political betters, and apathy is contagious. If the ideology becomes a mere fraud, sustained only by the self-interest of the elite and their sense of shared advantage, the Communist revolution is worn out.

NOTES

1. As commented extensively by Richard Lowenthal, "Development vs. Utopia in the Communist Polity," *Change in Communist Systems*, ed. Chalmers Johnson (Stanford: Stanford University Press, 1970), pp. 33–116.

2. Andrew C. Janos, "Systemic Models," in *Authoritarian Politics in Communist Europe: Uniformity and Diversity in One-Party States*, ed. Andrew C. Janos (Berkeley: Institute of International Studies, 1976), pp. 3–4.

3. Jacob Walkin, "Some Contrasts between the Tsarist and Communist Political Systems," *New Review of East European History* 16 (March 1976): 56.

4. As observed by Soviet dissident Dmitry Nelidov, "Ideocratic Consciousness and Personality," Document No. 1642 in *Arkhiv Samizdata*, September 1973.

5. George Feifer, *Russia Close-Up* (London: Jonathan Cape, 1973), p. 34.

6. Peter Wiles, "Leninism and Weltinnenpolitik," *Survey* 22 (Summer-Autumn 1976): 157.

7. As observed by Paul Cocks, "Bureaucracy and Party Control," in *Comparative Socialist Systems: Essays in Politics and Economics* ed. Carmelo Mesa-Lago and Carl Beck (Pittsburgh: University of Pittsburgh Center for International Studies, 1975), p. 219.

8. Benjamin Schwarts, "Modernization and the Maoist Vision," in *China Under Mao: Politics Takes Command*, ed. Roderick MacFarquhar (Cambridge: MIT Press, 1966), pp. 11–13.

9. Samuel P. Huntington, "Social and Institutional Dynamics of One-Party Systems," in *Authoritarian Politics in Modern Society*, ed. P. Samuel and H. Clement (New York: Basic Books, 1970), pp. 28, 29.

10. The thesis of Jerome Gillison, *The Soviet Image of Utopia* (Baltimore: Johns Hopkins University Press, 1975).

11. Max Eastman, *Marx, Lenin and the Science of Revolution* (1926; reprint ed., Westport, Conn.: Hyperion Press, 1973), p. 213.

12. Bertrand Russell, *The Practice and Theory of Bolshevism* (London: Allen and Unwin, 1920), p. 29.

13. Alexander I. Solzhenitsyn, *The Gulag Archipelago*, vol. 2 (New York: Harper & Row, 1976), p. 106.

14. Nikita Khrushchev, *Khrushchev Remembers* (Boston: Little, Brown, 1970), p. 229.

15. Paul Hollander, "Soviet Society Today," *Current History* 71 (October 1976): 137–38.

16. Ruth W. Mouly, "Values and Aspirations of Soviet Youth," in *The Dynamics of Soviet Politics*, ed. Paul Cocks, Robert V. Daniels, and Nancy W. Heer (Cambridge: Harvard University Press, 1976), p. 233.

17. *L'Express*, February 28–March 6, 1977, p. 38.

18. Mouly, "Values and Aspirations of Soviet Youth," pp. 223–24.

19. As marked by many observers, such as Leonid Vladimirov, *The Russians* (New York: Praeger, 1968), p. 44; and Leona and Jerrold Schecter, *An American Family in Moscow* (Boston: Little, Brown, 1975), passim.

20. John Barron, *KGB: The Secret Work of Soviet Secret Agents* (New York: Reader's Digest Press, 1974), pp. 197–98.

21. *New York Times*, January 3, 1977, p. 8.

22. *New York Times*, April 11, 1977, p. 3.

23. *New York Times*, April 5, 1976, p. 3.

24. Trond Gilberg, *Modernization in Romania since World War II* (New York: Praeger, 1975), pp. 246–48.

25. Anneli U. Gabanyi, *Partei und Literatur in Rumänien seit 1945* (Munich: Oldenbourg, 1975), pp. 189–90.

26. Peter A. Toma and Ivan Volgyes, *Politics in Hungary* (San Francisco: W. H. Freeman, 1977), pp. 149–50, 159.

27. Cited by A. Doak Barnett, *Uncertain Passage: China's Transition to the Post-Mao Era* (Washington: Brookings Institution, 1974), p. 7.

28. Lowell Dittmer, *Liu Shao-chi and the Chinese Cultural Revolution* (Berkeley: University of California Press, 1974), p. 46.

29. *New York Times*, March 24, 1977, p. A-27.

30. *Business Week*, May 12, 1975, p. 23.

31. B. V. Talantov, "Soviet Society," *Posev* (September 1969): 36.

32. Solzhenitsyn, *The Gulag Archipelago*, pp. 334–35.

33. As observed in the case of Hungary by Toma and Volgyes, *Politics in Hungary*, p. 148.

34. V. I. Lenin, "To the Rural Poor" (1903), *Selected Works* vol. 2, (New York: International Publishers, 1943), p. 279.

35. Sidney Harcave, *Years of the Golden Cockerel: The Last Russian Tsars, 1814–1917* (New York: Macmillan, 1968), p. 101.

36. Robert F. Byrnes, *Pobedonostsev, His Life and Thought* (Bloomington: Indiana University Press, 1968), pp. 345–47.

37. As by François Bundy, "Cultural Exchange and Prospects of Change," in *Detente*, ed. George R. Urban (London: Temple Smith, 1976), p. 57.

38. Khrushchev, *Khrushchev Remembers*, p. 323; idem, *Khrushchev Remembers: The Last Testament* (Boston: Little, Brown, 1974), p. 79.

39. Khrushchev, *Khrushchev Remembers: The Last Testament*, p. 532.

40. For example, Martin Esslin, "East-West Polarities," *Survey* 22 (Summer-Autumn 1976): 52; Paul Lendvai, *Die Grenzen des Wandels: Spielarten des Kommunismus im Donauraum* (Vienna: Europa Verlag, 1977), chap. 1.

41. Donald G. McRae, "The Future of East-West Relations," *Survey* 22 (Summer-Autumn 1976): 106–7.

42. Toma and Volgyes, *Politics in Hungary*, pp. 150–51.

43. Aleksei Myagkov, *Inside the KGB* (Richmond, Surrey: Foreign Affairs Publishing Co., 1976), p. 85.

44. Andrei Sakharov, "On Alexander Solzhenitsyn's 'A letter to the Soviet Leaders' " in *Kontinent*, ed. Vladimir Maksimov (Garden City, N.Y.: Doubleday, 1976), p. 6.

45. Jan S. Prybyla, "The Chinese Economy After the 'Gang of Four'," *Current History* (September 1977): 71; Roxane Witke, *Comrade Chiang Ch'ing* (Boston: Little, Brown, 1977), p. 303.

46. See, for example, Hedrick Smith, *The Russians* (New York: Quadrangle/New York Times, 1976), pp. 464–65.

47. *New York Times*, April 27, 1977, p. A-2.

48. *New York Times*, July 30, 1977, p. 3.

49. Maury Lisann, *Broadcasting to the Soviet Union: International Politics and Radio* (New York: Praeger, 1975), p. 129. This survey was published in 1965, a time of maximum openness in the Soviet Union, when there was a penchant for Western-style surveys.

3

POLITICAL PROBLEMS

THE NEW CLASS

The purpose of a revolution is to cast down a ruling class; its result is to set up a stronger ruling class. Large organization inevitably creates power differences, unequal status, and positions of privilege. The Communist system, in which the governing party, the administrative state, and virtually all organizations are tied together into one grand structure, is the most gargantuan of organizations. A ruling class could be avoided only if there were very strong institutions for responsibility and renewal of the elite. There are none.

The Communist party, reaching for power, proposes a dictatorship in the name of justice and equality, but there is no fixed limit to the period or extent of tutelage, and no serious thought of terminating it. The purpose of happiness for all lends itself to the creation of status and inequality.[1] The beneficiaries perpetuate their status: "Was there ever any domination which did not appear natural to those who possessed it?"[2] And in the Communist states they have peculiarly the means of doing so.

Ideological commitment can at best delay stratification. A religious order dedicated to charity and poverty is likely to find itself, in a few generations or sooner, supporting ecclesiastical princes. Populist revolutionary parties go the same way more rapidly. The Mexican revolution, for example, was once dedicated to social leveling; today Mexico suffers a degree of inequality exceptional even in Latin America because its one-party rulership has strong control of the state. Yet the Mexican governing party is much less closely organized than Communist parties, designed more to balance interests than to concentrate power.

Ideology served to keep Communist parties fairly close to the less privileged strata for a time. They maintained through propaganda an image of "with and for the people," even if the approach was paternalistic. But power separates and absolute power separates absolutely, as Yaroslav Bilinski remarked; the parties everywhere have grown apart from the masses they claimed to serve. The dream of collectivist equality cannot shut out the reality of hierarchic stratification.

In 1917 Lenin's party welcomed the masses and at first tried to reflect their aspirations. High leaders dressed and lived simply and mixed with unwashed workers. An early decree abolished all decorations, orders, and marks of distinction. The party remained fairly open and egalitarian in spirit through the difficult civil war. With victory, however, the party increasingly set itself up as a governing establishment above not only the peasant majority but also above the few proletarians remaining in the ravaged land. In the 1920s there were efforts to recruit bench workers into the party; by 1925 the party was looking down on worker members as backward; and workers who came into the party took administrative positions and cut themselves off from their class origins.[3] The subsequent course has been toward growing separation of the ruling class from the people.

In times of rapid socioeconomic change, the party is less rigid and less insulated. A dictator may be able to reshape the party, bring in new blood, and check the tendency to formation of a self-serving stratum. Stalin brought about a substantial renewal of cadres during the 1930s, the time of his Great Transformation. He struck violently at "familyness," the formation of local cliques. Khrushchev stirred up the party sufficiently to check, although not reverse, the aging of the upper echelons. He expanded membership and tried to institutionalize circulation by placing limits on the length of time leaders could remain in posts. Other strong chiefs have done as much or more. For example, Kim Il-song, consolidating his power during a cultural revolution in imitation of the Chinese, brought a large influx of new blood into the higher levels of the Korean party.[4] In Romania, Ceausescu carried out a broad renewal of the top ranks. But even for a Mao it proved difficult to attack entrenched party positions. To check party elitism, the leader must be very strong, have ideological authority, and use coercion if not terror. Such leaders have become increasingly unlikely in settled states governed by careerists.

Lacking catclysmic shake-ups, the Communist elite becomes more like a private club with unlimited public powers, a new nobility. Those who have invested their energies not in social change but in acquiring status have a stake in the system and their positions. The corporation of the elect becomes an in-group whose members are above all to be loyal, and being loyal are almost immune from expulsion. A KGB boss is quoted as saying, "Provided you defend it, the Soviet regime permits you to do almost everything."[5] Tenure is most important in the Communist world because outside the party, there is no status, perhaps no livelihood; and the security of one implies that of all.

Khrushchev's Secret Speech denouncing Stalin reassured the elites that there would be no more blood purges and that their rights would be respected.[6] Subsequently, he had the greatest difficulty in getting even outright enemies, the "Anti-party Group," expelled from their offices and the party. Since Khrushchev the party has settled down and stabilized on the basis of party loyalty, understood relations, and "faith in cadres." The atmosphere is relatively relaxed, and the party bosses are less driven and less threatened. There was a marked decrease of turnover in all categories of leading personnel in just one decade (1956–61 to 1966–71) in the central core, the ministries, the provincial secretariats, and the Central Committee.[7] Under the nomenklatura system, positions are practically a form of property.[8] Disgraced officials are spared punishment, and merely shifted from one post to another like unfortunate members of the family.[9] They are practically exempt from prosecution unless higher authorities decide to make them a scapegoat. To be stripped of real elite status is almost unknown, even if one is beset by political doubts.

Soviet society, having come to the end of the large-scale social mobility generated by rapid industrialization and urbanization, has become far more class-ridden than American.[10] The gateway to upper elitehood has narrowed since Khrushchev, and the participation of nonparty organizations in the formulation of policy has diminished.

Recent Soviet writers frankly see differences of status as inherent in socialist society and recognize higher and lower classes according to position, education and rewards.[11] There is no single elite, but elites within elites, circles of increasing power, privilege, and trust, divided into innumerable cliques yet sharing a similar mentality and common interests. At the top of the Soviet pyramid, political, economic, and military elites, and to some extent cultural and scientific, are substantially integrated. Each layer is selected by that above, until the top oligarchy selects itself or a dictator pushes to the summit and installs his own subordinates. There are no regular rules or fixed qualifications for advancement. The end of terror has not meant promotion by merit, as was sometimes assumed.[12] Individuals attach themselves, in a somewhat feudal way, to more powerful leaders, on whose goodwill their careers depend.[13] Cliques rest mostly on informal relations of trust and support.[14] It is taken for granted that superiors are powerful; relationships are strongly hierarchic, even in scientific institutes,[15] and the system is filled with obsequiousness looking up and severity looking down.[16] Consequently, "In Soviet reality, the altruistic type is exceptional and is doomed to martyrdom."[17] According to a former member of the system, "The purely party career has already become so unpopular and repugnant that intelligent and decent people strive to avoid it."[18]

Deformities of power are unavoidable in large bureaucracies, but the situation is worse in the Communist apparatus because the web of authority lacks most of the characteristics of regularized bureaucracy: clearly defined roles, objective criteria of appointment and promotion, and tenure during good behavior or for fixed terms.

A Communist of the old school, who defected after 58 years in the party, explained in a letter to Brezhnev:

> I understood that the Soviet Communist Party had long since ceased to be a political party, that it had been transformed into a mutual benefit society for the early fulfillment of the five-year plan.... What sort of socialism can one talk of in the Soviet Union when the place of the former capitalist and landowner exploiting classes has been taken by the privileged castes of the party and state bureaucracies? They are drowning in wealth, live isolated from the people, contemptuous of ordinary folk....[19]

Chairman Mao, who was more of a revolutionary romantic than Soviet leaders, always insisted that the party must be close to and learn from the masses.[20] To undo the "bourgeoisification" of the party, that is, the growth of a new aristocracy, was a prime purpose of his Cultural Revolution. But after it cadres resumed their positions and May 7 cadre schools, where officials were to be improved by physical labor and spartan living, evolved into executive resorts. Even under Mao, members of the Revolutionary Committees were acquiring limousines while the masses dreamed of a bicycle; to have a car was to be a ruler.[21] Ordinary Chinese hardly dared breathe in the presence of a member of the local Revolutionary Committee, and lesser leaders would freeze in the presence of higher.[22]

As a poem of the 1960s went, "I would like to be a tiny bolt/So they can put me where they want and bolt me in tightly/Whether on the arm of a powerful crane/Or in the simplest wheel."[23] The difference of standing between the "I" and "they" would seem greater than between horse and rider. It is not surprising that Deng Xiaoping was ousted in April 1976 because there was a popular demonstration in his favor.

Upon Mao's death, the ardent advocates of equality (for others) were disgraced, and the special virtue of manual labor was forgotten. Maoist egalitarianism gave way to policies of stability of cadres, special schools for better students, respect for knowledge and authority, and greater power for managers.

Like Mao's guerrillas, the Yugoslav partisans with Tito in World War II were a brotherhood as well as a party, a largely peasant group, unpretentious and dedicated. The inner circle of the party has become, in the phrase of Milovan Djilas, the New Class, with exclusive and egregious luxuries. People socialize with their own class. Worker's children have little access to the higher education that means advancement.[24] It is explicitly intended that the party should hold itself apart from the masses; in 1971 Tito accused the

Croatian party leadership of trying to get mass support.[25] The country has been dominated since World War II by a society of former partisan fighters numbering about 1,200.

The elitist traditions of Eastern Europe revive in the vanguard role of the party. Idealists drop out or are purged, and Balkan-style political connections regain their traditional importance. In party ranks, proletarians are replaced by managers and technocrats. Nearly two-thirds of the Polish party were reported to be bureaucrats,[26] and few of the elite really adhere to Communist values.[27] Romania has a very narrow aristocracy with total privileges. Stratification increases in Hungary, as the overwhelming majority of the population is outside the political system.[28] The size of the ruling sector of the party, the full-time professional apparatus, is a closely guarded secret as in all Communist states.

Unrestricted political power inevitably converts into material advantages. In the first years the Soviet party kept populist appearances and followed the rule of the "party maximum" that no person in authority in the workers' state should earn more than a skilled laborer. This self-denying ordinance never meant much, however, because most real income was in the form of perquisites. In the early 1930s Stalin attacked egalitarianism as "petty bourgeois," and the party maximum was abolished in 1932. Concurrently, the cadres were provided with more special stores, dining rooms, dachas, vacation resorts, gifts, and the like.[29]

Party salaries remain secret, but they probably are not high. General Secretary Brezhnev is said to be paid a paltry 1000 rubles per month. However, it also is reported that he and other members of the Politburo and the Secretariat have unlimited drawing privileges with the state bank.[30] Pay, in any case, is supplemented by irregular income of many varieties, and goods and perquisites that are unaccountable and more self-righteously defensible. Hence status in the Soviet Union and other Communist states is primarily rewarded by housing, limousines, servants, dachas, free transportation, exclusive entertainments (including productions considered unsuitable for the public), superior health care, access to information denied the masses, and foreign travel.[31] Party higher-ups are said to provide themselves with academic degrees in order to retire to placid and prestigious positions in institutes.[32] The elites are wholly at the service of the party, and the party cares well for them.[33]

Throughout East Europe the picture is similar, as new elites live like old aristocrats and semifeudal gentry in independent Yugoslavia and Albania as well as Soviet-dominated countries. The more recent Communism of Cuba has already provided its new class with luxuries—good apartments, appliances, cars, and so forth—that acquire added value in the general austerity of the island.

The way of life of Chinese upper brackets has been effectively shrouded. However, when Mao boiler suits were obligatory garb during and after the

Cultural Revolution, those of the commoners were cheap cotton and of the elite, fine wool. The expulsion from power of the radicals after the passing of Mao brought lurid accounts of regal living by the ideological egalitarians. Wang Hungwen was alleged to have gathered a stable of luxury cars.[34] Jiang Qing was credited with regal taste: she was ridiculously fussy about clothes, required a huge retinue on travels, demanded that everyone keep quiet in the village where she slept, and indulged in Western movies and books deemed sinful for the people.[35]

Communist luxury is more or less screened from view as a matter of principle. The automobile, however, makes class divisions more visible; it is very much a mark of status. The fact that Soviet automobile production has leveled at one-tenth that of the United States may indicate not only reluctance to invest in the infrastructure of roads, parking spaces, service stations, and so forth, but also disinclination to share the roads and the satisfactions of car ownership with the masses. Khrushchev reduced the number of bigwigs' chauffeured limousines, but under his successors they have been restored.[36] A luxury denied to the wealthy in Western societies is the lane reserved on main Moscow avenues for oligarchs' limousines to glide past traffic.

Just as ordinary people in the Soviet Union see little of the sumptuous existence of their betters, the latter are untouched by the life of the common folk. The elite, even of the lower levels, are better able than aristocrats of more open societies to ignore the conditions of their inferiors. They have no informative media; no one gains by telling them of the hardships from which they are sheltered.[37] For the oligarchs, like antique emperors, it is virtually impossible to view the real life of the people. For example, it is related that when Politburo member Mikhail Suslov was to visit a Leningrad market, customers were whisked to one side and replaced by KGB operatives, and shelves were loaded with goodies, all quickly removed after the official party passed through.[38]

The psychological separation of the elite is promoted by giving them access to foreign travel and to information withheld from the public. Awareness of being trusted furthers identification with the system and a sense of superiority. The party, it appears, wants its ruling servants to feel privileged.[39] If the party wants to learn about problems of the people, it is like the elephant investigating the life of the mice. Yet without good information, it is impossible to improve government.

Despite its privileges, an elite can remain vigorous if it is refreshed by a continued influx of new talents from below while the less capable decline in status. In the first decades of the Soviet party, flux and turmoil kept the corps of powerholders fluid. Further, a large number of Lenin's fellows, like Lenin, did not have children. Stalin strongly attacked familyness as detrimental to his authority; this mostly meant mutually self-supporting groups, but it applied no less to family connections. Khrushchev, on a much smaller scale, stirred, shifted, and brought in new blood. But under Brezhnev trust in cadres has been the slogan. The end of change and expansion means the end of mobility.

It is a firm principle of Marxism-Leninism that the party is self-selecting, the sole judge of its membership; to enter the party is always a privilege, never a right. A few parties, such as the Cuban, have made gestures toward permitting workers to elect party members, but nothing has come of this Marxist-logical intention. More important, promotion within the power structure is always by grace of superiors. It would be miraculous if a power elite that controls access to its ranks did not promote its own blood. The party is rarely likely to prefer worthy to well-connected applicants. Party rules favor insiders by requiring sponsorship, which is a serious commitment, by members of at least five years' standing. The offspring of faithful party folk may be assumed to be more reliable than those of nonparty families, and they probably have been involved in party affairs since childhood. An outsider clearly must have outstanding merits or persuasiveness to compete with the candidates closely related to party aristocrats. Meanwhile, the growing separation of elite and masses will make it more natural to look for reliability in the favored section.

Top elites associate with and marry one another.[40] Nepotism has not been conspicuous at the summit of the Soviet system, but it is certainly not excluded by Marxism-Leninism. Stalin's son Vasily, a worthless alcoholic, was made an air force general; and he treated ministers like dogs. Yuri Zhdanov, son of Stalin's close aide Andrei Zhdanov, became head of the science department of the Central Committee at age 24. Alexei Adzhubei, Khrushchev's son-in-law, was his father-in-law's closest adviser and seemed in line for a top position when Khrushchev was ousted. In the lower echelons, nepotism seems to be the rule, especially in Asiatic territories with traditions of clan solidarity.

The Albanian Central Committee of somewhat over 100 includes at least twenty relatives, among them five wives. In Bulgaria and other Balkan countries, not only families but people of particular villages stick together politically. Some fifteen relatives of Ceausescu have high posts—his wife, son, two brothers, three brothers-in-law, various nephews, and others.[41] In North Korea, the son of the leader has seemed to stand in the line of succession, and a dozen relatives and in-laws of Kim hold important positions.[42]

Thus far, there has been no Communist dynastic succession. Not only has there been insufficient time to establish a hereditary principle, but there are no institutions whereby a leader can bequeath power to his offspring. To the contrary, a deceased leader is fortunate not to be degraded postmortem. What the upper elite can and do transmit is a place in the magic circle of the establishment.

The obvious means of conveying status is through education. Although nominally open to all equally, in practice it serves as a sieve. A diploma is a principle ticket to high position. In Communist societies, as in any other, young people coming from a cultured background have a big head start in getting into better institutions. Tutoring, possible only for the well-off, has become an important and well-organized private business.[43] More important, political certification is requisite for entry to desirable institutions. Anyone with a tainted background can be excluded; conversely, those with suitable support can be assured that their applications will be favored. Well-placed Soviet officials, perhaps from district secretary up, regularly enroll their offspring appropriately. The most prestigious schools seem to be practically reserved for well-sponsored applicants. In Czechoslovakia, politically favored youths are frankly given every chance to enter a university. At a Chinese university "practically all" students were said to have parents in the party or the army.[44]

The fact that some nonelite get through the selective gateway legitimizes the status-perpetuating system. Discrimination is informal and personal, while rules and mechanisms are outwardly egalitarian. Beneficiaries consequently can claim and presumably believe that they enjoy only the fruits of merit. But status comes to be taken for granted; what elders fought for, the young accept as a natural right. Status is inherited not only through superior family background and educational opportunities, but also through friendships and relations among the powerful. So far as wealth may be accumulated, it, too, is inheritable in Soviet society. The new aristocrats are born to their class, not only spiritually but also physically isolated because of distrust of the masses and desire to avoid their envy.

The separation widens, the inclination to protect status grows, and its loss becomes more shattering. If the elite see their position weakening, they are less likely to open their ranks than to close them, feeling that loyalty is more than ever necessary. But the establishment of a new and narrower aristocracy very likely more corrupt and exploitative than the old ruling class, leads from Communism to ordinary tyranny.

QUALITY OF LEADERSHIP

The pyramidal structure of Communist power meets difficulties at the top, where the central ruling nucleus must choose itself or be selected by a dictator. The result is a somewhat anarchic situation that seems to require a single strong leader, although there is no ideological basis for autocracy and no regular way of picking an autocrat.

Communist parties, notwithstanding the ideology of class and historical materialism, have been eminently dominated by personalities. In the cases of Lenin, Stalin, Mao, Tito, Kim, Castro, Ho Chi Minh, and others, the leader seems virtually to stand for the party. It was the prime characteristic of Lenin's following before the revolution that it was Lenin's; no other party so adhered to a single individual. After the disappearance of each supreme Soviet leader, Lenin, Stalin, and Khrushchev, collective leadership prevailed for a few years and was held up as proper, probably mostly because the oligarchs had no desire to subordinate themselves to a new boss. But by much maneuvering a single person has been able each time to promote himself to supremacy. A cycle of single-to-collective-to-single leadership and back seems inherent in the system because of the mortality of the dictators, the lack of institutionalized means of replacing them, and the need for a cap on the pyramid of power.

A supreme figure is apparently necessary as a final decider and judge (especially in personnel matters), as a symbolic unifying figure, and as a spokesman of high policy and ideology. It is at the same time difficult to avoid the emergence of a supreme leader because there is no definite allocation of power. As oligarchs jostle to affirm their position, which means to improve it, oligarchy is unstable. Always in the Soviet Union and ordinarily in other Communist countries, the victor has been the ranking Secretary. On becoming primus, the leader, lacking in constitutional position or the assurance of a fixed term, naturally moves to make himself supreme, for security if not for satisfaction. The Communist system has an exalted leader both because it needs one and because it cannot avoid one.

Albania and Cuba are still guided by the chief of the revolution; others are led by successors or successors of successors. It does not make a great deal of difference in the way in which the leader is treated; adulation is the rule. Although Kim Il-song's revolutionary merit is obscure, his cult is notorious. Kimism is a higher stage of Marxism-Leninism. The cult is extended to his ancestors and family, and citizens swear personal loyalty to him, as did Germans to Hitler. Virtually no song or publication fails to pay tribute to the fountainhead of all knowledge. Of Ceausescu, "He is everything, the sun and the moon. He never listens to anyone, never consults experts, because he knows everything," a Romanian official said to a foreign journalist.[45] The report of the uninspiring Todor Zhivkov to the 1976 Bulgarian party congress was printed in advance, including such commentaries as "The report was often interrupted by spontaneous applause, and its conclusion was followed by stormy, prolonged, unabating applause which turned into an ovation."[46] In China, something of a cult of Chairman Hua, whose merits previously were obscure, began emerging within two months of the death of the deity of Chinese Communism. He was given the ritual title of "Wise Leader" and sometimes received space in the press comparable to Mao, although he seemed overshadowed in the government by the evidently greater ability of Deng Xiaoping.

Leonid Brezhnev, having become First Secretary in October 1964, was distinctly superior to his colleagues by 1966. Although he seemed personally rather unpretentious and appeals to Russians as an average Russian, the Brezhnev cult slowly gathered since then, especially after 1970. In the week after May Day in 1972, *Pravda* mentioned Brezhnev 18 times, and a year later, 371 times. By 1976 quotations from Brezhnev, whose writings have the dash of a legal brief, were almost as obligatory as those of Stalin had been and more conspicuous than the frequently snappier words of Khrushchev ever were. His seventieth birthday (1976) was celebrated in imperial fashion, with a documentary film, eulogistic books, medals, a ceremonial sword, and honors from leaders of vassal states. Called "*vozhd*" (leader) as Lenin and Stalin had once been, he was treated as "heir of Lenin" as though standing in immediate succession to the great founder without the intervening forty years of Stalin and Khrushchev.[47] In February 1978 there was bestowed on him, or he bestowed on himself, the Order of Victory, a decoration for commanders of large forces in the great war, although young Brezhnev was not a commander at all.

Leaders enjoy fixity. In Stalin's last years, despite his declining competence, there seems to have been no thought of getting rid of him (except perhaps during the final months, when he plotted the ultimate disloyalty to his long-time servants, a purge of the inner circle). Mao at times had little control of the party apparatus, and his policies (such as the people's communes, the Great Leap Forward, and the Cultural Revolution) were notably unsuccessful; yet he could not be set aside. The last public appearance of the aging god was in 1971. Thereafter he was increasingly incapacitated until his death in 1976, but he could not be replaced, and the majesty of his authority remained theoretically total.

It does not appear that any Communist leader has ever been removed simply for inability or failure of his policies. Exaltation and perpetuation of the leader, whether or not he has genuine merits, is some guarantee for stability and is in harmony with growing conservatism. Genuflection becomes a custom, and the verbal kowtow comes easily to minds dulled to critical thought. There need be no tremendous admiration nor deep loyalty; it is as easy and simple to accept the tin god as the earlier man of steel.

Decline of the quality of leadership seems inevitable in the absence of major upsets. Early leaders of Communist states have been outstanding for dynamism and energy, perhaps for intelligence and dedication. The group around Tito in the 1940s, for example, was remarkable for its intelligence, devotion, and imagination.[48] But in all ranks, careerists, bureaucrats, and servants replace idealists and drivers. Strong personalities are probably not wanted, and the selection process practically guarantees lack of imagination. The judgment of persons in positions of very great power, surrounded by dependents and admirers and constantly assured of their virtues and rightness, cannot remain unaffected, and the ability to appraise inferiors critically suffers. Moreover, persons who feel insecure in their positions—lacking institutional guarantees—are loathe to raise potential challengers to posts near them.

Lenin, a man of considerable confidence in his own position, gathered adherents who, although not major intellectuals of prerevolutionary Russian Marxism, were of outstanding ability, such as Stalin and Bukharin. He also accepted the brilliant Trotsky as a partner in the tumult of 1917. Stalin, stepping into the top place, at first worked with those who had been his equals under Lenin, such as Kamenev, Zinoviev, and Bukharin. When he had pushed these aside, he worked with his loyal followers and helpers, such as Molotov, Ordzhonikidze, and Kaganovich. As his power grew, he relied more on persons prepared to act as his creatures, such as Yezhov, Malenkov, Zhdanov, and Beria.

There also has been a marked loss of individuality, from Lenin through his lieutenants, Trotsky, Stalin, Zinoviev, and Bukharin, who were notable characters in their own right, to Molotov, Kaganovich, and Khrushchev, who were striking personalities, down to the anonymity of those around Brezhnev, such as Chernenko, Grishin, Kirilenko, or Romanov. Nowadays leaders are brought up to be a fuzzy carbon copy of their elders, and they become increasingly homogeneous in education and experience and decreasingly original.[49] It matters less who becomes leader, and the charisma that illuminates uncertain times fades as the state turns static and loses inspiration. The latter-day Communist leadership, in Weberian terms, is neither rational, legalistic, traditional, nor charismatic.

A concrete result of the difficulty of reallocating power is immobility and aging. It was postulated in Stalinist times that the system required frequent upheavals in order to function properly, and this probably was and is true.[50] New leadership has spelled temporary improvement, as in the entry into top place of Khrushchev and later Brezhnev. In Poland, Gomulka enlivened things in 1956, as did Gierek in 1970–71. But minirevolutions become less and less feasible with passing decades, and the capacity (and probably the desire) of leaders to bring new blood into the top ranks diminishes. Consequently the dictatorship of the revolutionary proletariat subsides into gerontocracy.

The policy of "faith in cadres" guarantees ossification and superannuation. Communist revolutions have been led by men in their thirties and forties, backed by comrades in their twenties and thirties, as in Russia, Yugoslavia, China, and Cuba. Age levels rise slowly as long as the state is fluid, but after it hardens the rulership ages rapidly. In 1976, the average age was 65. In Albania, despite sundry purges, the old guard of partisan days holds power, and Hoxha (born 1908) has been on top since 1941. The wartime resistance leadership, headed by Tito since 1941, likewise holds on in Yugoslavia. With the principal exception of the rejuvenation of upper levels of the Polish party in 1971, East European elites generally have been aging for many years. The Vietnamese party is still headed by leaders in the war against the French; the first party Congress in 16 years, held early in 1977, made practically no changes. The Politburo then averaged about 66, the Central Committee nearly 60 (data being uncertain).[51]

Up to 1976 it was indispensable to have been a veteran of the Long March, that is, to have been a party member since 1937 or before, in order to reach the top rank in China. The leader was still the incapacitated Mao, the bulk of whose quotations are taken from writings prior to 1949, and whose last important statement was emitted in 1957.[52] Mao was replaced as chairman by Hua, born in 1920, but much power seemed to rest with senior generals five to twenty years older under the leadership of Ye Jianying, 78, defense minister and vice-chairman of the party. Deng Xiaoping, who has seemed the most influential figure, was born in 1902.

The much commented aging of Soviet leadership has accelerated in the past decade, but it has progressed with few remissions almost since the revolution. In 1919 the average age of the Politburo was 41; thanks to Stalin's ouster of his rivals, it edged only to 46 in 1932, but rose to 59 by 1953, although Stalin catapulted current leaders, including Brezhnev, Kosygin, Suslov, and Gromyko, to high places when they were in their thirties. Khrushchev stirred up the leadership sufficiently that in 1967 the Politburo still averaged only 59, but thereafter it climbed steadily to 70 in 1980, when the top four, Brezhnev, Suslov, Kosygin, and Kirilenko, averaged 75.[53] The Politburo was rejuvenated by only three months through the limited changes made at the 1976 Twenty-Fifth Party Congress. Kirilenko, said to be in line to succeed Brezhnev although he is a little older, expressed this philosophy upon his seventieth birthday: "It is good that in our country this is considered only middle age." Brezhnev himself has expressed willingness to serve "to the last."

Since 1965 the few expulsions from the Politburo have been mostly from among the youngest members—Shelepin, Poliansky, and Shelest—until Podgorny, 74 but in better physical condition than Brezhnev, was removed in May 1977 to vacate the presidency for Brezhnev. He was in a sense replaced by Vasily Kuznetsov, named Brezhnev's vice-president in October 1977 at age 76. When Marshal Grechko left the Ministry of Defense by dying at age 73, General V. G. Kulikov was at 54 apparently considered too young to replace him;[54] the post went to D. Ustinov, 67, whom Stalin had placed in charge of arms production 34 years earlier. Perhaps older men are preferred because the younger are living testimony to the increasing debility of the oldsters. In 1956, Grishin became head of the trade unions at age 41; in 1967, the job went to Shelepin, aged 48; in 1976 it was taken by Shibaev, aged 61, a former oblast secretary of no trade union experience. In May 1977, Konstantin Katushev, at 50 one of the youngest men near the summit, was replaced as Central Committee Secretary by K. V. Rusakov, aged 68. Semichastny lost the headship of the police in 1967 to Andropov, who was ten years older. In 1974, N. A. Tikhonov was named to full membership in the Politburo at age 74.

The tenure of officials is cited by Soviet writers as a positive achievement. It supposedly makes for better use of expertise,[55] and stability of leadership should give a public image of unity and authority. It prevails through the system. The leadership of the Council of Ministers ages in step with the Politburo. Of living members of the Central Committee named in 1966, 81 percent were renamed in 1971; and in 1976, 89 percent. In 1939 averge age was 44. Each successive Congress has approved an older Committee: it averaged 50 in 1956, 56 in 1966,[56] and 60 in 1976. The aging of the Central Committee reflects the fixity of the official groups represented in it. Thus, in the 1971 report of election conferences of provincial parties, 137 out of 141 first secretaries were reelected; in party conferences between 1971 and 1974, only two first secretaries of 150 were dismissed for incompetence and one was demoted; at the 1974 conferences, only one of 150 was dismissed. All four of the unfortunates were non-Russians; two Ukrainians, one Georgian, and one an Uzbek.[57] In a mere six years after the fall of Khrushchev, the attrition rate of top party provincial (oblast) leaders was nearly halved.[58]

Communist leaders cannot easily withdraw from power because it has been their whole life. When relations are basically much more personal than legal or institutional, it is hard to hurt the faithful old colleague who always has tried to do a good job, even if his memory slips and he loses the thread of discourse, as Brezhnev sometimes did by the time he was elevated to the presidency in 1977. When those who are in charge of personnel are themselves getting on, everyone feels more comfortable to keep the old reliables around. It may also be, in view of the importance of the traumatic experiences of the past, that the older generation suspects (with some reason) that the younger is untempered and less worthy. The ruling nucleus in the Soviet Union, which came up in the years of the great purges, is unified by generational communalities.[59]

The quality of rulership is a grave problem for which the settled Communist state has no answer. Only an electoral system reliably avoids gerontocracy, and nowhere in the world do leaders have fixed terms without a constitutional process of legitimation, which is alien to the Communist system. Sooner or later the elders must pass; but they will not necessarily be replaced by much younger persons, as when a crown goes to a monarch's son. Leadership becomes not only increasingly feeble but also increasingly unrepresentative of society,[60] and an inherently rigid and uncreative system becomes more rigid and uncreative.

The makers of the Leninist Revolution did not intend to build a better state but to do away with the state. In the classless society, Marxism taught, there would be no superstructure of class control, hence no political state, only nonpolitical administration for the general welfare. Before the revolution, Lenin distinguished himself among Marxists by his insistence upon the "dictatorship of the proletariat" to put down the remnants of the older classes and to inaugurate the socialist order. But the supposedly proletarian dictatorship exercised by the party was to be a temporary improvisation. there is no Marxist-Leninist theory of the permanent state.

There has been no real inquiry in the Soviet Union, certainly not publicly and perhaps not privately, into the way political power should be managed, allocated, and renewed, how much power the party should have, how to assure that the most suitable persons are advanced, how power is to be shared between center and provinces, and especially how top leadership is to be chosen. These are not subjects for discussion because those in power have no desire to debate the limitation of their power. There are no known rules for selection by merit at any level; probably party politics select out moral character and integrity. Only occasionally, in the semivacuum left by the demise of a strong leader—especially after the ouster of Khrushchev—has it seemed possible to approach such matters in gingerly fashion; then there has been at best some understanding among the top elite, no public commitment or binding rules. There is no analysis of the way anyone, Lenin included, achieved power. At the height of de-Stalinization there was no evidence of discussion of how Stalin became able to commit his crimes or how he might have been restricted or removed.

Rulers have not been entirely oblivious to the problem. Khrushchev called at the Twenty-First Congress (1959) for rejuvenation of the party,[62] and he later instituted rules for rotation and limitation of terms. But these sensible regulations were never directed where most needed, at the top; and they were rejected by the party after Khrushchev. Brezhnev similarly has expressed awareness of the need for promoting new cadres,[63] but his actions have had the opposite effect. Communist leaders have no critical journalism and no published analysis of their system (except so far as they make use of Western studies) on which to base criticism. The social sciences are more or less limited to purposes directly serving the party. In China the study of history was taken away from the historians lest they draw critical political conclusions.[64]

The principal rules of the Communist structure, the status of the party, access to membership and to the inner circle of professionals, and the distribution of power near and at the top, are simply as they have silently and planlessly evolved in the effort of the party to assure and maximize its guidance of society, and in the drive of individuals to assure and maximize their positions within it. Marxism hinders understanding since it treats political conflict as a mere reflection of economic conflict. And if the state is to wither, why bother to think about its foundations?[65]

The only possible answer of the Communist to the problem of leadership is that the difficulty cannot exist because the leaders and the party are guided by Marxist-Leninist ideology. If cadres take their mission seriously, the system may function adequately, as many Communist states have functioned. But this implies that the situation is hopeless if ideology should fail.

IMMOBILITY

Authoritarianism is inherently conservative once the ruling group has brought under control what it needs to sustain itself. The Communist party, which set out to turn the world upside down, has become an instrument for the blocking of change. At least within the industrialized world, the most conservative states today are those that theoretically carry the banner of world revolution. The reversal is gradual, however. For some years, the capacity to remold society increases. Thus Stalin began his great transformation, collectivization, industrialization, and the general harnessing of the population some eight years after the Bolshevik victory in the civil war. Similarly, nine years after defeating the Nationalists, Mao was able to push his program of people's communes and the Great Leap Forward, which would have been beyond the capacity of the party shortly after the proclamation of the People's Republic.

But after the transformations mandated by the revolutionary program have been accomplished or have failed, the ponderous machine stalls. Thus in China there have been no new effective campaigns since the Great Leap of 1958–59, the Cultural Revolution having been not only destructive but also ineffective.[66] Khrushchev attempted many things, from partial decentralization of the economy to the planting of corn, but his big contribution, de-Stalinization, was negative. He proposed only patchwork reforms, and they were unsuccessful.

The Brezhnev government has undertaken no policy seriously hurting any important sector.[67] It has acted as broker rather than dictator and has avoided controversy, which means doing little. The efforts of Khrushchev's time to reshape the party structure have been given up. The biggest putative change, the economic reform of 1965, was hesitantly introduced, gradually watered down, and then forgotten. The party does not confront the past, as Khrushchev tried to do in de-Stalinization, or reconsider its tenets, but deals with problems from day to day by habitual methods.[68]

No individual seems to push anything in particular. At the Twenty-Third Congress (1966) it appeared that the party had lost not only the ability to act but also the ability to speak about problems.[69] There was no mention of either Stalin or Khrushchev, and practically no talk of any controversial matters. Subsequent Congresses have been even less animated. At the 1976 (Twenty-Fifth) Congress, the only sparks were contributed by a few foreign Communists.[70] No one remaining awake through the speeches could have guessed that the Soviet Union faced troubles of economic slowdown, agricultural failures, minority restiveness, growing crime and corruption, alcoholism, superannuation of leadership, and the like.

"Developed socialism," the state at which the Soviet Union allegedly has arrived in the Brezhnev era, suggests that there is little more to be done. There are no great expectations. When Stalin spoke, people stopped to listen because their lives might be affected. They half-listened to Khrushchev, who had some ideas. However, "with Brezhnev, no one listens at all," said a Muscovite as he and others ignored the loudspeaker in the park.[71] It was not even anticipated that the departure of Brezhnev would have any impact; the machine would doubtless grind on as before.

To be exciting, a book or film must be more or less anti-Soviet. Unlike youth in the West, Soviet youth (as organized) is wholly conformist. The Seventeenth Congress of the Komsomol (1974) saw no flicker of democracy or spontaneity and no discussion of controversial issues; even more than previous congresses of 1970 and 1966, it was an orderly party forum.[72] Even where it may seem agreed that there should be change, action is difficult. Khrushchev announced in 1961, "We are beginning to draft the new constitution of the USSR." After his political demise, the drafting commission renewed its labors under the chairmanship of Brezhnev, but the laboring mountain brought forth a mouse in June 1977. The new constitution proved to be a virtual copy of the old, with cosmetic changes and new propagandistic verbiage, plus the addition of a vice-president. The Stalinist words of the Soviet national anthem were dropped in 1956, but Soviet vocalists could only hum for their country at international events until 1977, when the respective commission produced verses slightly modified by the omission of Stalin.

The 50-year-old priority for heavy industry remains untouched. The collective farm system, well known to be inefficient, is unassailable. The Soviet state is nearly changeless; the few changes made are in the direction of further centralization when decentralization usually would seem more in order. The apparatus of party committees and departments, with local, district, and higher secretaries managing the government and other "transmission belt" organizations, remains frozen. The outward aspects of the state, with its ministries controlling the economy and administering the plan, are unaltered. The pages of *Pravda* or *Izvestia* look much as they did forty years ago, with columns of successes on the production line, exhortations to do more and better, and stories about evils and class struggle in the capitalist world. The language and vocabulary of the pseudo-revolutionary state softened only marginally as detente became the mode in Soviet foreign policy. It is never admitted that there has been any ideological change at all, just as it is never conceded that the party made any error. Lenin's works and thought remain canonical, and General Secretary Brezhnev expresses the official Marxist-Leninist view with no pretense of innovation.

The Soviet system is becoming like the old Russia of indolent quietism and horror of innovation. The Communist party is not designed for responsiveness to society. Consequently, when it ceases to move, it obstructs change. Its legitimacy increasingly rests on custom or fixity.[73] There are no independent organizations to crystallize opposition, and no levers by which independent forces can begin to pry open the closed and self-supporting political system.

It usually is necessary to change people in order to change policies; new leaders may bring new brooms. But the officials are increasingly fixed in Communist states. The personalities of those who rise through the machine, shaped by decades of indoctrination, become more stereotyped, challenging minds having been excluded by the selection process.[74] At the same time, the latter-day leader is surrounded by many senior party figures whom he cannot set aside; the immobile apparatus effectively rules.[75]

Stalin wisely warned in 1928, as he was becoming immune to criticism, that it would be disastrous if chiefs became immune to criticism.[76] Not only are Soviet leaders shielded from criticism, but genuine social and economic problems are either forbidden to discussion or can be treated openly only within circumscribed limits. All Communist systems, including the Yugoslav and Polish, make a fetish of secrecy. Almost any information, from disease statistics to telephone numbers, is likely to be considered a state secret. In some countries, secrecy even covers the identities of the principal officers of government, as in Laos and Cambodia. Quite inocuous information is withheld, such as the nature of the final illness of Chairman Mao. With far more reason, anything of a political nature is hidden in principle unless brought out (in possibly distorted form) by factional differences. Thus Stalin's contest for power and Khrushchev's differences with his colleagues shed considerable light on the inner workings of Soviet politics, as did the Cultural Revolution and the ouster of the Gang of Four for Chinese.

In the Soviet Union, the cost of living, wage scales, and the pay of bureaucrats are inadmissible subjects, along with so many others that the Soviet censors' manual has a 300-page list of prohibitions.[77] Problems cannot even be raised unless deemed convenient. The smothering blanket does not become smaller. Prices fixed in 1975 were kept secret, although those of 1955 and 1967 were published,[78] and sundry other economic data recently have been withheld, presumably because figures are unflattering. The 1976 yearbook of the *Large Soviet Encyclopedia* omitted the harmless little biographies of Central Committee members published since 1958. On the other hand, China, which was much more hermetic than the Soviet Union from the failure of the Great Leap until after the passing of Mao (1960–77), has become more communicative, releasing a fair amount of statistical data.

The party has difficulty in informing itself because information is distorted at each stage by the desire to please superiors. A Moscow police commander stated, "If I were to send in to police headquarters the genuine figures about crime in my precinct, I wouldn't last a day in my job."[79] Ideological fix, the doctrine of the superior knowledge of the party, compounds bureaucratic self-insulation. In times of Khrushchevian reformism (1956), the Central Committee was moved to improve intelligence by setting up an information sector. But people were irritated, it worked badly, and in 1971 it was severely limited.[80]

Immobility and inability to adapt imply the accumulation of tensions (or what Marxists call "contradictions") between the changing society and the unchanging regime. Inability to change inevitably leads to poor or irrelevant performance. For genuine stability, controlled instability is necessary. But as the system wears down, loses drive, and becomes less competent, change becomes at the same time more threatening, more difficult, and more necessary.

NOTES

1. The thesis of the bureaucratic ruling class of Communist countries unhampered by the political and economic checks at least partially effective in other countries is developed in extenso by Ota Šik, *Das Kommunistische Machtsystem* (Hamburg: Hoffman u. Camp, 1976).

2. John Stuart Mill, *The Subjection of Woman* (London: 1869), p. 229.

3. Roger Pethybridge, *The Social Prelude to Stalinism* (London: Macmillan, 1974), pp. 3, 304.

4. Joungwon A. Kim, *Divided Korea: The Politics of Development, 1945–1972* (Cambridge: Harvard University Press, 1975), p. 315.

5. Aleksei Myagkov, *Inside the KGB* (Richmond, Surrey: Foreign Affairs Publishing Co., 1976), p. 58.

6. Arrigo Levi, "The Evolution of the Soviet System," in *Dilemmas of Change in Soviet Politics*, ed., Zbigniew Brzezinski (New York: Columbia University Press, 1969), p. 138.

7. Jerry Hough, "The Soviet System: Petrification or Pluralism," *Problems of Communism* (March–April): 32.

8. Walter D. Connor, "Differentiation, Integration, and Political Dissent," in *Dissent in the USSR: Politics, Ideology, and People*, ed. Rudolf L. Tokes (Baltimore: Johns Hopkins University Press, 1975), p. 146.

9. Leonid Vladimirov. *The Russians* (New York: Praeger, 1968), p. 143.

10. Dimitri K. Simes, "The Soviet Succession: Domestic and International Dimensions," *Journal of International Affairs* 32 (Fall–Winter 1970), p. 217.

11. Murray Yanovitch and Wesley A. Fisher, *Social Stratification and Mobility in the USSR* (White Plains: New York International Arts and Sciences Press, 1973), pp. 5, 8.

12. As by Barrington Moore, Jr., *Terror and Progress, USSR: Some Sources of Change and Stability in the Soviet Dictatorship* (Cambridge: Harvard University Press, 1954), p. 189.

13. T. H. Rigby, "Politics in the Mono-Organizational Society," in *Authoritarian Politics in Communist Europe: Uniformity and Diversity in One Party States*, ed. A. Janos (Berkeley: Institute of International Studies, 1976), p. 37.

14. William S. Odom, "The Party Connection," *Problems of Communism* 22 (September–October 1975): 24–25.

15. Hedrick Smith, *The Russians* (New York: Quadrangle/New York Times, 1976), p. 249.

16. Robert G. Kaiser, *Russia: The People and the Power* (New York: Atheneum, 1976), chap. 4.

17. Abraham A. Krensler, *Contemporary Education and Moral Upbringing in the Soviet Union* (Ann Arbor, Mich.: University Microfilm Intl., 1976), p. 228.

18. Vadim Belotserkovsky, "Letter to Future Leaders of the USSR," in *Demokraticheskie alternativy*, ed. Vadim Belotserkovsky (Achberg: Achberg Verlapanstalt, 1976), p. 284.

19. *New York Times*, October 7, 1976, p. 8.

20. James C. Hsiung, *Ideology and Practice: The Evolution of Chinese Communism* (New York: Praeger, 1970), p. 94.

21. Simon Leys [pseud.], "Chinese Shadows: Bureaucracy, Happiness, History," *New York Review*, June 9, 1977, p. 17.

22. Orville Schell, "A Reporter at Large," *New Yorker*, March 7, 1977, pp. 54, 78.

23. Cited by Klaus Mehnert, *China Returns* (New York: Dutton, 1972), p. 218.

24. William N. Dunn, "Revolution and Modernization," in *Comparative Socialist Systems*, ed. Carmelo Mesa-Lago and Carl Beck (Pittsburgh: University of Pittsburgh Center for International Studies, 1975), p. 174.

25. Bogdan Raditsa, "Nationalism in Croatia since 1964," in *Nationalism in the USSR and Eastern Europe in the Era of Brezhnev and Kosygin,* ed. George W. Simmonds (Detroit: University of Detroit Press, 1977), p. 466.

26. J. Fiszman, "Poland: Continuity and Change," in *The Changing Face of Communism in Eastern Europe*, ed. Peter A. Toma (Tucson: University of Arizona Press, 1970), p. 79.

27. Ivan Volyges, in *Political Socialization in Eastern Europe: A Comparative Framework*, ed. Ivan Volyges (New York: Praeger, 1975), pp. 7–8.

28. Peter A. Toma and Ivan Volyges, *Politics in Hungary* (San Francisco: W. II. Freeman, 1977), p. 156.

29. Roy A. Medvedev, *Let History Judge: The Origins and Consequences of Stalinism* (New York: Knopf, 1971), pp. 539–40.

30. John Dornberg. *Brezhnev: The Masks of Power* (London: Andre Deutsch, 1974), p. 289.

31. See Hedrick Smith, "How the Soviet Elite Lives," *Atlantic*, December 1975, pp. 39–50. For vivid descriptions of the privileges of the new class, see Ilia Zemtsov, *Partiia ili Mafiia* (Paris: Editeurs Reunis, 1976), and Alexander Yanov, *Detente after Brezhnev: The Domestic Roots of Soviet Foreign Policy* (Berkeley: Institute of International Studies, 1977), p. 2. For a broad study, see Mervyn Matthews, *Privilege in the Soviet Union: A Study of Elite Life-Styles under Communism* (London: George Allen & Unwin, 1978).

32. Pravdin, "Inside the CPSU Central Committee," *Survey* 20 (Autumn 1974): 102.

33. Vladimirov, *The Russians* p. 151.

34. *New York Times*, April 13, 1977, p. A-5.

35. *New York Times*, November 3, 1976, p. 3; *Peking Review*, February 4, 1977, p. 15; Roxane Witke, *Comrade Chiang Ch'ing* (Boston: Little, Brown, 1977), p. 439.

36. A. Katsenelinboigen, "Colored Markets in the USSR," *Soviet Studies* 29 (January 1977): 77.

37. See Kaiser, *Russia*, chap. 4; Dornberg, *Brezhnev*, p. 290.

38. *The Samizdat Bulletin*, no. 36, April 1976.

39. Kaiser, *Russia*, p. 370.

40. Smith, "How the Soviet Elite Lives," p. 49; Vladimirov, *The Russians*, p. 155.

41. As detailed by *Weltwoche*, August 11, 1977.

42. Tai Sung An, "Korea," *Yearbook of International Communist Affairs*, ed., Richard F. Staar (Stanford: Hoover Institution Press, 1976), p. 318.

43. Eighty-five percent of entrants at Moscow University's Mechanics and Mathematics Department in 1969 received private instruction. *Komsomolskaia pravda*, August 27, 1969.

44. *New York Times*, May 14, 1978, p. 4.

45. *New York Times*, May 20, 1979, p. 7.

46. *New York Times*, April 3, 1976, p. 4.

47. *New York Times*, December 20, 1976, p. A-3.

48. Dennison Rusinow, *The Yugoslav Experiment, 1948–1974* (Berkeley: University of California Press, 1977), p. 343.

49. As observed by T. H. Rigby, "The Soviet Politburo: A Comparative Profile, 1951–71," *Soviet Studies* 24 (July 1972): 21.

50. For example, see Moore, *Terror and Progress, USSR*, p. 188.

51. William S. Turley, "Vietnam since Reunification," *Problems of Communism* 26 (March–April 1977): 38.

52. Mehnert, *China Returns*, p. 242.

53. Rein Taagepera and Robert D. Chapman, "A Note on the Aging of the Politburo," *Soviet Studies* 29 (April 1977): 296–305.

54. *New York Times*, May 24, 1976, p. 3.

55. Joel C. Moses, *Regional Party Leadership and Policy-Making in the USSR* (New York: Praeger, 1974), p. 9.

56. Daryl P. Hammer, *USSR: The Politics of Oligarchy* (Hinsdale, Ill.: Dryden Press, 1974), p. 421.

57. "Results of the Kraikom and Obkom Party Elections, January-March, 1974," *Radio Liberty Dispatch*, April 1, 1974.

58. Moses, *Regional Party Leadership*, pp. 185, 192.

59. John D. Nagle, "A New Look at the Soviet Elite: A Generational Model of the Soviet System," *Journal of Political and Military Sociology* 3 (Spring 1975): 11.

60. Blackwell, "Career Development in the Soviet Obkom Elite," *Soviet Studies* 24 (July 1972): 39.

61. For Poland, see Jan T. Gross, "Crisis Management in Poland," in *Perspectives for Change in Communist Societies*, ed. Teresa Rakowska-Harmstone (Boulder, Colo.: Westview Press, 1979), p. 156.

62. Wolfgang Leonhard, *The Kremlin since Stalin* (New York: Praeger, 1962), p. 336.

63. Peter Frank, "The Changing Composition of the Communist Party," in *The Soviet Union since the Fall of Khrushchev*, ed. Archie Brown and Michael Kaser (London: Macmillan, 1975), pp. 112–13.

64. Witke, *Comrade Chiang Ch'ing*, p. 461.

65. Zvi Gitelman, "Beyond Leninism," *Newsletter on Comparative Communism* 5 (May 1972): 34.

66. Harry Harding, Jr., "China after Mao," *Problems of Communism* 26 (March–April 1977): 18.

67. Hough, "The Soviet System," p. 32.

68. Peter Reddaway, "The Development of Dissent and Opposition," in *The Soviet Union since the Fall of Khrushchev*, p. 121.

69. Giorgio Galli, "A Bureaucracy under Fire," in *Soviet Politics*, p. 58.

70. R. G. Wesson, "The Twenty-Fifth Congress of the CPSU," *Current History* 71 (October 1976): 119–22.

71. *New York Times*, December 19, 1976, p. 7.

72. Otto Luchterhandt, "Der XVII Komsomolkongress," *Osteuropa* 25 (January 1975): 30.

73. Its great claim becomes the maintenance of order and unity. Richard Lowenthal, "The Ruling Party in a Mature Society," in *Social Consequences of Modernization in Communist Societies*, ed. Mark G. Field (Baltimore: Johns Hopkins University Press, 1976), p. 105.

74. Betram D. Wolfe, *An Ideology in Power: Reflections on the Russian Revolution* (New York: Stein and Day, 1969), p. 188.

75. Roy A. and Zhores Medvedev, *Khrushchev: The Years in Power* (New York: Columbia University Press, 1976), p. 183.

76. Roy A. Medvedev, *Let History Judge*, p. 538.

77. George R. Urban, ed., *Detente* (London: Temple Smith, 1976), p. 89.

78. *Business Week*, February 28, 1977, pp. 98, 102.

79. *New York Times*, March 5, 1978, p. 16.

80. Pravdin, "Inside the CPSU Central Committee," pp. 97–98.

4

PROBLEMS OF MANAGEMENT

PRODUCTIVITY

The prime excuse for the Communist state's negation of freedom has been that it was rapidly modernizing and building up the economy in order to bring the predicted era of abundance. Freedom was seen as a low-priority luxury. It was widely believed that the Communist system had a special recipe for accelerated industrial growth by planning the use of resources and compelling people to work for the future. This seemed evident in the early 1930s when the Stalinists were reporting fabulous increases in basic production while the Western world was writhing in depression.

With fluctuations, however, the Soviet growth rate has tended to subside since then. Partly because of the purges, it was rather unimpressive in the late 1930s. After World War II, reconstruction was vigorous, assisted by reparations and the forced cooperation of Eastern European countries. But the mobilization state became demobilized, and the last years of the Khrushchev era were lackluster. The Brezhnev-Kosygin regime raised the growth rate of industrial production for a few years, but the performance of the Soviet economy over a decade was not much above the world average.[1] Recently, economic growth seems to have come virtually to a halt. The Tenth Five-Year Plan for 1976–80 is the most modest yet, contemplating an increase of national income by 24 to 28 percent, which implies a per capita increase of 3 to 4 percent yearly. Housing and automobile production are to increase hardly at all. Yet modest goals have not been met. Official statistics tell of little or no growth in coal, steel, and various other basic indicators, while it appears that oil production soon will begin to decline.

Soviet factory labor is only half as productive as American, not so much for lack of adequate equipment as for poor organization and motivation. Moscow workers typically do half a day's work by Western standards.[2] Waste is enormous. For example, coal miners take only the richest deposits beause natural resources usually are not counted as a cost; 30 percent of coal mined is lost in shipping and processing.[3] According to a defecting official, 70 percent of fish caught is wasted because of planning rigidities and poor coordination.[4]

Agriculture is the weaker flank of the Soviet economy. Under Stalin, the state squeezed the peasantry to promote industrialization. Since 1965, agriculture has received heavy investment and has become, as in the West, a subsidized sector. Yet the country, a leading grain exporter under the tsars, regularly imports large quantities of grain. The lag continues because of weakness of incentives and overcontrol through the oversize farms, which are little dictatorships under the party-appointed chairman.

It is true that climate handicaps Soviet agriculture. But fields in Finland have yields of 50 to 100 percent more than comparable areas across the Soviet border.[5] The tiny household plots permitted collective farmers are many times as productive as the collective fields. In 1978 they provided two-thirds of the potatoes (most of the "socialized" potatoes being lost or damaged in picking), two-fifths of the eggs, and one-third of the meat and vegetables from less than 1.5 percent of the arable land.[6] The authorities still send army battalions and hundreds of thousands of students into the fields at harvest time.[7] After more than 40 years of mechanization, nearly 70 percent of collective farm labor is manual, and the percentage has improved only trivially in recent years.[8] Most vegetable production is said to be lost in transportation and distribution. Housing has improved in Soviet cities over the past decade, but eating has not.[9]

Soviet farms use twice as much grain to produce a pound of meat as do U.S. producers. The Soviet Union invests in agriculture several times as much as the United States without improving productivity.[10] In modern societies, output per unit of invested capital increases with the advancement of technology, but in the Soviet Union it has fallen in agriculture as in industry. The return from a ruble invested in agriculture fell by half in a decade, from 1.43 rubles in 1965 to 0.74 rubles in 1974.[11] The ratio of Soviet output to fixed capital fell from 1955 to 1975 by 60 percent.[12] According to a Soviet report, in 1975 40.8 percent of construction and assembly jobs undertaken were never completed; ten years earlier the figure was 1.7 percent.[13]

The system impedes technological innovation, much as change is resisted in the political sphere. For many years the Soviet state reportedly has produced several times as many scientists and engineers as the United States, yet it becomes more and more dependent upon imported technology. Despite the increasing politicization of institutes,[14] the prestige of science and engineering is still high, and huge sums are spent on them, yet results are meager. It was not always so. By 1938 the Soviet Union was the world's largest producer of tractors; Soviet farm machinery today is inferior in design. In 1935, the Soviets had the world's largest airplane and in 1954 an intercontinental jet bomber; recently, they have been wanting to buy wide-bodied jet technology from the United States, and they have tried in vain to break into the world civil aviation market. They made a strong effort to achieve priority in supersonic aviation, but they have had to discontinue the limited service offered by their imitation of the Concord. In 1954, they claimed the world's first nuclear power station; recently they have been seeking technology abroad.

The Soviet Union produced its first fission bomb in 1949, years ahead of U.S. expectations, and a fusion (hydrogen) bomb in August 1953, nearly seven months ahead of the United States. Soviet basic and applied physics and chemistry were at that time rated equal to America's by the Department of Defense.[15] The Soviets produced ICBMs in 1957. Their space program began with the first sputnik in October 1957 and continued to set records for several years; but the momentum wound down, and recently it has done little new. Computers long have been the grand hope of the planners, yet the Soviet Union is about a decade behind the United States in technology and has only about one-tenth of the U.S. stock. The latest Soviet guidance systems captured by the Israelis in the 1973 war used vacuum tubes, outdated in the West twenty years before.[16]

Khrushchev retreated from Stalin's drive for autarky, and the procurement of technology abroad increased fairly steadily after 1955, especially since the advent of officially promoted detente in 1971. From 1971 to 1975 Soviet machinery imports nearly quadrupled (in current dollars). The largest single import item, oddly for the country that calls itself the world's biggest steel producer, is rolled steel.[17] Since 1955 the Soviet Union, in its relations with the West, has become increasingly an exporter of raw materials, decreasingly of industrial products. Raw materials comprise 70 percent of Soviet hard currency earnings, 40 percent coming from petroleum alone.[18] Soviet indebtedness to the West may imply serious problems if the current petroleum export surplus gives way to a need for petroleum imports. All problems are compounded by heavy spending for military strength, which consumes at least two or three times as large a proportion of the national income as in the United States. To maintain a steady rise of defense expenditure in an economy that is growing slowly or not at all may require severe cuts of the standard of living.

It is no longer possible for Soviets to tell themselves confidently that they are better off year by year. If the Soviet economy is leveling off, it is at the modest level, in consumer goods and service, of a Third World Country, not an advanced industrial state. Fresh vegetables regularly disappear from October through May. Such basic and cheap staples as cabbage are often in limited supply and deficient quality in Moscow markets; meat was for the privileged in January 1980. Seventy percent of Soviet roads are impassable during the spring thaw. The vast Soviet Union has less paved highway than Ohio.[19] In 1977 there was an average of one filling station per thirty miles on the Moscow-Leningrad highway. There are only one-tenth as many telephones per capita as in the United States, far fewer even than in Hong Kong. The standard of living is low. Soviet store salesmen, a relatively poorly paid group, were raised in January 1977 to 71.60 rubles monthly, the price of a modest suit. Pensions earned after 25 years are about $33 per month for farmers, $55 for workers (with no food stamps), while prices except for a few subsidized items (rent, basic food) are high. The claim to have no inflation was true under Stalin; for some years prices were regularly reduced. But nowadays prices are frequently increased, in part openly, in part disguisedly. The proud boast that there is no unemployment in the socialist economy also has become falsified. Not only is there redundant labor in industry and underemployment in agriculture but also an outright lack of jobs in many places, especially Asian areas, where there are not enough new openings for the expanding work force.

Other Communist economies have shown a similar picture of more or less rapid growth followed by slowdown. When the Eastern European governments were new, industrial production rose rapidly under the Stalinist whip; but it has slowed markedly in recent years, and the return on investment has shrunk. The gap of living standards between Eastern and Western Europe generally has increased during the last decade. By 1979, the satellite economies were suffering chronic power shortages and inflation of 20 percent or more.[20] Even East Germany, the industrial pride of the Soviet bloc, has come into a time of economic troubles and stagnation with disaffection and political uncertainty.

To meet these difficulties Eastern European countries set ideological preferences aside to increase trade with Western Europe and the United States after 1970. They also have sought assistance in many forms, from joint enterprises to loans. Bulgaria solicited large credits from West Germany while proclaiming the "crisis of world capitalism," and Poland was able to raise its standard of living after 1970 thanks to large loans from both the Soviet Union and Western countries. But bills fell due, and by 1979 Polish authorities had to admit that the standard of living was declining, and there was little hope of improvement.

In China and Cuba the story has been somewhat different. In both, mismanagement and excess of political interference kept the economy from expanding for many years. The first years of the Chinese People's Republic (1949–57) showed excellent results, but under the Maoist priority for ideology there was subsequently very little growth of GNP per capita or the standard of living. The successors of Mao, with non-Communist candor, admitted backwardness, large-scale unemployment, even malnutrition of a substantial fraction of the workers. It was officially reported that only about one-third of all investment from 1950 to 1971 actually increased productive capacity. There are many beggars where tourists do not go, and grain rations are lower than twenty years ago.[21] Mainland China and Taiwan started from comparable levels in 1949; per capita income in Taiwan is now at least five times higher.

Castro's Cuba during its first decade was one of the very few countries to show a shrinkage of per capita real income. After the expensive failure to come near the goals of the 1970 sugar harvest, the government settled down, management was made more systematic, and production improved substantially. But by 1977, after the collapse of sugar prices, the economy was again admittedly in difficulties. Nearly everything was rationed, and rations were slim—an ounce of coffee per week, six pounds of rice per month, a pair of pants *or* a shirt per year, and so on, while a huge black market offered nearly everything at millionaire's prices. Yet Cuba was receiving a Soviet subsidy estimated at several million dollars per day.

There are many reasons for this disappointing performance. Far too much is drawn to the center for even modern computers to handle. For example, a Moscow office tries to control some 10 million prices, and apartment builders in Vladivostok must have plans approved in Moscow. The problem of getting and processing the needed information becomes worse as technology complicates interchange and production. Political priorities hinder study; in the Soviet Union there is no market research like that carried on by thousands of firms in the United States.

Industry has to satisfy not an impersonal market but administrative bosses, and there is no necessary penalty for inefficiency. It is difficult to displace workers either because of the technological obsolescence of their jobs or because of poor performance. There is not much to be gained from extra exertion, hence a certain lethargy is common. Anyone who works hard is apt to get a raised assignment and is subject to ostracism by fellow workers. *Die Zeit* reported (September 27, 1974) that ethnic Germans emigrating from the Soviet Union to West Germany found it difficult to shed habits of indolence. Planners have no way to determine just what should be produced in what quantities, how prices should be set without a free market, or how good management is to be rewarded. Politically named and motivated administrators cannot be expected to make the right economic decisions. There are no rewards for risk taking and only irregular penalties for poor management. The basic requirements of continued industrial advance seem to include research unhampered by dogma, a free flow of technical and economic information and criticism, rules of management conducive to initiative and innovation, recruitment of elites on the basis of competence, and security of management from political injuries.[22] But the Communist state cannot furnish these without ceasing to be Communists.

Political regulation may be desired for various reasons but it is burdensome for the economy, and in the past state-controlled economies have seldom proved capable of much innovation and growth. The Industrial Revolution was made possible by the relatively liberal and commercial atmosphere of eighteenth-century England, and loosely structured Japan could industrialize in the nineteenth century whereas bureaucratic imperial China could not. Attempts to socialize the economy have turned out badly in recent years in Burma, Sri Lanka, Egypt, Tanzania, Ghana, Zambia, Guinea, and so forth; nowhere in the Third World has state enterprise proved productive. There is no reason to suppose that state control of the economy will prosper better in the Communist state unless it benefits from ideological mobilization, not much of which remains.

Russian history shows several spurts of modernization, all stimulated by needs of defense and all followed by stagnation. The Leninist-Stalinist spurt was generated by political renewal as well as war, but it too seems to be running its course. Assuming no major upsets, there seems no way to prevent slowdown turning into stagnation and very likely regression. In the past decade many countries have shown that it is possible to get poorer in the age of technology. As though resigned to this fate, the system that proclaimed itself the way to abundance has turned around to preach the virtues of modest living and attack consumer psychology as an insidious bourgeois intrusion, leading to individualism and greed. Soviet authorities have found that rural people do not really want automobiles but prefer motorcycles with sidecars.[23] True happiness, the people are taught, lies in working not for oneself but for the collective.

The world of the future is likely to be trying, and all nations face severe problems of adjustment. But the Communist states are more rigid and less capable of innovation than the industrialized West.

DEVIANCE

In its better days the Communist state was notable for good order. Austerity was spartan; the law was harsh but effective; and such Western vices as speculation, pornography, narcotics, and street crime were hardly conceivable. In some ways Communist states still impress visitors as very orderly, but the past decade has seen a marked decline in the effectiveness of the state, probably in all Communist countries. Fear of authority has waned. People feel freer to ignore exhortations and injunctions, and the anarchic private universe grows at the expense of the party-controlled sphere.

The irregular economy also seems to grow steadily at the expense of the planned economy. Industrial managers cannot hope to fill quotas without going outside official channels for materials or equipment that the planners fail to provide. The profession of fixers (*tolkachi*) is legion. Plants overstate needs or fudge reports to get surplus materials to bargain for other materials (possibly for private advantage); Soviet writers admit that such exchanges are a "production necessity."[24] Frustrated inventors peddle their inventions privately.[25] In 1934 the Soviet government could get workers to put in multiple shifts at the cost of health and nerves. Nowadays workers come late, leave early, take off for a feast in honor of a deceased comrade, and resent anyone's asking why.[26] Materials and parts are pilfered; reports are inflated to earn bonuses; salable products are written off as spoilage, and so on, all despite an enormous expenditure of manpower to enforce the rules.[27] In 1976 there were reportedly 437,000 People's Control Groups in industry and 367,000 in agriculture fighting violations of economic discipline.[28]

The private, more or less illegal economy in the Soviet Union seems to amount to 20 percent or more of the official economy.[29] Private entrepreneurs, usually illegal but tolerated, offer all manner of services the state cannot adequately provide, especially repairs. All manner of goods are smuggled, unofficially (illegally) produced, or "diverted" from official channels.[30] Dachas are widely rented, patients pay unofficially for better health care, and most salespeople in shops supplement meager incomes by withholding desirable merchandise.[31] Many jobs, as in retail trade, have booome luorative and henoo are sold for thousands of rubles.[32]

Collective farm workshops may be operated practically as the private business of the chairman. Private entrepreneurs get big and bold; huge operations have allegedly flourished, especially in the Caucasus region. Freewheeling Georgian exporters of agricultural produce to central Russia even built a new road across the mountains to bypass official checkpoints.[33] The inefficiencies of official distribution are such that a load of fruit (illegally) transported to Moscow is worth a modest fortune. Private citrus growers seemed to have a monopoly and refused to sell to the state.[34] The Georgian boss Eduard Shevarnadze complained after four years of cleaning up, "Unfortunately no sphere of the republic's life has been untouched by the negative tendencies of the private ownership psychology."[35]

This may be considered part of normalization.[36] Maoist China, at least so far as the outside world knew, seemed free of such unsocialist behavior. After 1976, however, there were many reports of speculation, black marketeering, and labor indiscipline. Prostitutes reappeared.[37] Youth gangs and shoplifters were reported, and bank robbers apparently were regarded as folk heroes in the Robin Hood tradition.[38] Rusticated youths returning illegally to the cities became vagrants or outlaws. Chinese buyers at the Canton trade fair expected watches or even automobiles from Western sellers. According to a Chinese party paper:

Saboteurs, embezzlers, speculators, murderers, arsonists, grafters, swindlers, criminal gangs and others seriously have disrupted public order and engaged in beating, smashing, and looting, stirred up incidents, incited work stoppages, incited the looting of goods, and interrupted railroad transport.[39]

In the Soviet Union, the automobile creates a big gray-black market of its own; there is a secondary extralegal market in repairs, accessories, and tires, as well as parts, ordinarily obtainable only for a gratuity. The prohibition against selling used cars above official prices forces everyone to disregard the law. It seems impossible to prevent private cars from using official gasoline. According to a writer in *Izvestia*, more than one-third of private motorists drove on state-owned gasoline in 1972–73.[40] Recorded gasoline sales fell during 1970–76, despite a severalfold increase in the number of automobiles.[41] The automobile also facilitates private contacts, communications, and exchanges.

Officials who allot desperately needed housing at low rents have a valuable commodity for which they can extract something. Builders leave new apartments poorly finished, both in order to fulfill their plans more easily and to permit private carpenters and plumbers to finish up and correct defects. In a different fashion, teachers may leave gaps in their instruction so that their tutoring, or perhaps their influence, is more necessary for admission to desirable institutions.[42] In the absence of telephone directories, telephone numbers are salable. Censorship makes much literature, records, and so on black market merchandise; a Moscow postal censor could get rich by selling confiscated materials.[43] A Soviet paper wrote, after describing the thriving business of a "secondhand" market where most sales were improper by Soviet standards, "Is it no cause for alarm that they [young people] come under the influence of the morality that dominates the market, the morality that stresses monetary gain and the acquisition of material goods?"[44]

Under Stalin, when the parallel economy was trivial, one had to work for the state in order to live. Under Khrushchev it became necessary to pass various antiparasite laws, decreeing the obligation to work and prescribing exile to Siberia or confinement in a labor camp for those who refused. Dropouts perform private services, engage in trade ("speculation"), or work irregularly, when they please and at individually negotiated rates. Many go to the far north to work at high pay on odd jobs during the summer and pass the winter with the vodka bottle, in part, it seems, to escape the regimentation of Soviet life. Their number has been guessed at two million.[45] The magnitude of economic nonconformism is suggested by the large and rapidly growing gap between the Soviet adult population and the number of registered persons (who automatically go on the voter lists). The difference was 3.4 million in 1962, over 6 million in 1966, and 9.4 million in 1975.[46] Although these figures include those in mental institutions and labor camps, the majority, and especially most of the 6-million increase from 1962 to 1975, must be persons without regular employment and legal housing.

Mores evolve contrary to official desires. In ten years the divorce rate increased from 3 to 30 per 100 marriages. There apparently has been a deterioration of health care, because the infant mortality rate, after reaching a low in 1971 (at 22.9 per 1,000, compared to recent rates of 16 per 1,000 in the United States), has increased nearly 50 percent. The death rate for males over thirty, after declining up to the mid-1960s, has been rising since.[47] Much of the lower life expectancy for men is attributed to ever growing alcoholism.[48]

Despite continual exhortations to sobriety out of concern for productivity, if not health and tranquility, per capita sales of alcohol increased about fivefold for 1940–73. Universal testimony of the growth of drunkenness confirms statistical data that the Soviet Union leads the world in consumption of hard liquor.[49] Workers are permitted to stay on the job as long as they can stay on their feet, and "enterprise directors rarely enforce this law [authorizing discharge for drunkenness at work]."[50] The state can hardly outlaw hard liquor because that would give the market to the private entrepreneurs using stolen grain, sugar, and potatoes. In any event, it has been estimated that they produce half of the vodka consumed.[51] Moreover, the sale of alcohol is an important source of revenues (more than 10 percent of the budget) for the Soviet state, as it was for the tsarist; and outlets push it to fulfill their quotas.

The problem is similar in Eastern Europe. For example, per capita liquor consumption in Czechoslovakia nearly doubled from 1965–75. In Poland alcohol accounted for 24 percent of marketed goods by the early 1970s. Hungarians spend as much for alcohol as for meat.[52] Bulgaria and other Eastern European countries have shown similar trends.[53]

Rising alcoholism often is attributed to the tedium of the too thoroughly organized life, satiation with the political message, and the dullness of official art and literature. It is part of a growing disrespect for the norms of Communist society, manifestations of which are multiform and innumerable. Soviet youths shirk job assignments upon graduation, flee the farms, and shun manual labor. In 1970–73, 600,000 agricultural specialists were graduated, of whom 3,000 reported for farm work.[54] Muscovites take removable parts off cars before entrusting them to repair stations. Theft and crimes by officials have grown over the Soviet period, despite more laws and harsher penalties.[55] In Eastern Europe there has been a general rise of violent crime during the postwar period.[56]

Small bribes apparently are expected for almost any kind of official service in the Soviet Union, from a certificate of place of residence to nomination to a ministerial post in a Soviet republic, even for a bedpan in a hospital.[57] Tips are a necessity for nurses because of their low pay, 70 to 90 rubles per month. To bury the dead it may be necessary to pay not mere tips but hundreds of rubles in unofficial fees.[58] There are countless ways in which a foreman can help or hurt workers because of complex regulations, which offer countless opportunities to require tribute.[59] On a higher level, pardons are said to be for sale at prices that ordinary criminals cannot afford. A bad augur for the future of education and science is the sale (or award because of political standing) of higher degrees.[60] It seems that 170 of 200 students admitted to a Tbilisi medical institute resorted to bribery.[61] To get into law school cost about $20,000.[62]

The party from time to time attempts a cleanup, especially where corruption is associated with minority nationalism; corruption and black-marketeering are especially notorious in the more Asian Transcaucasus. It is too prevalent to be uprooted. To denounce abuses to authorities is risky, attitudes are condescending, and punishments are frequently light.[63] An official who tries to enforce the law is apt to find himself jobless.[64] Press organs can only call for more party control. Deviance is corrosive, although it has little direct political effect. A French journalist remarked, "I think the main worry of the regime is not the dissidents, it is the chaos, the disorder, the corruption spreading everywhere."[65]

In the words of a Soviet dissident:

> There flourishes here an unparalleled freedom from responsibilities; nowhere else are there more opportunities for shirking work, stealing from the state, and taking words for deeds than in Russia. Society demands little and man demands little of himself.[66]

Corruption, strictly speaking, is mostly for the lower elite; the upper level enjoys indefinite material privileges as perquisites in the mingling of public and private property.

OPINION CONTROL AND DISSIDENCE

The party has less to say to the people and says it less effectively. The press, broadcasting, all organized meetings, art, and literature are completely at the disposal of the authorities to be used for their purposes. However, so little that is merely interesting or amusing appears in the media that their utility as propaganda is seriously diminished. Soviet newspapers have only four pages, except *Pravda* and *Izvestia*, which usually have six. It is probably fair to say that the Soviet press in general seems to be written for persons of limited reasoning powers. Intellectuals despise it.[67] There is no attempt to arouse popular interest in the party and its activities except in a formal way. Censors are said to insist on woodenness of language.[68] Leaders are built up as statues, not personalities. People learn from the grapevine about such things as shortages or availability of goods, disasters, and interesting entertainment.

In the first years after the revolution and civil war, Soviet literature had a vibrant message, as seen in the poetry of Mayakovsky and such novels as Dmitry Furmanov's *Chapayev*, Isaac Babel's *Red Cavalry*, Mikail Bulgakov's *White Guard*, and Fyodor Gladkov's *Cement*. In the agitated

1930s, despite the imposition of Stalin's Socialist Realism, some powerful works appeared, such as Nikolai Ostrovsky's *How the Steel is Tempered*. The war evoked moving accounts by Konstantin Simonov, Ilya Ehrenberg, Alexander Fadeev, and others. But in the quiet years, conformist Soviet literature has remained largely a desert.

Within the official canon—simple, even simpleminded presentations emphasising socialist values, conflicts only between the proper good and evil, no individualistic characters—it no longer seems possible to produce much of genuine interest. There is consequently great demand for foreign, especially Western productions, legally or illegally obtained. As an incentive for turning in used paper, Soviet authorities offered six translations of Western works and one Soviet book, a satirical work published in 1928 by Ilf and Petrov.[69] Smuggled books, mostly nonpolitical, are a major black market commodity.

Few new Soviet writers appear; the Writers' Union ages along with the Central Committee.[70] To refute the admittedly widespread notion that Soviet literature was in a decline, the youth newspaper pointed to a galaxy of bright new poets; all of those named were over 40.[71] Politburo member Grishin criticized Soviet literature for "an absence of bright characters and modern heroes... the topic of class struggle is seldom broached."[72] There are no more stirring ideological films like those that made Eisenstein famous in the 1920s and 1930s. The most interesting recent productions are those that are as critical as censorship permits. Thus, a recent motion picture portrayed class distinctions, snobbery, and excessive concern with material goods; another starred a high-school history teacher who had trouble changing his course to suit the party line.

Previously forbidden themes such as personal love, alcoholism, despair, and loneliness, are allowed to creep into Soviet movies and literature (often for restricted distribution or small editions) in order to keep some life in the arts or to entertain the elite. Having fought Western music for many years, the authorities first permitted imitations, then spent hard currency to import Western rock recordings.[73] However, to the extent to which mass media become lively and appealing, they escape party control and undermine "partyness" by diverting from prescribed norms of thinking.[74]

In the 1960s Akademgorodok, the then new science city in Siberia, was vibrant; now it is party managed and gray. In Soviet education, "The inwardly secure and cowardly bureaucracy, fearing all fresh ideas lest there be something 'subversive' in them, thus artificially creates another sphere of criminal activity."[75] Enthusiasm being dead and fear having abated, the intellectuals see the party as having betrayed the ideals to which they were educated. According to published Soviet polls of the 1960s, government officials, journalists, and scientists evinced most disenchantment.[76] Few go into overt opposition, which they regard as quixotic and hopeless; many see themselves superior to the self-seeking party and its outdated message. They speak properly for official and public purposes and work dutifully for the state; in private they express themselves in the language of new philosophies and Russia's future, perhaps read uncensored works or write for the desk drawer, possibly send articles abroad to be published anonymously. Many fall into cynicism and take pleasure in pornography.[77]

The few who have become more forthright are following a Russian tradition since the days of Pushkin. Intellectual antagonism to the regime revived in the relatively slack atmosphere of the mid-1920s. Independent expression was crushed by Stalin, but total conformity ended as soon as the terror was removed. Returnees from the labor camps, accustomed to free speech and disrespect for authorities, also undercut the legitimacy of censorship.[78]

During the Khrushchev years there was little undercover literature or bitter protest because Khrushchev tried to infuse life into the Communist dream, was willing at times to engage in a dialogue with the intellectuals, and encouraged hopes for improvement. In the uncertainty of leadership shortly after his removal in October 1964, freedom of opinion came to a (relatively) high point. From the summer of 1965, however, the Brezhnev-Kosygin government started to reideologize and to arrest dissident intellectuals, especially those with minority nationalistic tendencies. The trial of two writers, Daniel and Siniavsky, early in 1966 for publishing non-Soviet (but not necessarily anti-Soviet) works abroad was intended to intimidate but had the opposite effect.[79] *Samizdat* (self-publisher), privately circulated literature, memoranda, letters, and so on, had been in evidence from about 1960; from 1966 it began to assume importance.

In 1967, Soviet opposition to Israel in the June war galvanized pride in the Jewish state, and catalyzed the self-awareness of the Jewish community, which furnished a substantial portion of the scientific and literary elite. In April 1968 a regular underground publication, *Chronicle of Current Events*, began giving factual accounts of repressions every two months. Defying the police for many years, it helped to sustain morale and tie together victims of the state. On August 28, 1968, 15 rebels mounted a demonstration against the invasion of Czechoslovakia, the first open anti-Soviet protest in Moscow in 40 years.

Since then the Soviet government and a small sector of the intelligentsia have been engaged in guerrilla warfare, with the government from time to time escalating its search-and-destroy missions. The opposition, armed with little more than moral force, has suffered many casualties and gained no great victories. Yet the number of sympathizers increased manyfold in a decade.[80] By the mid-1970s there were a dozen or so fairly regular *Samzidat* publications on the model of the *Chronicle*, and tens of thousands of pages of documents have reached the West. Many of the finest Soviet literary talents have emigrated, voluntarily or under compulsion, creating a new Russian expatriate community of recently exiled writers, scientists, and artists.

The dissidents include a small, probably declining sector of neo-Leninists or neo-Marxists (headed by Roy Medvedev), liberal-humanitarians (headed by Andrei Sakharov), growing numbers of religious-nationalists (headed by Alexander Solzhenitsyn), and seekers for more freedom in various directions.[81] Neo-Stalinists and extreme Russian nationalists are discreetly tolerated or even supported in high circles. Motives of dissent are varied, from disgust at falsification to friction with authorities over a trip abroad or irritation with arbitrary management of work and careers. The deadness of cultural and political life repels many; for some, the desire is less to oppose the system than to escape it. A major cause of discontent is the offense to moral dignity of having to repeat and live by what they feel to be a lie.[82] Many believe that to fight for world peace requires opposing the Soviet system. Russian pride plays a part. One dissenter wrote, "It seems to me that every political prisoner must daily feel upon himself the breath of history and his participation in it."[83]

Because of the lack of messianic convictions, the general desire of the elite for security, the preference for appearances of legal and constitutional norms, and concern for the Soviet image abroad, the police no longer execute dissidents as traitors, or even send them to labor camps without some sort of real or supposed evidence of law breaking. The commonest charge is the dissemination of anti-Soviet propaganda, which is anything the party dislikes. The freedom of the press promised 'y the constitution is frankly interpreted as "freedom to express through the press opinions serving the objective interests of the toilers and having as their goal the strengthening of the socialist system."[84]

Repression consists of a great variety of pressures, from friendly warnings through loss of jobs to arrest and confinement in a work camp or perhaps a psychiatric ward. It is capricious, ignoring some and hitting others savagely. It is fairly effective. Of the 15 demonstrators against the invasion of Czechoslovakia in 1968, only two were living free in the Soviet Union in 1976. A series of arrests and trials in 1977 and 1978 went far toward decapitating the movement. All members of the group monitoring compliance with the Helsinki agreements were removed by mid-1978, and 1979 saw a stiffening of persecution. Repressions are harsher in the provinces, out of sight of foreign journalists and diplomats; no one in Omsk would dream of taking the liberties assumed by a few in the capital.

The importance of the movement is difficult to estimate. The number of persons involved is not negligible. The University of Amsterdam has collected data on some 10,000. According to an émigré Soviet psychiatrist, 700 to 1,000 were confined in hospitals.[85]

For every person prepared to speak out, there must be a hundred, perhaps a thousand, sympathizers. It is likely that most Soviet intellectuals are skeptical in some degree. Scientists know they are valuable and have little respect for the party hacks who give them orders. They resent restrictions on travel and on communication with the generally more advanced centers of the West. True scientists are by definition independent minded, and to be independent minded is to be at odds with the government. The Academy of Sciences refused to expel such leading nonconformists as Sakharov and Veniamin Levich and to elect a leading Central Committee member, Sergei Trapezhnikov.

The movement may be significant mostly as the symptom of a broad weakening of control over the minds of citizens. It has publicized the repressive actions of the state and injected the idea of respect for law and individual rights into the atmosphere.[86]

Many persons are slightly rebellious without being politically involved. Theater directors, ballet dancers, and cinema producers are told how they should carry out their art by persons who know less about it; professionals are frustrated by censorship. Bolshoi stars are allowed all manner of foreign luxuries, but have to attend frequent ideological sessions and are permitted no creative latitude. The official Artists' Union is even more dominated by hacks than the Writers' Union, but a few painters want to invent and experiment with modern styles. A group of some 50 to 100 in Moscow and Leningrad has carried on a not always unsuccessful battle against censorship and Socialist Realism, painting as they please and stowing their canvasses or selling them privately. When they have managed to exhibit, people flock in, although the announcement is made only by word of mouth. Russian traditionalist painter Ilya Glazunov has won immense popularity. Authorities compromised by permitting some nonconformists to form a special section of the Artists' Union and to show their works. Writers engage in all manner of games, evading censorship in many little ways, such as allusions to classics or conditions abroad. In a bold case, a poetic lament for the death of the last tsarina was slipped into a Leningrad literary journal.[87]

It is second nature for intellectuals to be critical of the power holders of their society, unless there are strong claims on their loyalty. Material rewards draw and hold conformist mediocrities, but strong and original talents seem more and more to find themselves at odds with the structures that frustrate inventiveness and self-assertion. Soviet art schools reportedly reject exceptionally talented applicants because they create problems.

A sector of society turns toward the moral negativism of pre-Communist Russia; and similar movements of protest have appeared in Eastern Europe, their strength varying from powerful in Poland to very weak in Romania, Bulgaria, and Albania. Many hopes were crushed by the Soviet occupation of Czechoslovakia in 1968, but people have lost much of their fear. In Poland a half dozen organized opposition groups put out a score of uncensored publications more or less tolerated by the police, while students of Warsaw University have a "counter university" with lecture courses on forbidden topics of history and politics. East Germany has awakened from passivity to many expressions of discontent; the state often has preferred to exile nonconformist writers. Even in Romania there have been strikes and riots.

The Chinese have shown how apparent conformity may be deceptive. Visitors in the later years of Mao returned convinced that the people thought only of serving the state and the Great Helmsman, and that the Cultural Revolution had reshaped Chinese psychology. But when Mao's successors for reasons of their own permitted a "Democracy Wall" and some latitude of criticism, it appeared that many of the generation raised under Maoism were eager for freedom. Numerous underground or unsanctioned journals sprang up. In a few months China displayed something the existence of which no one in the West had suspected: a vigorous civil rights movement. The authorities, having promised complete freedom of posters and unofficial papers, turned around to rein in the movement, reassert the primary right of the party, and close Democracy Wall.

Communist regimes generally have ceased to demand that people display enthusiasm for the state, only requiring that they accept and fear it. Yet a regime must rely on the intellectuals to sustain the ideology, which always requires reaffirmation. However, it is more difficult to manage the new intelligentsia than to destroy the old. Partly because the struggle with the old regime is almost forgotten, it is harder to cope with those who were raised under the new system and see themselves as equal members of the new society. Coercion becomes more difficult as the ruling elite draws away from the dirty-handed masses and congratulates itself on its culture and education, qualities that distinguish the leading critics, while the children of the elite take pride in their non-Communist sophistication.

The dissident movement, however, seems not to be a revolutionary force. Like other political fashions, it has its waves of enthusiasm and discouragement. It surged in the Soviet Union in 1965–66 as a reaction to the withdrawal by Brezhnev of much of what Khrushchev had conceded, particularly after the Daniel-Siniavsky trial; disillusion made for bitterness.[88] There was a revival after the August 1968 invasion of Czechoslovakia. Detente in 1971 and afterward nourished new hopes. The Helsinki agreements of 1975 provided a document signed by the Soviet Union on which to base a case for civil rights. But people state their principles, agitate, expose themselves, and suffer consequences. There may be some slight concessions, but many are punished; and nothing is changed.

Samizdat seems to have become less political since the early 1970s. It recently has consisted mostly of complaints of personal injuries and protests against denial of the only right Soviet citizens may realistically claim, that of emigration. Writers beg the indulgence of the state and call upon the government only to moderate its conduct. They are rather timorous (with reason), and take a legalistic approach with authorities who are prepared to override law. They (necessarily) renounce the use of force against a regime that freely uses force and rejects peaceful change. They cannot even discuss means of action against the government.

The movement exists to a considerable extent on the sufferance of the KGB, which has its own reasons for keeping it alive but not allowing it to grow; the KGB may well create enemies to unmask.[89] They therefore do not crush the movement, as would be easily within the physical capacity of the state. A Romanian writer said: "Here everyone must make his peace with the security force sooner or later. I have done so. At least you stay out of jail."[90] Unlike the nineteenth-century Populists, the contemporary dissidents have no confidence in the masses and look down on mere workers. Sakhavor and his wife Elena Bonner, for example, gratuitously branded a workers' protest group as "not entirely healthy."[91] The workers are said to see the dissidents as members of the intelligentsia and hence parasites. They are tragic figures in a materially hopeless but morally satisfying battle.

They have no vision of the humane society or the road to it. The dissidents lack an ideological basis and carry on individual and incoherent moral struggles, with minimal means of communication.[92] The leaders are removed, by prison or exile, and the followers are immobilized by the fact that they are employed by the state. There are no calls for strikes or demonstrations; there is hardly any coordinated antistate propaganda. Samizdat speaks to the converted—it is dangerous to pass it to others—and asks for sympathy, not action. There are criticisms of distortions, failures, and abuses of the system, but few or no specific demands for change. Unofficial artists are commonly escapist and nostalgic. There is little to engage enthusiasm or mobilize the readiness to self-sacrifice. East Europeans know that they can do little more than keep sparks alive in hopes that Soviet armies one day will go home. Russians fear the anarchy that would come from a collapse of the system. Many of the dissidents disarm themselves by accepting basic premises of Marxism-Leninism, that is, the evil or at least decadence of capitalist society, the dangers of (Western) imperialism, and the necessity for socialism. Dissidents often insist that they are not trying to change the system, only asking it to live up to its own promises.

But if the dissidents have no means of casting down the system, they peck at its foundations, the myths and morale that distinguish Communism from less total and less demanding forms of government.

FISSURES IN SOCIETY

As the cement of the Communist system is eroded, cracks appear or reappear, despite all efforts to maintain a surface of solidarity. Community feelings are replaced by apathy, separatism, and factionalism. When the party can no longer focus life on its purposes, people turn to separate identities, to the family, ethnic groups, or religious competitors.

Various sectors, such as the armed forces, police, ministerial bureaucracies, managerial groups, trade union bureaucracy, and so on, become able in some degree to defend their own interests and develop their own approaches, which are at least a little different from those of the party apparatus. Organizations acquire institutional momentum, and as rigidity sets in they become difficult to move from outside. Even under Stalin, there apparently was some contention for power among leading groups; and Stalin seems to have played off party, state apparatus, military, and police for his own benefit. Disagreements, however, were kept veiled. Under Khrushchev it increasingly appeared that various interests could assert themselves.[93] A study of the publications of important groups showed clearly that they were able to express somewhat varying views, although no clear relationship between interest groups and decisions could be demonstrated.[94]

In the absence of either a positive mission or dynamic leadership, bureaucratic infighting is certain to increase, although it is mostly hidden because it is neither licit nor useful to appeal to a broad constituency. It seems that both military and security forces have capacities for pressing their own interests, arguing, for example, over whether navy or rocket forces should get a larger share of the defense budget. There even have been hints of independent actions of the KGB. Polish security forces have shown that they could pursue policies against the state when they desired.[95] The immobility of the Brezhnev regime may be ascribed largely to the ability of various sectors to prevent anything they dislike.

Sometimes there are notes in the Soviet press of discord within the apparatus. Thus, in January 1977 electric power personnel, vegetable growers, fishing interests, and dairy farmers were waging a "paper war" in the courts over the distribution of water in the Volga delta.[96] *Pravda* wrote of an order limiting timber cutting along the Volga, "But it is difficult to say whether the order will in fact be observed.... Kuibyshev foresters have to persuade the officials of the ministry to carry out their own order, since there is a notable tendency to violate it."[97]

Local organizations seem to gain de facto autonomy in the face of de jure centralization. As words and commands lose impact in the more relaxed society, local officials undoubtedly protect themselves and their cliques. Familyness can no longer be crushed as in Stalin's day. It also must be expected that the old divisions and non-Communist forces overlaid by the revolutionary ethos and social transformations reassert themselves and penetrate the ruling apparatus. Thus nationalism and religion, which is closely allied with nationalism in the Soviet Union and Eastern Europe, gradually recover strength and become divisive forces as they were prior to the revolution.

The makers of the new order regarded religion as backward and hostile, because it necessarily contradicts the essence of the Marxist-Leninist state, its philosophy and its legitimacy. On securing power, they assumed that the church would wither when deprived of support in the classless society and that the new truth would free minds of superstitions. Without waiting for the withering, however, they used a whole armory of pressures and compulsions to squeeze religion out of the national life. In all Communist countries except Poland they have had considerable success. But for a decade or more the tide seems to have reversed.

Observers agree that there has been an upsurge in Christian, Muslim, and Judaic religiosity in the Soviet Union. The state has introduced and solemnized Communist marriage celebrations and other ceremonies of life's turning points, a confession of failure of the rationalistic Marxist-Leninist approach. But a large part of the population accepts the risks and difficulties of religious weddings, christenings, and funerals. In a tribute to the attractions of Easter, the Soviet authorities schedule popular television and cinema programs, including Western imports, to draw people away from the traditional services; the crowds, however, are undiminished.

In the Soviet Union there are about 30 million Orthodox faithful, 5 million Catholics, 2 million Baptists and other Protestants, as well as millions of Muslims, all including many party members and their children.[98] Soviet sources have estimated that there are about 50 million adult Soviet religious believers or near-believers and have expressed fears of growing attachment of the youth to religion. Officials speak of the fashion for religion, hoping it is only a passing phase. It was claimed that official figures in 1972 showed nearly one-third of Moscow infants were baptized.[99] The proportion must be considerably larger today.

The attractions of the church and its mystique seem to grow, partly because it offers an alternative and an escape from the organized official existence. As Marxism-Leninism becomes increasingly vacuous and as a nationalistic conservative mentality grows, many intellectuals look back to the traditional Russian faith. The writer Vladimir Maksimov said in exile, "For the past two or three years there has been a great movement under way among us, people turn away from Marxism, they recover faith, radical faith."[100]

Although the largest church, the Russian Orthodox, is tolerated and tamed—the state has considerable control over the hierarchy—religious affiliation remains deviant. Religion is the least dangerous form of dissent; and religious rejectors of Communism are perhaps a thousand times more numerous than civil rights advocates. Many Orthodox are much more militant than the higher ecclesiastics. The discountenanced independent Baptists claimed an underground network of half a million to a million souls.[101] More or less forbidden sects have become bolder; various groups of

Pentecostals, for example, have demanded to leave the Soviet Union. Some church groups have illegal presses.

In Eastern Europe, religion has been subject to pressures of varying intensity, most in Albania, least in Poland, followed by Hungary. In 1974, nearly 700,000 Bibles were going yearly into Eastern Europe, a quantity five times greater than in 1966.[102] Church and state long have been engaged in a careful duel for the allegiance of the people. The state, while holding most of the material weapons, has been at times on the defensive. Official policies have softened in several countries. Hungary permitted an evangelical tour by Billy Graham in 1977, and the state radio regularly makes time available for religious broadcasts. The East German government, long abrasively atheistic, has promised full religious freedom, allowed religious programs on television, and sought church (Lutheran) cooperation in meeting social problems.[103]

The Catholic Church in Poland is the only really strong independent organization in any Communist country. With the support of close to 90 percent of the population, it carries on some of its historic mission of preserving Polish identity under foreign domination, and it thrives as never before. In the 1950s, the authorities were closing churches and seminaries, but now there are twice as many churches (14,000) as before the war, and 19,000 priests compared to 11,000. Nearly all children in the lower grades receive religious instructions as do close to half of those in secondary school. The Sunday sermon is the chief form of uncensored expression, and church-sponsored publications are the chief non-Communist (although censored) outlet. The church gives expression to popular complaints, and it has become a sort of umbrella for discontented intellectuals. It lends discreet support to workers' demands and the call for civil rights; for itself it wants legal recognition and freedom of broadcasting and publishing.

Relations of the government with the church are ambiguous. The party remains officially atheistic; but it cannot afford to attack frontally, because in case of disturbances, it could not count on the army. At the same time it would like to have the cooperation of the church in combating alcoholism and keeping up social discipline. Party leaders confer occasionally with church authorities; and they tried to make the Pope's visit in June 1979 their celebration also, turning attention away from economic hardships. The party seems resigned to coexisting permanently with the church; and the church has no desire to promote revolution, only to secure its own autonomy.

Religion in Poland speaks for a national cause against a somewhat alien political system, as it does in Hungary, Czechoslovakia, and elsewhere in Eastern Europe. Likewise, within the Soviet Union religion and minority nationalism are inseparable. For example, the Lithuanian protest against Russian domination finds expression in Catholicism; Jews reassert Judaism and loyalty to Israel as an ethnic affirmation; Islam for Central Asians represents the badge of difference from the Russian superiors. As a Soviet paper wrote,

> Islam, like any religion, often plays the role of "custodian" of reactionary national customs and traditions and arouses feelings of national exclusiveness... all this creates artificial differences in relations among peoples and separates them along religious lines.[104]

The problem of Soviet minority nationalism seems to become graver. The Russian Revolution began as a truly internationalist movement with a strong commitment to the equality of all peoples and the priority of the proletariat as a class over the claims of nationality. National origin was unimportant; Georgians, Jews, Poles, and Balts shared equally in high party councils and provided Lenin's firmest support. Until the mid-1920s a mostly non-Russian group formed the core of the party.[105] They were replaced during Stalin's transformations by a younger generation of largely Russian background and slight education. The Soviet Union has now become as Russian dominated as the tsarist empire was before it. The key positions are filled by Russians, who exclusively man the nucleus of power, the Secretariat of the Central Committee. Representatives of minorities (other than Slavic) are few in high political circles, and they represent mostly tokenism. Lenin was saved by Latvian units; now no Latvian units are allowed.

The state thus faces a problem of the management of the minority peoples by the Russian core, which constitutes less than half the population. Nationalism has revived since the late 1960s,[106] just as religion has revived, and for the same reasons.[107] There are numerous frictions over jobs for Russians or natives, use of Russian or the minority language, freedom to cultivate the local culture, control of local economic resources, and the growing gap between economic levels.

The powers of the central government are ample to assume the dominion of the central authorities, and the minority republics have been stripped of most of the little administrative autonomy that survived Stalinism. The answer to centrifugal forces is more centralization, although more centralization means more inefficiency and alienation. The minority sections of the parties are bound to obedience to the center. A Russian Second Secretary dominates minority republics, the military district commander is always a Slav, and only Russians (and Ukrainians) have all-Union political careers.[108] The economies are tied together, Russians fill the cities in minority areas (except the Caucasus), cadres and professionals are shifted around, the army is used as a melting pot, interethnic marriages are encouraged, and all manner of propaganda decries "bourgeois nationalism." There is enormous attention to the teaching of Russian, which is regarded as a means toward the merger of nationalities. Russian is taught in all non-Russian schools from the first grade up. The better schools everywhere are Russian, and it is necessary to become Russified to hope for a good career.

Official doctrine calls for "rapprochement" of the nationalities progressing to "merger," with a single culture (theoretically "enriched" by all the peoples but necessarily mostly Russian) in the single socialist Soviet nation. But according to the 1970 census, the percentage calling themselves Russians dropped during 1959–70 from 54.6 to 53.4 percent, the percentage of persons calling Russian their native language fell from 59.5 to 58.7 percent, and the percentage of Russians decreased in all Asian republics.[109] Under Soviet conditions, adherence to a non-Russian language amounts to an assertion of self-will.[110] According to a Soviet ethnographer, the percentage of persons in Central Asia not mastering the Russian language has been increasing; she called for reduction of the birthrate in Turkmenistan as well as intensified teaching of Russian.[111] Soviet Muslim communities are undeniably becoming more self-aware and drawing more apart from the Slavic majority.[112] Among non-Russian nationalities, endogamy is overwhelmingly the rule, and intermarriage is no threat to any major group.[113]

To promote the growth of an entirely Russian-speaking intelligentsia, in 1970 most minority republics decreed, by order of the central Ministry of Higher Education, that textbooks in higher institutions were to be in Russian. A few, including Georgia, especially proud of its language and ancient culture, managed to resist until 1976. The policy was implemented, despite protests, and the Georgian First Secretary addressed the Georgian party congress in Russian. But in April 1978 about 5,000 persons shouted against omission of reference to the Georgian language in the new draft constitution of the republic; the omission was rectified.

Despite the pressures, or perhaps in part because of them, there seems to be a revival of minority cultures and self-awareness, even among the party cadres.[114] Tendencies to nepotism, stability of cadres, corruption, bending of the law, and enfeeblement of ideology all improve the ability of the locals to go their own way. The Armenians, Uzbeks, and various other minority peoples have expelled borrowed Russian words from their languages.[115] Some Georgian nationalists allegedly have come to the position that they would welcome U.S. armed forces as liberators.[116] According to a Soviet writer, Ukrainians call themselves Ukrainian with increasing conviction, and more children of mixed Russian-Ukrainian marriages choose Ukrainian nationality.[117] A decree forbidding change of the nationality stated in Soviet passports can only have been aimed at persons desiring to drop Russian for a minority (probably Jewish) nationality.[118] Nationalist agitation has been almost incessant in Lithuania in recent years. In Estonia it is inadvisable to speak Russian if one wants service in a store or restaurant, and that area—the only part of the Soviet Union exposed to non-Communist television

(Estonian being close to Finnish)—has won a certain latitude in literature and art, which the Moscow government permits as the price for the high productivity of the republic.[119]

High party leaders sometimes stray into nationalist deviations. For example, Piotr Shelest was dismissed from his overlordship of the Ukraine in 1972 because he ventured to make concessions to Ukrainian sentiments, promoted the language, and tried to defend a slight autonomy.[120] There have been repeated scandals and cleanups in the ruling apparatus of various minority republics in the 1970s, especially Georgia, Azerbaidzhan, Armenia, and Central Asia. Mismanagement and corruption are charged, even though the principal concern is probably political deviation, somewhat as priests are accused not of practicing religion but of seducing girls or speculating in candles.[121]

Russification does not seem to solve the problem. The more highly educated Russian-speaking Tatars have been found to be the more nationalistic.[122] Modernization makes feelings more acute; the articulate nationalists are professionals and intellectuals of the cities.[123] Soviet Jews, who once furnished a large percentage of the leadership of Lenin's state, who speak Russian and were long voiceless and subdued, have turned away from a Soviet state grown anti-Semitic. Despite all manner of obstacles, hundreds of thousands have applied to emigrate; they submit to loss of jobs, manifold molestations, a long waiting period, heavy fees, and abandonment of property. In Stalin's day it was inconceivable that people should be allowed to leave the workers' state for personal reasons, but emigration of Jews has been allowed to increase to over 50,000 in 1979. Unfortunately, the desire to leave brands Jews as traitors in the official view; hence discrimination against them increases and more are driven to desire to emigrate.[124] Ethnic Germans, whose families had been in Russia for centuries and many of whom retained little German, also clamored to depart despite harassments like those suffered by the Jews.

Most other Communist states are fairly homogeneous. However, pressures of the Slovak minority were disruptive in Czechoslovakia in 1968 and had much to do with bringing Alexander Dubček to power and making possible the attempted liberalization. In recent years the Hungarian minority in Transylvania has become vocal after decades of silence, despite the Romanian insistence that all have to be true Romanians.

Yugoslavia has a minority problem comparable to that of the Soviet Union. The Serbs constitute only 40 percent of the population, the remainder being divided among a half dozen antagonistic nationalities. Tito's revolution, like Lenin's, was broad in spirit and truly pan-Yugoslav. Communism seemed to have solved the ethnic problem when the country was divided into six republics and two regions, and antagonisms were to be dissolved by providing much autonomy under party guidance. But first loyalty went not to the federation but to the ethnic republic. Separatist feelings rose in the late

1960s, and in 1971 only about 2 percent of the population called themselves Yugoslav.[125] In 1970 Croatia, richest and second most populous of the republics, launched a campaign for control of its resources. Other republics followed, until it appeared that Yugoslavia might be converted into a loose conglomeration. President Tito had to call upon army and police to defeat the nationalists and the liberals, technocrats, and intellectuals who supported them.

Like the desire for intellectual and religious freedom, the urge of national minorities for more autonomy is a major cause of disaffection. It is easy for Ukrainians, Georgians, and so forth to imagine that ills would be cured if only foreign domination were thrown off. Arbitrary government is doubly irritating when orders come from alien people far away, and the claim that all should be loyal to the party of the proletariat seems no longer relevant. The situation is worse for the Russians because the Central Asians, whom they despise, have a much higher birthrate and the percentage of Russians in the population declines steadily.

The nationality problem, like intellectual dissent and the religious revival, seems likely only to weaken the Soviet state, not destroy it. The central leadership has all the advantages of centrality and unity. The minorities are inherently at odds. Abkhazians riot against Georgians, and the Russians stand as arbiters over both. Ukrainians are involved in the system by giving them a role in the management of Central Asia. Baltic forces probably will be willing to suppress disloyal manifestations by Georgians, and vice versa; Asiatic troops were brought in to handle the Novocherkassk riots of 1962. Concessions of form are helpful; Central Asians are supposed to be grateful for being allowed to keep their language and customs. Economic bonds are promoted so that any real separation would threaten chaos, if not poverty. There are a host of cultural and poliical entanglements. Those who dream of cutting their homeland off from Moscow face the problem of breaking out of the tightest web the party has been able to weave. Estonians and other small nationalities, although wishing to preserve their heritage and increase their autonomy, seem to have little idea of independence—although their ambitions might grow if Soviet power crumbled.

The Soviet system claims to have solved the nationality problem. In a sense it has done so in keeping order and at least outward tranquility in a world where relations between unequal peoples are endlessly troubled. Communism functions, moreover, in such lands as Czechoslovakia and Hungary, where it is even more of a foreign imposition than in the Ukraine or Georgia; people bow to and respect force. Only the Leninist system could conceivably hold all these people together. It is possible, then, that the multinational character of the realm reinforces the Communist order. The lesser peoples are helpless, while for the Russians Communism is the means of sustaining their superior position and the status and livelihood of hundreds of thousands of officials.

Yet the minorities represent an unsolved and probably unsolvable problem for the Soviet state. This may be considered the last of the great multinational empires, since the Austro-Hungarian, British, French, and other imperial edifices have been dissolved. The Soviet Union, with a hundred-odd nationalities, also may be seen as the largest of the many multinational Third World states, like India, Pakistan, Indonesia, Nigeria, and other African and Asian states composed of dozens of more or less inimical national or ethnic groups. For the Soviet Union as for the majority of Third World nations, ethnic divisiveness is a long-term cause of weakness and major impediment to democratic government.

NOTES

1. Abram Bergson, "Toward a New Growth Model," *Problems of Communism* 22 (March–April 1973): 1–9.

2. Lena and Joseph Schecter, *An American Family in Moscow* (Boston: Little, Brown, 1975), p. 72.

3. Donald R. Kelley, "Economic Growth and Environmental Quality in the USSR: Soviet Reaction to 'The Limits of Growth'," *Canadian Slavonic Papers* 18 (September 1976): 279.

4. *Christian Science Monitor*, April 25, 1977, p. 2.

5. D. Gale Johnson, "The Soviet Grain Shortage," *Current History* 68 (June 1975): 248.

6. *New York Times*, April 17, 1978, p. 2.

7. *Krasnaya zvezda*, November 16, 1976, p. 1.

8. *Sociological Research* (July-September 1976), in *Current Digest of the Soviet Press* 28 (January 1977).

9. Peter Kenez, "Russia Revisited," *New Leader*, March 27, 1978, p. 11.

10. *New York Times*, December 11, 1976, p. 23; James R. Millar, "Prospects for Soviet Agriculture," *Problems of Communism* 26 (May–June 1977): 7–8.

11. *Vestnik selskoi nauki*, no. 10, 1976, p. 3.

12. Central Intelligence Agency, Directorate of Intelligence, *Soviet Economic Problems and Prospects* (Washington, July 1977), pp. 1, 4.

13. *Finansy SSSR*, August 8, 1977, p. 17.

14. According to a defecting physicist, "Science in the Soviet Union is completely dependent on the KGB and the party." *Los Angeles Times*, May 1, 1979, p. 13.

15. Stanley A. Blumberg and Gwinn Owens, *Energy and Conflict: The Life and Times of Edward Teller* (New York: Putnam's, 1976), pp. 272, 291, 386.

16. Kosta Tsipis, "The Calculus of Nuclear Counterforce," *Technology Review* 77 (October-November 1974): 41.

17. *New York Times*, March 7, 1977, p. 70.

18. Marshall Goldman, *Radio Liberty Research*, RL 9/77, January 10, 1977.

19. Paul Hollander, "Soviet Society Today," *Current History* 71 (October 1976): 137.

20. *New York Times*, November 1, 1979, p. A-2.

21. *Los Angeles Times*, October 21, 1979, p. 1.

22. Richard Lowenthal, "The Ruling Party in a Mature Society," in *Social Consequences of Modernization in Communist Societies*, ed. Mark G. Field (Baltimore: Johns Hopkins University Press, 1976), p. 86.

23. *EKO*, no. 2 (March–April 1977); 170–76, in *Current Digest of the Soviet Press*, 29 (May 18, 1977).

24. *Ekonomicheskaia gazeta* 34 (August 1973); *Current Digest of the Soviet Press* 26 (August 16, 1973).

25. *Sotsialisticheskaia industriia*, November 18, 1975.

26. *Pravda*, September 20, 1974, p. 2.

27. *New York Times*, April 13, 1976, p. 17.

28. *Kommunist* 18 (1976): 23–37.

29. Robert G. Kaiser, *Russia: The People and the Power* (New York: Atheneum, 1976), p. 341.

30. A general account is given by Dimitri K. Simes, "The Soviet Parallel Market," *Survey* 21 (Summer 1975): 45–52.

31. A. Katsenelinboigen, "Colored Markets in the Soviet Union," *Soviet Studies* 29 (January 1977): 70, 71, 76, 79.

32. Ilia Zemtsov, *Partiia ili Mafiia?* (Paris: Editeurs Reunis, 1976), pp. 33–35.

33. *Izvestia*, March 23, 1973.

34. *New York Times*, January 31, 1976, p. 10.

35. *New York Times*, May 11, 1976, p. 31.

36. Typically, there is nothing about corruption in G. Warren Nutter, *The Strange World of Ivan Ivanov* (New York: World Publishing Co., 1969); in the roughly comparable book of Hedrick Smith, *The Russians*, published seven years later, corruption in manifold forms is a principal topic.

37. *New York Times*, July 26, 1976, p. 11 and September 6, 1976, p. 26.

38. *New York Times*, August 23, 1976, p. 1.

39. *New York Times*, March 28, 1977.

40. *Izvestia*, January 1, 1975.

41. *U.S. News and World Report*, January 31, 1977, p. 54.

42. Kaiser, *Russia*, p. 35.

43. *Materialy Samizdata* 24 (July 28, 1976).

44. *Komsomolskaia pravda*, March 18, 1973: *Current Digest of the Soviet Press* 25 (August 29, 1973): 21.

45. Viktor Yakhot, "Refugees from Civilization," *Radio Liberty Special Report*, RL 78–77, April 5, 1977.

46. *Radio Liberty Research Bulletin*, 67/77, March 23, 1977, pp. 3–5.

47. *New York Times*, June 21, 1975, p. 8.

48. *Literaturnaya gazeta*, June 7, 1978, p. 11; *Current Digest of the Soviet Press* 30 (July 12, 1978): 16.

49. Vladimir G. Treml, "Alcohol in the USSR: A Fiscal Dilemma," *Soviet Studies* 27 (April 1975): 165. On this subject, see also David E. Powell, "Alcoholism in the USSR," *Survey* 16 (Winter 1971): 123–37; and Walter D. Connor, "Alcohol and Soviet Society," *Slavic Review* 30 (September 1971): 570–88. It should be recalled that alcohol consumption has risen considerably in the West also in the last generation.

50. *Literaturnaya gazeta*, April 5, 1978, p. 10; *Current Digest of the Soviet Press* 30 (May 10, 1978): 12.

51. *EKO* 4, 1974, p. 37, cited by *Radio Liberty Bulletin*, 467/76, November 10, 1976.

52. *New York Times*, July 24, 1978, p. D-8.

53. Walter D. Connor, "Deviance, Stress, and Modernization in Eastern Europe," in *Social Consequences of Modernization in Communist Societies*, pp. 188, 189. See also J. L. Kerr, "The Case of Alcoholism," in *Social Deviance in Eastern Europe*, ed. Ivan Volgyes (Boulder, Colo.: Westview Press, 1978), chap. 8.

54. *Trud*, May 11, 1974.

55. Peter H. Juviler, *Revolutionary Law and Order: Politics and Social Change in the USSR* (New York: Free Press, 1976), pp. 169, 172.

56. Connor, "Deviance, Stress and Modernization in Eastern Europe," p. 187.

57. *International Herald Tribune*, January 18, 1974, cited by *Radio Liberty Bulletin*, RL 67/77, March 23, 1977, p. 4; Konstantin Sims, "The Machinery of Corruption in the Soviet Union," *Survey* 23 (Autumn 1977–78): 39.

58. *Izvestia*, August 31, 1976.

59. Leonid Vladimirov, *The Russians* (New York: Praeger, 1968), p. 54.

60. Borris Rabbot, "A Letter to Brezhnev," *New York Times Magazine*, November 6, 1977, p. 56.

61. *New York Times*, May 7, 1978, p. 22.

62. *Newsweek*, October 10, 1977, p. 67.

63. *Pravda*, March 24, 1975, p. 4; *Current Digest of the Soviet Press* 27 (April 16, 1975): 22.

64. *Literaturnaya gazeta*, April 26, 1978, p. 13; *Current Digest of the Soviet Press* 30 (June 21, 1978): 17.

65. Michel Gordey interview, *Atlas* 24 (May 1977): 10.

66. Leonid Rzhevsky, "A Typology of Cultures Based on Attitudes toward Death," *Survey* 22 (Spring 1976): 52.

67. George Feifer, *Russia Close-Up* (London: Jonathan Cape, 1973), p. 28.

68. Alain Besancon, *The Soviet Syndrome* (New York: Harcourt, Brace, Jovanovich, 1978), p. 32.

69. *Sotsialisticheskaya industria*, September 14, 1974, reported by *Radio Liberty Dispatch* 318, October 2, 1974.

70. Wolfgang Berner et al., *The Soviet Union 1973* (New York: Holmes and Meier, 1975), p. 29.

71. *Komsomolskaya pravda*, December 17, 1976, p. 2.

71. *New York Times*, May 9, 1979.

73. *Christian Science Monitor*, September 28, 1976, p. 17.

74. Maury Lisann, *Broadcasting to the Soviet Union: International Politics and Radio* (New York: Praeger, 1975), p. 116.

75. Dimitri Pospielovsky, "Education and Ideology in the USSR," *Survey* 21 (Autumn 1975): 38.

76. Gayle D. Hannah, "Soviet Public Communications in the Post-Stalin Era, in *Change and Adaptation in Soviet and East European Politics*, ed. Jan P. Shapiro and Peter J. Potichny (New York: Praeger, 1976), pp. 138, 142. The publication of such polls was terminated.

77. Cf. Yuri Kuper, *Holy Fools in Moscow* (New York: Quadrangle, 1974).

78. Hannah, "Soviet Public Communications," p. 138.

79. Frederick C. Barghoorn, "The Post-Khrushchev Campaign to Suppress Dissent," in *Dissent in the USSR: Politics, Ideology and People*, ed. Rudolf Tokes (Baltimore: Johns Hopkins University Press, 1975), p. 52. See also Lewis S. Feuer, "The Intelligentsia in Opposition," *Problems of Communism* 19 (November–December 1970): 1–16; and Frederick C. Barghoorn, *Detente and the Democratic Movement in the USSR* (New York: Free Press, 1976).

80. Peter G. Grigorenko, *The Grigorenko Papers* (Boulder, Colo.: Westview Press, 1976), pp. 7–8.

81. Peter Reddaway, "The Development of Dissent and Opposition," in *The Soviet Union since the Fall of Khrushchev*, ed. Archie Brown and Michael Kaser (London: Macmillan, 1975), pp. 128–31. See also Abraham Brumberg, "Dissent in Russia," *Foreign Affairs* 52 (July 1974): 785.

82. A. Surrobov, "Longing for History," *Arkhiv Samizdata*, Doc. no. 1,641, 1973, p. 3.

83. K. Liubarskii, "Dear Friends," *Materialy Samizdata* 16, 77, June 21, 1977; *Arkhiv Samizdata*, no. 2,931.

84. M. A. Fedotov and E. I. Kozlov, "Constitutional Bases of Freedom of the Press in the USSR," in *Present Problems of State and Law in the Developed Socialist Society*, vol. 40 (Moscow: All-Union Juridical Correspondence Institute, 1975), p. 33.

85. *International Herald Tribune*, August 31, 1977, p. 1.

86. Valery Chalidze, "How Important is Soviet Dissent?" *Commentary* 63 (June 1977): 59, 61.

87. *New York Times*, April 28, 1977, p. A-9; *Aurora*, November 1976.

88. O. S. Fedyshyn, "Khrushchev's Liberalization and the Rise of Dissent in the USSR," in *Nationalism and Human Rights*, ed. Ihor Kamenetsky (Littleton, Colo.: Libraries Unlimited, 1977), p. 73.

89. Aleksei Myagkov, *Inside the KGB* (Richmond, Surrey: Foreign Affairs Publishing Co., 1976), pp. 74–75.

90. *New York Times*, September 3, 1977, p. 3.

91. David K. Shipler, "Crisis for Russia's Dissidents," *New York Times*, July 23, 1978, p. 34.

92. As remarked by Amalrik shortly after leaving the Soviet Union. *Le Monde*, June 30, 1976, p. 2.

93. As indicated by studies collected in H. G. Skilling and F. Griffith, eds., *Interest Groups in Soviet Politics* (Princeton: Princeton University Press, 1969).

94. Milton G. Lodge, *Soviet Elite Attitudes since Stalin* (Columbus, Ohio: C. E. Marrill, 1969).

95. Jacek Kuron, interview in *Der Spiegel*, January 17, 1977, p. 78.

96. *Literaturnaya gazeta*, January 5, 1977, p. 11; *Current Digest of the Soviet Press* 29 (February 9, 1977).

97. *Pravda*, December 19, 1976, p. 3.

98. *New York Times*, January 3, 1977, p. 1.

99. *Veche* no. 5, May 25, 1972; *Arkhiv Samizdata*, doc. 1230, p. 44.

100. *Die Zeit*, April 1974.

101. *The Samizdat Bulletin*, no. 25, May 1975.

102. *Christian Science Monitor*, November 26, 1974, p. 9.

103. *New York Times*, July 3, 1978, p. C-4.

104. *Turkmenskaya iskra*, May 30, 1976, p. 1; *Current Digest of the Soviet Press* (July 7, 1976): 1.

105. Roger Pethybridge. *The Social Prelude to Stalinism* (London: Macmillan, 1974), p. 4.

106. Alexander Yanov, *The Russian New Right: Right-Wing Ideologies in the Contemporary USSR* (Berkeley: University of California, Institute of International Studies, 1978), pp. 11–12.

107. For the conditions and attitudes of Soviet minority peoples, cf. Zev Katz, Rosemarie Rogers, and Frederic Harned, *Handbook of Major Soviet Nationalities* (New York: Free Press, 1975); and George W. Simmonds, ed., *Nationalism in the USSR and Eastern Europe in the Era of Brezhnev and Kosygin* (Detroit: University of Detroit Press, 1977).

108. John H. Miller, "Cadres Policy in Nationality Areas," *Soviet Studies* 29 (January 1977): 15, 25.

109. Rein Taagepera, "The 1970 Soviet Census: Fusion of Crystallization of Nationalities," *Soviet Studies* 23 (October 1971): 216–21.

110. Rakowska-Harmstone, "Study of Ethnic Politics," p. 26.

111. R. Goletskaya, "Directions of Demographic Politics," *Voprosy ekonomiki* 8 (August 1975): 151, 152.

112. Michael Rywkin, "Central Asia and Soviet Manpower," *Problems of Communism* 28 (January–February 1979): 13.

113. Wesley A. Fisher, "Ethnic Consciousness and Intermarriage," *Soviet Studies* 29 (July 1977): 399–400.

114. Rakowska-Harmstone, "Study of Ethnic Politics," pp. 21, 27, 29.

115. Ibid., p. 28; James Critchlow, "Nationalism in Uzbekistan in the Brezhnev Era," in *Nationalism in the USSR and Eastern Europe*, pp. 308–9.

116. *New York Times*, May 15, 1976, p. 9.

117. Yaroslav Bilinski, "Impact of Western Ukraine," in *The Influence of East Europe and the Soviet West on the USSR*, ed. Roman Szporluk (New York: Praeger, 1976), p. 215.

118. *New York Times*, October 14, 1974, p. 9.

119. Tönu Parming, "Nationalism in Estonia since 1964," in *Nationalism in the USSR and Eastern Europe*, p. 123.

120. Jaroslaw Pelenski, "Shelest and his Period in Soviet Ukraine (1963–1972): A Revival of Controlled Ukrainian Autonomism," in *Ukraine in the Seventies*, ed. Peter J. Potichnyi (Oakville, Ont.: Mosaic Press, 1975), pp. 283–99.

121. Stevan Hegaard, "Nationalism in Azerbaidzhan in the Era of Brezhnev," *Nationalism in the USSR and Eastern Europe*, pp. 190–91.

122. *International Herald Tribune*, October 13, 1976, p. 4.

123. Teresa Rakowska-Harmstone, "The Dialectics of Nationalism," *Problems of Communism* 23 (May–June 1974): 10.

124. Papers by Jews, previously numerous, have practically disappeared from mathematical journals. See *Science* 202 (October 20, 1978): 294.

125. George J. Pripic, "Commentary," in *Nationalism in the USSR and Eastern Europe*, p. 470.

5

FOREIGN INFLUENCES

TRADE

If the Communist state were encapsulated, it would age. But its difficulties are multiplied by interaction with a wealthy and powerful outside world, the ideas and practices of which are totally at variance with the Marxist-Leninist foundations. The leaders of the Soviet Union and the states that follow its example might prefer to live behind an impenetrable wall. But they cannot cut themselves off from the alien, basically disliked exterior universe. They can no longer even claim full control of their economies, as they depend on foreign markets and credits and import foreign inflation.

In the nineteenth century the tsarist empire required continual importation of technology for military and economic strength, while the elite desired to keep up, so far as feasible, to the material standards of the advanced world. It is far less possible nowadays to opt out of a world in which interdependence is ever more the price of progress. Since Stalinism reached its height about 1949, the Communist states have tended, at times hesitantly, at times more eagerly, to increase exchanges of all kinds, including tourism, cultural contacts, and trade. Especially since about 1970 and the official adoption of detente, the Communist states, particularly the Soviet Union, have become ever more involved with and dependent upon the world economic system.

Stalin wanted to phase out foreign trade, but Brezhnev at the 1971 party congress looked frankly to Western technology to raise the Soviet standard of living. Since then, Soviet foreign trade has grown twice as fast as industrial production, and trade with the West has expanded faster than with other Communist countries. By 1977, Soviet trade outside the bloc (mostly with

Western countries) was over half the total for the first time since the beginning of the cold war. The Soviet Union has made large investments directed toward foreign trade, such as gas pipelines, containerization facilities, and plants for processing imported materials.[1] For the sake of trade the Soviets were prepared at Helsinki in 1975 to accept potentially embarrassing commitments to cultural and personal freedoms. The importation of technology is important beyond its magnitude; the marginal productivity of capital goods from the West may be eight to fourteen times greater than that of the rest of the industrial capital stock.[2]

Business relations with the West extend greatly beyond exchange of goods. West German, U.S., and other corporations are involved in the construction of hundreds of industrial projects; thousands of foreign engineers and technicians work in the Soviet land for months or years. The Communist state has borrowed heavily abroad, and when new credits are sought hitherto secret information must be divulged.[3] Italians designed Moscow supermarkets, and a German engineer was hired to manage Soviet expositions.[4] Soviet rubles and the government paper *Izvestia* are printed on German presses. Soviet distributors copy Madison Avenue techniques.[5] The Soviet elite enjoy Pepsi-Cola bottled in Novorossisk.

To earn foreign currency, the state also reaches abroad. In 1978 there were 84 Soviet firms in the non-Communist world, mostly selling Soviet products, but also engaged in sundry money-making operations.[6] Soviet banks operate in many countries, not only financing East-West trade, but also lending locally on a large scale.[7] Soviet exporters work with Western traders, sometimes joining Western consortiums and cartels. Soviet shipping lines have undercut competition not only in East-West trade but also between non-Communist states. The Soviet Union has made a big business of trucking traffic to Western Europe, capturing a large share of Japan-Western Europe traffic by hauling containers across Siberia.

East European countries have been even more eager for trade with the West. All the bloc countries except Bulgaria increased the share of their trade with the West from 1967–76, in most cases precipitously; all but Hungary showed a declining percentage of trade with the Soviet Union. Since 1975 they especially have reached westward, with even orthodox Bulgaria welcoming American businessmen and going as far as possible into debt to capitalist nations. The recovery of the Polish economy after 1970 was based to a large extent on Western trade and credits. To get hard currency, Poland lures U.S. retirees.[8] In various East European countries, such as Hungary, it seems to be assumed that a new hotel requires Western participation. In 1977 Austrian, Italian, and American banks had offices in Budapest. Contrary to Soviet desires, the dollar is widely used in Eastern Europe.[9] East Germany has become more and more dependent on West German credits and trade concessions. In a form of economic assistance, West Germany has ransomed political prisoners for about $20,000 each, more for persons of technical training, to a total of several hundred million dollars. The Western mark is a coveted second currency in East Germany.[10]

China, in the imperial tradition, has stressed self-reliance much more than the Soviet Union. During the Cultural Revolution it drew back into virtual isolation, as the leftists around Mao, subsequently known as the "Gang of Four," tried to restrict trade and foreign contacts in general. But the result was economic slowdown. After Mao's death, the government of Hua Guofeng and Deng Xiaoping pushed economic development and foreign trade with extraordinary fervor. Huge trade agreements were made with any industrial country prepared to offer suitable credits, and thousands of Japanese and other foreign technicians were invited to help. By 1979 China was offering inducements to foreign corporations to set up operations in China with guarantees of profit remittance and tax exemptions, and foreign corporations were invited to bid for petroleum development. The Chinese offered to place advertisements for foreign corporations in any paper except the party organ *Ren Min Ribao.* China began exporting laborers to the Mideast and elsewhere, keeping four-fifths of their earnings for the state. Hundreds of Hong Kong firms established operations in China to take advantage of wages that were only a small fraction of Hong Kong levels.[11]

The effects of trade with non-Communist states and increasing dependence upon them are controversial. Communist rulers, faithful to their materialist philosophy, enter trade relations to serve their own interests. Lenin frankly invited greedy capitalists, for a handful of silver, to contribute to the building of socialism and hence to their own destruction, just as Count Witte, industrializing Russia in the 1890s, saw the Western nations hurting themselves by their willingness to furnish Russia the means of power.[12] Contemporary Soviet writers repeatedly urge maximum use of Western knowledge in the struggle for victory. Western writers contend that the Communists get the better of the transaction because they acquire advanced technology at much less than the original cost of development and often on generous credit terms. It also is argued that purchasing innovation and modernization from the West relieves the Communist state of the necessity of economic reforms to make its own system innovative; that is, it saves it from the penalties of its own vices and reduces the strength of internal liberalizing forces.[13] Foreign trade, which is more necessary for Communist economies because of their rigidities, lessens the need to reduce the rigidities.

To participate in the world economy, however, means entering the enemy camp, adapting in some ways to Western institutions and capitalist modes. Large scale equal and friendly relations with theoretically class hostile powers becloud the ideological picture and contradict the consecrated confrontation. Commerce fosters commercial values, which are ipso facto "bourgeois." The Communist system is made for isolation in a hostile world and is strained by contacts and compromise.[14] The citizen of a Communist country must wonder why a supposedly superior economic system should need goods from inferior states, or, even more, why foreign goods generally should be of far better quality. The more they trade with the capitalist powers, whose economic superiority is apparent, the more ridiculous the idea of the Communists leading a world revolution becomes. It is excessively Machiavellian to say that we buy your goods to revolutionize your workers.

Communist governments know this and publicize foreign trade only so far as it indicates their goods are wanted abroad. Foreign commercial representation is kept as inconspicuous as possible in all Communist countries except (partially) Yugoslavia. American businessmen find dealing in Moscow wearisome and expensive.[15] The government tries to isolate foreign trade from the rest of the structure.[16] Soviet merchant seamen in foreign posts are subjected to restrictions that must be irritating and humiliating for intelligent people. Soviet truck drivers in Western Europe are forbidden to talk to the natives, are authorized for only one trip at a time, and are forbidden to seek non-Soviet medical attention without special permission.[17]

The effectiveness of such measures is questionable, even if they could be strictly enforced. Calls for vigilance in connection with exchanges of all kinds become routine, and all well-informed Soviet citizens prize Western manufactures, often beyond their merits. The transfer of technology comes mostly through movement of persons, which the Communist regime most dislikes.[18] It is impossible to prevent many influential persons from coming into close contact with foreigners and absorbing impressions of the freedom and practicality of the representatives of the other world; the make-believe is vulnerable to reality.[19] Not infrequently they, like their tsarist predecessors, carry back in their coat pockets works of dissidents. Many of the Soviet elite profit psychologically, socially, and economically from travel to the West and the precious foreign goods they bring back; they are subject to moral corruption and gain a stake in detente.[20] That Soviet officials like to live and work abroad may be a reason for the recent proliferation of Soviet multinational corporations.

Many Russians become accustomed to Western methods and manners, and trade promotes habits of peaceful, realistic, nondogmatic dealings. It is no longer customary for Soviet negotiators to burden business negotiations with propaganda talks. Trade with the West becomes a career and a commitment for many influential citizens. Soviet economic ministries want more freedom to trade; the ideologists protest.[21]

Although foreign trade in some ways relieves the Communist regime of pressures to liberalize its economy, growing vested interest in foreign trade and technology becomes a habitual dependency increasingly costly to disrupt.[22] When credits are at stake, the government has reason to hesitate in repression, perhaps to bend so far (in the Soviet case) as to permit emigration of tens of thousands of Jews. Norway called off a new trade agreement with

Czechoslovakia because of reprisals against Charter 77 signers. Democracy Wall in Beijing probably owed its existence to China's need for credits and technology.

Currency and pricing problems, endless red tape and slow decision making, the layers of bureaucracy between buyers and users, and the lack of incentives for risk taking all reduce the ability of the Communist system to make the best use of import opportunities. Yet the Soviet Union needs goods Eastern Europe cannot supply, East Europeans need goods that the Soviet Union cannot provide, and in order to import they must have competitive exports. Hungary, for which foreign trade approaches half of GNP, can hardly return to centralized planning. The need to compete in world markets pushes even Czechoslovakia back a little toward the economic reform crushed by the Soviet occupation.

Communist leaderships must know that large-scale trade with capitalist powers vitiates their ideological picture and raises questions for their form of society; the commercially integrated world is not congenial to the self-regarding autocracy. It is not clear how fully they analyze this problem, the ramifications of which may not be brought to their attention. At any given time, immediate material benefits seem to outweigh distant and conjectural political drawbacks, much as a smoker may find that the pleasure of the moment overrides fears of future cancer.

CONTAGION OF IDEAS

Since Stalin's time, there has been an enormous growth of awareness of the outside world in the Soviet Union, and contacts between Soviet citizens and Westerners have become hunreds of times more frequent.[23] Some are fostered by Soviet authorities despite their negative implications: sports for international prestige, tourism for revenues, and cultural exchanges and scientific travel for the acquisition of knowledge. Other interactions the authorities cannot very well prevent, because of cost or attractiveness. For example, the jamming of foreign radio broadcasts has been largely given up in the Soviet sphere because it was expensive or ineffective or both. All but the most fundamentalist Communist states admit selected Western literary works and movies. They sometimes make a virtue of necessity and congratulate themselves on publishing far more Western literature than the West publishes of theirs.

In Stalin's day, the Iron Curtain was penetrated only by persons on official business and a few journalists; since then, ever larger numbers of persons have been traveling in both directions. In 1975, over two million visitors came to the Soviet Union from bloc countries, over a million from the West, the largest number from neighboring Finland, followed by West Germany, France, and Britain. Several million tourists yearly enjoy the sights of Romania, Hungary, Bulgaria, and other bloc nations. Tourism is an important source of the foreign exchange for which Communist states always thirst. Hence it, like trade, builds an interest in international tranquility and a good reputation; tourism it more sensitive than trade to public opinion.

The presence of tourists accents the fact that Soviet or East German citizens are not free to visit Paris and Rome. For the most part, foreign tourists are segregated, have no knowledge of the local language, and bring with them little in the way of political ideas. They cannot be entirely isolated from the local population, however, and crowds of tourists make problems for the authorities. Many citizens earn a nonsocialist living by trading currency, buying clothes, and so on. Newspapers imported for foreigners become partially available to natives. Along with sightseers come the persons of emigre background, relatives or expatriates, who can mix with and speak convincingly to the local people. They are especially embarrassing for East Germany, particularly after the 1972 agreements facilitated visits by West Berliners and West Germans. Because of the growth of nonconformism in 1976 and after, the East German government began to scrutinize applications more critically. Party and state officials were forbidden to have contact with West Germans.[24] Other East European countries, such as Romania, have taken steps to confine tourists to official accommodations.

Politically more significant is the granting or denial of permission to view life abroad. Policies vary; Albania and Asian Communist countries permit no outward personal travel at all. Yugoslavia is quite free; millions go and only a few blacklisted persons are denied passports. A million-and-a-half Soviet citizens traveled to Communist countries in 1975, and nearly a million (nearly all on official business and in organized groups) to non-Communist countries. East European Soviet bloc countries encourage movement within the bloc but restrict travel to the West, slackly, as in the case of Hungary and Poland, or strictly, as in the case of Romania and Bulgaria. The chief restriction on travel from Hungary to the West is the cost.

East Germany, whose people can fit easily into West Germany, is by far the most restrictive of the economically advanced Communist countries. Prior to the closure of the border with the Berlin Wall in August 1961, the hemorrhage of skilled personnel severely taxed the economy. At substantial cost and at the expense of its image in the world, the government built a fortified line along the entire border and thereby nearly ended the crime of "republic-flight." But the dilemma of the Communist state whose citizens are much aware of the outside world and feel themselves part of advanced civilization is stark. By denial of the right to emigrate, the state affronts the dignity of its citizens, lowers the credibility of its propaganda, and adds a new discontent, arbitrary denial of an important freedom enjoyed by peoples of civilized states. East German youths, obsessed with the idea of travel to the West, form the bulk of those who attempt to escape, often at the cost of their lives. The state has made it a punishable offense for a person of working age to apply for permission to leave.[25] In May 1978 East German officials were forbidden to travel to West Berlin even for business purposes. Nothing could contribute more to making West Germany seem a paradise.

The problem is less grave for the Soviet Union but nonetheless bothersome. Foreign travel is a privilege of the elite and a reward for conformity. It is feared both that Soviet citizens going to the West may absorb undesirable ideas, and that they may decline to return. The weight of these considerations is indicated by the fact that recently over twice as many have been permitted to travel to Japan (93,000 in 1975) as to France (40,000). The latter country is much more attractive and accessible to the bulk of the Soviet population; but Russians are much more likely to meet emigres in France, to read the local press, talk with people, and perhaps decide to stay. For the sake of prestige and money, ballet companies and orchestras are sent abroad, despite the fact that some frustrate the KGB and defect. The inability to travel remains a major grievance of those left behind. They long to visit cities such as Paris, London, and New York, not only for their snob appeal and material satisfaction, but also for the opportunity to buy goods not to be found at home. Since permission to leave is a reward of conformism, those who are favored must continue to conform in order to remain eligible. Selective issuance of passports is an instrument of party control.

Cultural exchange programs between Soviet and Western governments, especially the United States, have sponsored a growing number of visits, although the bureaucratic framework may actually have inhibited the travel of scholars, scientists, and artists.[26] The Soviet Union has tried to extract maximum benefit by sending physical scientists (90 percent of Soviet participants) to bring back useful knowledge, while most Americans going to the Soviet Union are in the humanities or social sciences. Soviet scientists and engineers who have benefited from the exchange program have evidently been impressed not only by U.S. technology, but also by the easy ways of U.S. scientists. They have been particularly critical of their own government, especially its restraints on travel and communications.[27] Only in scientific publications is there criticism of restrictions on foreign travel.[28] Because of fear of contagion, the Soviet Union formerly held aloof from world sports; the Olympic Games were scorned as a variety of bourgeois deceit. It was revolutionary when in 1952 a Soviet team went to the Helsinki Olympics. The Soviets did very well, approaching the American totals of medals and points. The leadership seems to think that the glory harvested at such events—the Soviet Union being an athletic superpower—is well worth the cost. Hardly any nation now sends more athletes abroad.

There are permanent Western correspondents in all Communist countries except Albania, Bulgaria, and the smaller Asian lands. Although their reports primarily influence foreign opinion, they have internal effects. Dissidents see their best chances in coming to the attention of the Western press. By contacts with journalists, they keep informed, find moral encouragement, and bring ideas to the attention of their fellow citizens via foreign radio broadcasts. Some 240 foreign correspondents in Moscow are a leaven in the intellectual atmosphere of the capital and a problem for the controllers. Journalists, like other foreigners, are housed in closely watched little ghettos. Theoretically, they should have official authorization for any contact with Soviet citizens, and every effort is made to hinder communication. The Soviets believe, or write as though they believed, that the Western press is an agency of propaganda like their own.

The economically more advanced Communist states are under pressure to admit Western publications. In Yugoslavia, leading Western papers and newsmagazines are freely and consistently available on newsstands, ordinarily without restrictions. Poland, Czechoslovakia, and Hungary have in recent years permitted fairly easy access to a few West European papers. The Soviet Union has claimed to do so but in fact has allowed only trivial numbers of such publications as *Le Monde* or the *London Times*, available only to a few foreigners. From the Soviet point of view, foreign news, even through the lens of Soviet journalism, is inherently a little unhealthy; and party authorities have tended to cut down on it. But it is of much interest, perhaps because it is more varied than domestic reporting. The Soviet press is apt to give more actual news of the world abroad than of the Soviet Union, concerning which there are only official pronouncements and more or less propagandistic reports. The magazine *Za rubezhom*, devoted to material from and about the outside world, has been exceptionally popular. Since 1957 China has published a *Reference News* of translations from the foreign press for officials and others. This is a classified paper that is kept out of foreign hands. Communist officials rely on the Western press for news of the world, including Communist countries. East European leaders questioned Western reporters and read Western papers to learn whatever they could about the ouster of Podgorny from the Soviet Politburo in May 1977. The Soviets had told them nothing.[29]

In Yugoslavia, Western movies and television shows appear practically to the exclusion of Soviet and East European ones.[30] Western films commonly dominate the Hungarian screen, despite the fact that there is pressure to show Soviet productions, which are cheap and obtainable in exchange for Hungarian films. Three-quarters of the movies shown in Poland are Western, while Polish movies are sometimes censored in East Germany.[31] The Soviet Union has been more resistant to audience pressure on the basis that Soviet films are good enough, but it imports foreign productions, especially those carrying an anticapitalist message. Cuba shows many U.S. movies while endeavoring to counter their ideological impact by interpretive commentaries. In 1978 the Chinese government began importing Western films for audiences starved of entertainment under Mao. English lessons on Chinese television have been extremely popular.

States have less discretion concerning the admission of foreign radio broadcasts. Asian Communist countries have few private radios, but shortwave receivers are easily available in the Soviet bloc. It is not clear why the Soviet state provides its citizens with shortwave receivers of Western propaganda; one reason may be that the radio industry is close to the military, politically powerful, and desirous of selling its wares. In any event the Voice of America, BBC, Deutsche Welle, the U.S.-financed Radio Liberty and Radio Free Europe, and others beam many hours of programs to Eastern Europe and the Soviet Union. Listening is not specifically forbidden, although passing on what one hears may be ground for prosecution in the Soviet Union. Jamming was first reduced and then halted by Khrushchev in 1963. It was resumed in 1968 at the time of the invasion of Czechoslovakia, a story that Soviet media did not know how to handle.[32] In the upswing of detente in 1973, jamming was again stopped except for Radio Liberty, whose programs are more penetrating and embarrassing than the blander output of strictly governmental stations. Jamming at best is much more expensive than broadcasting, and of limited effectiveness.

The dullness and uninformativeness of Soviet media create a big audience for foreign radio. Typical estimates are that one-quarter to one-half of the Soviet urban population listens with some frequency. According to a poll of Soviet citizens permitted to travel abroad, those of or near elite status listen most: Soviet officials, students, engineers, and technical workers.[33] The percentage among students was 77 percent. The Soviet press has frequently attested to the popularity of foreign broadcasts by reviling them, but any analysis of them implies encouragement to hear the other side.

Surveys of East Europeans abroad indicate large proportions of adult populations to be listeners, ranging from half in Bulgaria to three-quarters in Czechoslovakia. The audience is largest in times of crisis. Hungarian papers print Austrian television programs, and store clerks in Budapest sell radios by showing how well they receive Radio Free Europe.[34] Nearly everyone in East Germany is said to watch West German television. Estonia is in a parallel situation, and it is said that Estonians regularly tune first to Finnish TV for news.

The effect of foreign influences and ideas through these and various other channels cannot be assessed unless and until freedom of expression comes to Communist countries. It is difficult to convey a positive political philosophy by radio; the principal effect probably is to arouse skepticism. The dissident movement, however, could hardly exist without moral support and intellectual nourishment from abroad. Its morale rests on the knowledge that the informed opinion of advanced countries sympathizes with them and their cause. Even if Western verbal support means more intense repression, it helps them to reject the Soviet contention that they must be insane to oppose the state. As one said, "World opinion is what keeps us going, keeps us alive."[35] The Soviet press agrees. Jewish agitation for emigration is attributed to foreign Zionists, and dissidents are called foreign agents. A Soviet journal called them "a tiny group of nonentities who represent no one and nothing, are far removed from Soviet realities, and exist only because they are supported and eulogized by the West."[36] Brezhnev has warned that U.S. support for human rights in the Soviet Union might bring a new cold war.

Soviet dissidents learn about one another's activities more via foreign radio than directly.[37] The only means for protesting Soviet workers to get broad attention is via the Western media. The Polish government could not isolate and quash the riots of December 1970 because the whole nation became immediately aware of them through foreign broadcasts. It was perhaps for the same reason that the government reacted so promptly to placate the rioters of June 1976. Dissidents are also heartened by news of parallel protests in various countries. Soviet intellectuals, who were keenly interested in the attempted democratization of Communism in Czechoslovakia in 1968, expressed solidarity with the authors of Charter 77 in 1977.[38] The Czechs in turn were fortified by knowledge of movements in the Soviet Union, Poland, East Germany, and Romania.

Many groups in the West of all political persuasions, even Communist parties, decry repressions of protesters in the Soviet bloc. Andrei Sakharov was left in freedom for many years, despite his continual provocations of Soviet authorities, because the American scientific community stood behind him. The concern of such countries as Austria, Netherlands, and Norway made it difficult for the Czechoslovak government to deal severely with protesters in 1977. The foreign minister, Bohuslav Chnoupek, backed by the technocrats, was said to urge moderation for the sake of the country's international reputation.[39]

Human rights have become an international concern supported by moral pressure, and pacts and international documents have been very helpful to dissenters. The United Nations Declaration of Human Rights has been cited countless times, and the U.N. Human Rights Year gave the impetus for the appearance of the *Chronicle of Current Events* in 1968. The 1975 Helsinki agreement, promoted and signed by the Soviet Union, included, as a balance to Western recognition of the European political status quo, "basket three," which set forth the right to travel, the right of families to be reunited, the obligation to give journalists multiple entry visas, the desirability of freer flow of information, and respect for "fundamental freedoms, including freedom of thought, conscience, religion, or belief." In May 1976 a group was set up in Moscow, with branches in the Ukraine and Lithuania, to monitor fulfillment of the Helsinki agreement. The Soviet government has more effective means of handling its domestic critics than did the tsarist regime, but modern intellectual rebels have an advantage over their predecessors, international backing and publicity. Unable to isolate Moscow from the world, Soviet authorities have tried to check the flow of information between Moscow and the provinces.[40] The competition of foreign broadcasts also forces the Soviet media to be faster, more interesting, and more informative than they might otherwise be. Many events in the Soviet land have been reported by the Soviet press only after foreign publicity made it impossible to ignore them. Censorship slows news down so that the Soviet version may be late in reaching the public.[41]

If few rebel against the system, tens of millions dissociate themselves from it morally by preference for things Western. Hungary now has allowed jeans production there by Levi Strauss. There is something of a blue jeans youth international in the Communist world, not only in Eastern Europe but in the Soviet Union; tens of thousands use them in Moscow, although they are never to be seen in stores.[42] The Soviet state, like Hungary, surrendered to the extent of contracting for a U.S. manufacturer to build a factory for making two million pairs per year. Foreign books as well as clothes are a status symbol in the Soviet Union and an open sign of protest.[43] Youths want American lapel pins, soft drinks, and T-shirts with Mickey Mouse or American collegiate initials.[44] Western popular music means modernity. Since 1977 American rock groups have received wildly enthusiastic welcomes in various Soviet cities. Some young Estonians in the late 1960s and early 1970s followed their Western counterparts into the New Left movement.[45] East Germans are said to be unconditional admirers of things Western.[46] The Soviet state yields to foreign styles; it has taken up tennis and was recently building its first golf course near Moscow. Commercials on Soviet television look increasingly like U.S. ones, and Radio Moscow pushes pop songs to compete with the BBC. A Soviet toothpaste box carries a blurb in English: "Refreshes and cleans the mouth cavity well."[47]

The Russians, long accustomed to borrowing from the West and looking up to it, have come to measure their successes by comparison with the West. In the nineteenth century, educated Russians became ashamed of political backwardness. Nowadays, claiming to be progressive, the Soviet state talks of individual rights, freedom of opinion, equality before the law, and freedom of peoples, and pretends to respect them. Stalin killed millions without concern for foreign reaction. Now a prison camp inmate may be spared a beating if his plight is likely to be publicized abroad.

The Soviet leaders themselves seem basically to admire and envy the West, which they are much more fully informed about than are their subjects. The Soviet elite have an increasingly undogmatic appreciation of U.S. life and politics, although this is kept out of schools and the popular press.[48] Nikita Khrushchev, a man of peasant background and crude Stalinist education, came to believe, at a time when foreign contacts were much less pervasive, that the Soviet Union, as a great modern state, should be able to open its borders, admit foreign publications, and permit a choice in elections.[49]

A Polish paper expressed fears that detente might "make for a 'softening' of attitudes, a weakening of resistance vis-a-vis imperialism... a temptation to transfer the tactics of compromise to the ideological sphere."[50] The mystique and messianism of Communism-cum-nationalism are dissolved as bourgeois propaganda sows skepticism, individualism, worship of alien ways, and private ownership psychology, according to a Soviet military writer.[51] Repeatedly Soviet authorities warn their people against contamination by foreign visitors and radio, the consumer mentality, and other vices spread by the West. In 1971 Tito blamed Western influences for the decline of party spirit and the "rotten liberalism" of Croatia.[52] A deviant East German functionary saw the dullness of official propaganda leaving a vacuum for Western influences and forcing the state to treat the workers more decently. The beneficiaries of the system are vulnerable, too, because of their anxiety for respectability and passion for modernity.[53]

Modernization entails communication and the desire for more. Claiming to build the socialist society of the future, the Communist state cannot produce attractive and sophisticated native films, television shows, literature and styles, much less a full range of consumer goods. Yet as it begins to permit these things from abroad, its myths appear fraudulent and its special destiny a hoax. The ideological shield sinks, while low creativity makes foreign styles more attractive, just as the difficulty of innovations makes foreign goods and technology more desirable. The state cannot really afford to admit or to exclude foreign influences. When Nicholas I tried to isolate Russia, he succeeded mostly in weakening it. His successor opened the gates and improved the economy at the price of division and undermining the moral basis of the state.

THE INTERNATIONAL ENVIRONMENT

In various other ways the Communist state is affected by the surrounding alien world. For example, erosion of the solidarity of the formerly wholly obedient world Communist movement and the independent, more or less prodemocratic stance of some parties, especially of Western Europe and Japan, faces the Soviet leaders with a dilemma. They can either admit a right of pluralism in the movement they sponsor, or they can cut relations with important nonruling parties, with consequent loss of influence and prestige. Dissidents in the Soviet bloc can quote leaders whose credentials as Marxists-Leninists have not been revoked by Moscow.

Moreover, the Leninist revolutionary movement has been compelled to evolve by the realities of the international system. The revolution in 1917 initially saw itself not as heir of the Russian state but as the spearhead of the greater revolution to sweep Germany and Western Europe. The Soviet state has continued to this day to regard itself, officially or propagandistically, not as a mere state like "bourgeois" states, but as the leader of a movement of world revolution or (more recently) "world revolutionary transformation."

But the Leninist movement took possession of state power and made itself the successor of the tsarist empire, with a position in the world system of independent interacting sovereignties not unlike that of the old empire. To end the war in 1918 it had to negotiate peace with Germany. To buy and sell and to enjoy the prestige of belonging to the modern world after the civil war, it had to enter into formal relations with outside powers. By 1924 it had secured diplomatic recognition and entrée to the councils of the powers.

Since then the Soviet Union has tended usually to become more and more involved in dealings with other sovereign powers. But to deal as equals with powers regarded as ideologically hostile and morally inferior represents a degradation of principles and falsifies the pretense to special virtue and a supreme mission to reshape the world. This pretense and mission are fundamental to the legitimacy of the Communist state, and they cannot be entirely surrendered; but the mission is indefinitely postponed and ignored in practice. Throughout Soviet history, the state has gradually tended to behave less and less like a cause.

International interaction continually abrades the specialness of the Communist polity. Persons in high positions cannot fail to observe that states do not behave as they theoretically should and that Marxist-Leninist predictions are falsified. The Leninist theory of imperialism, for example, has shown itself to be a miserably bad guide. The need to carry on foreign relations brings to the Communist capital a sizable corps of cultured outsiders, who communicate with influential officials and leading personages. Delegations sent abroad for practical purposes can be partially insulated from the alien philosophy and way of life only at a cost to their effectiveness. Top leaders get to know foreign counterparts, possibly establish some personal understanding with them, and gain some sense of varying or contrary views. Until Khrushchev began his many foreign travels in 1955, Communist leaders did not travel to "bourgeois" lands. It is clear from his memoirs that Khrushchev learned a great deal from his meetings with foreign statesmen, especially his visit to the United States and talks with Eisenhower. Brezhnev has been as peripatetic as his health has permitted. The excursions abroad of Hua Guofeng are a landmark in the history of Chinese Communism. Leaders of the strictest Communist societies, such as North Korea and Albania, stay home except for a possible outing to an allied Communist state.

General secretaries abroad shed much of the rigidity of their ways at home. For example, in Bonn, Paris, or Washington, Brezhnev has emerged from the dour seclusion of the Kremlin to become a jovial backslapping politician, chatting freely with foreign journalists, and revealing a hundred minor facts about himself and his personal life that are withheld from the Soviet people.

The foreign travels of Communist leaders, proudly reported at home, do not harmonize with the broad thesis of inevitable and mortal class struggle; it is unconvincing to treat peaceful relations as simply an armistice in the ongoing contest. The Leninist state thrives on conflict and confrontation, but real conflict would endanger the very comfortable existence of the ruling elite. Peceful coexistence is easier, pleasanter, and more profitable. If consistently pursued, however, it leaves the Communist state with no credible enemies and tends to deprive the regime of its special character. For the Communist state to choose relaxation is to admit fatigue.

Prestige and the advantages of international intercourse require the Soviet Union and other Communist countries to join a host of multilateral bodies. In some, they may seek only advantages for themselves; in others, however, their presence is meaningless unless they are working for generally shared goals. International organizations, moreover, are models of the pluralistic society—forums of open debate, voting, compromise on issues, and independence of members. No regime can totally isolate its own society from its role in the international society.

Disagreement among Communist states also erodes the ideological world view; and Communist states, so far as independent, are at least as prone to quarrel violently as are non-Communist ones. When Yugoslavia broke away from the Soviet bloc in 1948, the Soviet interpretation was that the Titoists, recently admirable Communists, suddenly and for no reason explainable in Marxism had become fascists. For Yugoslavia the break was even more disillusioning; the great socialist model had unaccountably turned away from true socialism. Yugoslavia found itself seeking support in the capitalist West against threats from the noncapitalist East. Despite considerable willingness to swallow inconsistencies, the Yugoslavs inevitably downgraded and loosened their ideological fixations. Many persons in East Europe also were led to questioning of dogmas; if two supposedly socialist powers were at odds, truth ceased to be self-evident.

The Sino-Soviet split and the departure from the Soviet sphere of the majority of its population shattered the myth that international conflict was due solely to capitalism and that the end of economic-exploiting classes would bring eternal harmony. It also deflated the sense of inevitable victory. With the Soviet Union, China, and lesser states joined in a mighty union, it was easy to believe that the avalanche could only grow. With the two giants become each other's worst enemy, the world victory of Communism could come only over the corpse of the Soviet or the Chinese version. China, which previously berated the Soviets for abandoning violent revolution, sought accommodation with the United States, its former archenemy. The Soviet Union felt impelled to move toward better relations with the United States because of improvement of U.S. relations with China. China, fearing a Soviet attack, acquired a new interest in the international order. Romanian differences with the Soviet Union over Bessarabia, with Hungary over Transylvania, and with Bulgaria over Dobrudja contributed to the strongly nationalistic character of Romanian Communists.

The international contest implies a striving for power, prestige, and national interests, contrary to the basic ideas of the solidarity of the proletariat or the brotherhood of Communists. Soviet behavior on the world stage has been rather realistic from the beginning, but pretenses of standing behind the workers' movement and Communist parties were maintained, with decreasing intensity, into the Khrushchev era. Khrushchev, however, embraced Egyptian President Nasser as a brother while Nasser held Egyptian Communists in jail. Since Khrushchev, the Soviet leadership has weighed the interests of foreign parties lightly. For example, the Soviet Union at various times supported de Gaulle, Pompidou, and Giscard d'Estaing against the French Communists. In the Third World the Soviets, paying little attention to local Communists or the "socialist" convictions of national leaders, have been ready to assist almost anyone willing to cooperate with them for the destruction of Western influence.

A basic purpose of Communism is national strength, and Russian economic development historically has been a function of military exigencies. Needs of defenses and desires for domination force the system to be competitive; the Soviet leadership in effect asks to be judged by its strength. But the maintenance of strength ultimately engages the vital forces of society. The international interplay of powers, with the stakes of security, prestige, or domination, is basically realistic and anti-ideological. Real economic reform is more likely to come because economic failure means weakness than because of an inability to supply consumer goods. Purposeful systematic change in the Soviet Union is most likely if influential persons, especially in the armed services, become convinced that the party leadership has become too feeble or that the Communist order no longer can provide strength to play its proper role in the world.

The outside world in many ways tends to dissolve the specialness of the Communist political system: through trade, cultural penetration, the infiltration of alien ideas, the divergence of Western Communist parties, and feedback from participation in the international system. Such influences are effective to the extent that the once powerfully motivated revolutionary state loses dynanism.

NOTES

1. Marshall Goldman, "Cooperation in the Field of Economics: The Soviet Side and Basket Two," *Radio Liberty Research* RL 9/77, January 10, 1977, p. 1.

2. Philip Hanson, "Technology Transfer to the Soviet Union," *Survey* 23 (Spring 1978): 87.

3. Daniel Yergin, "Politics and Soviet-American Trade," *Foreign Affairs* 55 (April 1977): 538.

4. *Die Zeit*, June 24, 1974, p. 16.

5. *Business Week*, September 8, 1975, p. 41.

6. Herbert E. Meyer, "This Communist Internationale Has a Capitalist Accent," *Fortune* 95 (February 1977): 134.

7. *New York Times*, June 26, 1976, p. 31.

8. *Wall Street Journal*, February 25, 1977, p. 42.

9. *New York Times*, December 29, 1976, p. 6.

10. Helmut Zimmermann, "The GDR in the 1970's," *Problems of Communism* 27 (March–April 1978): 38.

11. *Wall Street Journal*, July 9, 1979, p. 6; *Time*, April 30, 1979, p. 75.

12. Zygmunt Nagorski, Jr., *The Psychology of East-West Trade* (New York: Mason and Lipscomb, 1974), p. 6.

13. As discussed, for example, by William Hayter, "Sovereignty, Appeasement, and Detente," in *Detente*, ed. George F. Urban (London: Temple Smith, 1976), p. 36.

14. Daniel Yergin, "Politics and Soviet-American Trade," *Foreign Affairs* 55 (April 1977): 523.

15. *Business Week*, June 25, 1979, p. 46.

16. John A. Armstrong, "The Soviet-American Confrontation: A New Phase?" *Survey* 21 (Autumn 1975): 45.

17. *Christian Science Monitor*, August 25, 1976, p. 3.

18. Joseph S. Berliner, *The Innovation Decision in Soviet Industry* (Cambridge: MIT Press, 1976), p. 515.

19. Boris Rabbot, "A Letter to Brezhnev," *New York Times Magazine*, November 6, 1977, p. 56.

20. As observed by Alexander Yanov, *Detente after Brezhnev: The Domestic Roots of Soviet Foreign Policy* (Berkeley: Institute of International Studies, 1977), pp. 3–4.

21. Jack Brougher, "Soviet Foreign Trade: A Greater Role for Trade with the West," in *Soviet Economy in a New Perspective*, Joint Economic Committee of the Congress of the United States (Washington, D.C.: GPO, 1976), p. 679.

22. Meyer, "This Communist Internationale," p. 137.

23. As noted by Alexander Dallin, "The Fruits of Interaction," *Survey* 22 (Summer–Autumn 1976): 45.

24. Zimmerman, "The GDR in the 1970's," p. 37.

25. *Der Spiegel*, May 2, 1977, p. 52.

26. François Bondy, "Cultural Exchange and the Prospects of Change," in *The Influence of East Europe and the Soviet West on the USSR*, ed. Roman Szporluk (New York: Praeger, 1976), p. 67. On the history and difficulties, see Robert F. Byrnes, *Soviet-American Exchanges 1958–1975* (Bloomington: Indiana University Press, 1976).

27. Robert F. Byrnes, "Soviet-American Academic Exchanges," *Survey* 26 (Summer–Autumn 1976): 30, 34.

28. Yakov M. Rabkin, "Measuring Sciences in the USSR: Uses and Expectations," *Survey* 22 (Spring 1976): 76.

29. *New York Times*, June 2, 1977, p. A-6.

30. Bogdan D. Denitch, *The Legitimation of a Revolution: The Yugoslav Case* (New Haven: Yale University Press, 1976), p. 3.

31. Peter Michielsen, "The Irrepressible Poles," *Atlas* 24 (July 1977): 50.

32. Maury Lisann, *Broadcasting to the Soviet Union: International Politics and Radio* (New York: Praeger, 1975), p. 114.

33. Ibid., pp. 126, 164.

34. Gayle D. Hollander, "Political Communication and Dissent in the Soviet Union," in *Dissent in the USSR*, p. 246.

35. *Time*, February 21, 1977, p. 22.

36. *New York Times*, March 2, 1977, p. A-6.

37. Theodore Friedgut, "*The Democratic Movement*," in *Dissent in the USSR*, pp. 127, 130.

38. *New York Times*, March 2, 1977, p. A-61.

39. *New York Times*, February 7, 1977, p. 4.

40. Valery Chalidze. "How Important is Soviet Dissent?" *Commentary* 63 (June 1977): 60.

41. Lisann, *Broadcasting*, p. 94.

42. Peter Kenez, "Russia Revisited," *New Leader*, March 27, 1978, p. 10.

43. Chalidze, "How important is Soviet Dissent?" p. 61.

44. *New York Times*, May 24, 1975, p. 8.

45. Tönu Parming, "Nationalism in Estonia since 1964," in *Eastern Europe in the Era of Brezhnev and Kosygin*, ed. George W. Simmonds (Detroit: University of Detroit Press, 1977), p. 119.

46. *Le Monde*, January 21, 1978, p. 7.

47. *Christian Science Monitor*, July 18, 1978, p. 3.

48. S. Frederick Starr, "The Russian View of America," *Wilson Quarterly* 1 (Winter 1977): 115.

49. Nikita Khrushchev, *Khrushchev Remembers: The Last Testament* (Boston: Little, Brown, 1974), p. 84.

50. *Wojsko ludove*, May 5, 1972, cited by Vernon Aspaturian, "Has Eastern Europe Become a Liability to the Soviet Union?" in *The International Politics of Eastern Europe*, ed. Charles Gati (New York: Praeger, 1976), p. 27.

51. *Kommunist voorushennykh sil*, no. 3, February 1977, pp. 9–23; *Current Digest of the Soviet Press* 29 (March 2, 1977): 5.

52. Dennison Rusinow, *The Yugoslav Experiment, 1948–1974* (Berkeley: University of California Press, 1977), p. 309.

53. *Der Spiegel*, August 22, 1977, p. 38.

6

LIMITS OF LIBERALIZATION

To judge from lamentations in their press, leaders of all Communist states have been dismayed by many shortfalls from expectations, such as the stubbornness of religion and minority nationalism, the growing ravages of alcoholism, rising crime rates, unruly youth, Western styles, and so forth. In response, they have made countless exhortations, launched innumerable campaigns, and essayed myriad remedies. But substantial reforms would cut into the structure devised to sustain the power of the party, and the capacity for reform declines. No European Communist state has made important political changes for a decade. Patchwork reforms have been mostly in the direction of centralization, that is, extending the edifice, or shifting secondary authorities, neither hurting nor helping very much. No Communist state has proposed (with the partial exception of Yugoslavia) any sacrifice of the authority of the center, and any reforms have been reversible.

Relaxations have often been undone or at least checked as the system reverted toward previous norms, such as in the Soviet Union, Poland, East Germany, and elsewhere. Maoist China had its Hundred Flowers period, when criticism was made free for a few months. The Cultural Revolution was the most violent attempt yet made by a Communist system to purify and renew itself. Both were reversed when they got out of hand. In 1968, Czechoslovakia briefly experienced the most rapid change of atmosphere and philosphy ever seen in the Communist world. It was possible because of the coalescing of many groups in the desire for freedom, including writers, economists, students, workers, Slovaks, and so on.[1] External force having cut it short, one can only guess whether the reform wave would have subsided into a reassertion of party dictatorship as inevitable troubles appeared.

Yugoslavia, upon breaking with Stalinism, embarked upon a broad devolution of power to local bodies ("self-management") and to the workers whom the party professed to represent ("workers' control"). In the latter 1960s it seemed as though a basically different, looser society might emerge; again the experiment was partly reversed by centralist forces, and party control remains unchallenged.

SOVIET UNION

The greatest of Soviet reforms was Lenin's New Economic Policy (NEP) introduced at the end of the civil war in 1921. The economy was in abysmal condition, with industrial production only a small fraction (perhaps one-fifth) of prewar and agriculture down to subsistence. The total controls introduced during the civil war ("War Communism") had broken down, and such trade as existed was mostly illegal. Lenin, against the wishes of most of the party leadership, freed trade, allowed the peasants to produce for sale, and encouraged small private enterprises to manufacture for the market. By inviting the people to cooperate in the reconstruction of Russia for their own benefit, Lenin probably saved the Soviet state. Production rose rapidly, and by 1928 average income and the standard of living were back to prewar levels.

Economic reform, however, was accompanied by political antireform, the stiffening of dictatorship. The remnants of organized opposition were outlawed, and the Menshevik and Socialist Revolutionary parties, which had helped the Bolsheviks during the civil war, were liquidated. Centralization, reduction or abolition of local autonomy, and strengthening of the party and state apparatus were the order of the day. Exceptionally, in 1925–27 some electoral freedom was permitted in order to get more peasant cooperation with local soviets; but non-Communists were elected, so the experiment was terminated and never repeated.[2]

By 1929 the party's instruments of rule had been set in place and Stalin's leadership was practically unchallenged. At the same time there had grown up a prosperous private sector of the economy; small manufacturers, traders ("speculators"), and successful farmers had become comparatively wealthy without any share in political power. Prudence might have dictated leaving them at work while exploiting them by taxation. The party stalwarts, however, envied them their possessions, hated them for their non-Communist outlook and mode of life, and feared them as potential claimants for a place in the state. They were also the principal support of more moderate, non-Stalinist sectors of the party. Moreover, the popular discontent that endangered the Bolsheviks in 1921 had been dissipated, and the economy was sufficiently prosperous to permit risks. Hence Stalin inaugurated a course of radical change to subdue the peasants by collectivization, an old goal for which the party had lacked cadres, organizations, and will to carry out earlier. He also destroyed the private trading and manufacturing that had grown up during the NEP years and mobilized everything for his economic plans.

The stern Stalinist system was rather effective in building heavy industry and in the war and postwar reconstruction. But its rigidity became increasingly suffocating in peacetime, and after Stalin and Khrushchev tried to open up slightly. Having partly demolished the exalted image of his predecessor, he decreed an extensive devolution of economic administration to the provinces, held "debates" on major questions, and made some liberal changes in party procedures. However, his decentralization was mostly undone even before he left office. The debates apparently did not decide much, the proposal to hold referenda was never implemented, and the changes in the party rules were annulled.

Not long after coming to power, Khrushchev's successors decried an economic reform designed to make profitability a major, or the major, factor in managerial decisions in industry. It was implemented and watered down at the same time, additional freedom under the plan being removed by additional extraplan controls. Where the reform was really applied, results were excellent. It was allowed to fail because managers proceeded to produce what was profitable at unrealistic state-fixed prices instead of what party authorities wanted them to produce, and because party bosses at middle and lower levels resisted giving up supervisory powers. If managers were able simply to buy and sell on the market, a whole hierarchy of profitable bureaucratic dependencies would collapse. An effort to promote efficiency by freeing wages similarly failed because party bosses resisted allowing workers to collect higher pay. Subsequent reforms have been mostly efforts to promote efficiency by combination.[3] But where the Soviets most urgently want results they permit freedom. Thus they let cartels mine gold as they see fit and pay very high prices for the output.[4]

The present system, under which Moscow tries to set millions of prices and enterprise managers are held to hundreds of mostly unenforceable indicators, is clearly ineffective. But any scheme for the autonomy of enterprises or guidance of production by strictly economic considerations would represent a major ideological retreat. A market-oriented economy would require freedom of information, and it would deprive a large part of the party apparatus of its justification for existence.[5] It would conflict with the Marxist-Leninist axiom that all property is collective and that no interests contrary to those of the party should exist. Centralization is desirable per se, and it is seen as strength.[6] Controllers regard reformers who would allow more autonomy or more reliance on market mechanisms as antistate, hence antisocialist. If consumers decide what is to be produced, the Kremlin does not. Relaxation of economic planning might permit oppositional factions to develop an economic base; it also could be dangerous for Soviet hegemony over its satellites.[7] The usual reaction to difficulties is to try to improve remedies under party control, that is, to centralize and extend controls, to amalgamate and eliminate competition as wasteful. Control of the economy is the basis of the political monopoly.[8]

In agriculture, there has been a long contest between advocates and opponents of turning land over to small groups of peasants who earn according to what they produce. It has been repeatedly demonstrated that the result of devolution is greatly increased production.[9] But it is seen as individualistic and ideologically bad, and collective and state farm administrations and ministerial bureaucracies are opposed.[10] A collective farm manager in Kazakhstan, I.N. Khudenko, who was very successful in an experiment in deregulation, drastically cutting labor costs and raising productivity, was hounded to prison for his pains.[11] An incidental reason that the bureaucratization of agriculture cannot be relaxed is that most peasants are non-Russian, hence potentially dangerous. From time to time, when meat or potatoes or garlic are in short supply, peasants are encouraged to produce more on household plots and bring it to town to sell. But they are never given any real security; perhaps they cannot be, because the authority of the party is unchecked.

Pressure for reform is overwhelmingly economic; not only are economic shortcomings pressing and tangible, but also the safest criticism is that the mechanism should be modified in order to raise the production graphs. Political reform is unmentionable. There have been controversies within the party as to who should exercise power, but there has never been a move toward sharing power with nonparty groups. Elections would become more interesting if there were some choice among party-approved candidates, but this would imply giving voters some authority and cause deputies to owe their position partly to the voters instead of wholly to the party. Censorship cannot be relaxed, even if the party were prepared to tolerate some criticism, because fissures in Soviet society would come to the surface. Moreover, too many shameful affairs of the past await exposure, beginning with German financing of Lenin's revolution and ending nowhere. It has thus far been impossible to rehabilitate even such victims of Stalin as Bukharin and Rykov, who were among those closest to Lenin. The party has difficulty even studying the possibility of reforms. Social science can be used only to learn how to manipulate, not to analyze the system itself, because the reality is too discordant with the precepts. Information gathering is suspect. In the 1960s there was an effort to learn about habits and preferences of Soviet radio listeners. The results were not flattering to the Soviet media, and opposition rose in party circles on the ground that the party should lead, not follow the masses; moreover, polls implied a right to divergent opinions.[12]

EASTERN EUROPE

Since the 1960s Soviet-dominated Eastern Europe (Romania chiefly excepted) has been aware of the widening economic gap with the West.[13] It was widely recognized that rationalization required more managerial initiative, more economic incentives, more competition among state producers, and more freedom for small-scale private enterprise. For this reason all Soviet bloc states have essayed economic reforms of varying depth, usually accompanied by some political and cultural relaxation; and reform movements have had more effect than in the Soviet Union, probably mostly because of more Western background and influence in the satellites. Bulgaria, for example, undertook some economic decentralization in 1966–68. It soon shrank back in fear of political consequences,[14] but in 1976–78, it was again tinkering with reform to reinvigorate the economy. Collectivized peasants were permitted to enlarge their personal plots, and incentive wages were introduced. Paradoxically, despite heavy investments, labor productivity was lower in high-priority branches of industry than in low-priority enterprises, because the former were more politicized.[15]

The East German New Economic System, conceived in 1963, brought about widespread delegation of management in the following years to let lower echelons make necessary decisions while achieving the purposes of the planners. The use of profits as main indicator of plan fulfillment was abolished in 1965 on the ground that it led to production that was not according to national priorities; but it was restored in 1967. The system brought rapid industrial growth, but recentralization began in 1969 and by 1970 the country was roughly back to the status quo ante of 1963.[16] Profitability was rejected as an economic indicator, and nothing was put in its place.[17] Small-scale private enterprise was encouraged a little longer, and in December 1971 there were 12,000 private or semiprivate enterprises employing 16 percent of the labor force. After 1972 only 1,000 remained, with 2 percent of the labor force.[18] The regime of Erich Honecker, who succeeded Walter Ulbricht in 1971, also reduced the political role of the technocrats who earlier had seemed to be moving into high decision-making circles.

Poland has been through two major cycles of decompression and recompression since de-Stalinization set the stage for change in 1956. Wladyslaw Gomulka, whose election as First Secretary represented defiance toward the Russians, began as a popular liberalizer. Writers and artists secured the greatest freedom in the Soviet bloc, perhaps more than in Yugoslavia. There were economic reforms and decentralization; among other changes, Workers' Councils were set up to bargain with management, and local administrations were given more latitude. The private sector of the economy was allowed to boom. But after a few years censorship was rehardened, and the freewheeling discussion that gave interest to Polish intellectual life was brought to an end. Ministries recentralized. Elected local officials lost power to appointed administrators.[19] Non-Communist parties became demoralized and political clubs disappeared.[20] The Workers' Councils turned into a token pretense of industrial democracy, used mostly by managers to increase production or to assist in bargaining with the ministries.[21]

Edward Gierek took over after the disorders of December 1970 with less of a commitment to liberalization than Gomulka once had. However, he at first promoted relaxation, more attention to popular desires, democratization, and broad consultation. Wider public participation seemed to be the panacea for social and political ills.[22] There was a general demand for reform in industry, the trade unions, the bureaucracy, and the party.

But Gierek gradually retreated from consultation; the party, instead of talking with the people, talked with itself. The administrative apparatus again withdrew powers from local government. A 1973 law enlarged party control of all facets of the electoral process. Indoctrination was stepped up, the press became grayer, and fidelity to the Soviet Union was again the order of the day.[23] The party settled back to old habits, and economic growth slowed down. A heavy capital tax was levied in 1974 on the already overregulated and burdened small-scale private enterprises;[24] new income and property taxes were introduced at the beginning of 1976. Party secretaries, made redundant by the abolition in May 1975 of some 300 districts, pressed for collectivization of agriculture to make new positions. The workers were thus again ready to riot when the government tried to raise food prices in June 1976.

The new, less serious disturbances led to a new, less serious reform wave. Private farmers received various concessions, and pressures toward socialization were dropped. Private production was called upon to relieve shortages: taxes were reduced, social security benefits were extended in the private sector, and entrepreneurs were allowed more freedom to hire workers. But there were no political changes to suggest any guarantee against whims of official policy or the caprices of minor bureaucrats, and the private sector languished. In 1978 and 1979 shortages grew and the GNP declined, but Gierek told the nation at the party congress of February 1980 that it must merely drink less and work more; no basic changes could be made.[25]

Since the dolorous experience of 1956, Hungary has found its way to the widest relaxation in the Soviet bloc. Janos Kadar, in a policy of national reconciliation, introduced a New Economic Mechanism in 1968–69. Private small-scale enterprise in trade and industry was allowed more scope, and the profit motive was introduced for state enterprises. Planning is slack; firms bid against one another for talent, introduce new products, and manage as they see fit so long as they manage efficiently.[26] Trade unions bargain over wages and working conditions, although they may not strike. Central price fixing was much reduced. Emphasis was shifted to production for the market; consumers benefited from fuller shops and better merchandise; the standard of living rose substantially. Management of collective farms also has been loosened, and peasants were encouraged to produce on their private plots. These include an exceptionally large proportion (18 percent) of cultivated land and account for half of agricultural production.[27] Some peasants have become rather rich by local standards.

There has also been some political relaxation. The government opened the frontiers more than those of any other country of the bloc, depoliticized life, and made gestures of democratization.[28] There are sometimes more electoral candidates (all party approved) than places to be filled, people talk fairly openly, and the press criticizes administration, although not policies or principles. There is no censorship, only authors' and publishers' responsibility for what they publish; everyone knows the limits of dissent. Hence there is little samizdat. The result was popular acceptance of the government as the best to be expected, and some satisfaction with the materially improved life. Many persons, not only bureaucrats and party bosses but managers fearful of competition, trade union leaders, and wealthy profiteers, like things as they are.[29]

Yet the New Economic Mechanism has come under pressure since 1972, especially with the decline of growth after 1974. Because of state-induced shortages, some got rich by speculation in scarce goods or by production for a starved market. Small-scale artisans or entrepreneurs earn much more than regular state workers, and workers moonlight to the neglect of regular jobs. Since rationalization and competition imply freedom to discharge workers, unemployment has come to the socialist market economy. Workers demand equalization of wages instead of payment for productivity.[30] Party cadres see dealers and adventurers buying villas the loyal party servants cannot afford. Some prices rise sharply, despite enormous expenditures on subsidies, and inflation outpaces wages for many. More private money-making means more money for bribery and corruption. Party people denounce their society as unequal, bureaucratized, bourgeoisified, and consumer oriented.

The political reforms also lose allure. There are few contests, even formal ones, for seats in the powerless parliament, and little pretense of a campaign.[31] The new middle class, prospering from the limited economic freedom, is indifferent to the political order that no one expects to be able to change. Local officials sabotage official policy for improving relations with the church and harass small farmers and private artisans. The number of private entrepreneurs declines from year to year.

YUGOSLAVIA

Yugoslavia demonstrates how far a Communist party can go in adopting non-Communist forms without renouncing the essence of power.

After 1949, fully convinced that reconciliation with Stalin was impossible and economically hard-pressed, Tito undertook to build popular support and to justify independent Communism. The Titoists went back to Marx's notion of a society managed by "free associations of producers,"[32] and the role of the party was reassessed. Thus Yugoslavia in 1949–52 developed its own Communism, characterized by doctrines of "self-management" and "workers' control."

Towns, communes, provinces, and national republics composing Yugoslavia were given considerable autonomy. The workers, supposedly the ruling class under socialism, were told that they should manage, through their elected representatives, the factories and other enterprises in which they worked. Such measures were at first taken seriously by neither workers nor party officials. But they gradually acquired significance, and self-management became practically an ideology, the essence of Yugoslav socialism. Mandatory planning of the economy was abandoned. Collectivization of agriculture was mostly undone, and the peasants were allowed to sell their crops. Borders were opened. The press was given considerable latitude so long as it refrained from criticism of high figures and party policy. People were permitted to form private organizations, provided they did not oppose the Communist party (renamed "League of Yugoslav Communists" to differentiate it from the Soviet party). The party, membership in which was opened to almost anyone, was to refrain from Leninist-style control and to limit itself to general and long-range guidance.[33] Many organized pressure groups grew up. The "socialist market economy" introduced in 1965 was practically free to serve the consumer.

The constitutional structure took on an importance unique in the Communist world. Votes in parliamentary bodies were sometimes contrary to the wishes of higher authorities. Electors had a choice of candidates, although all had to be approved by the League. Most governmental functions were turned over to the six republics (and two districts) that make up the federal state. Their major banks acquired substantial political power.[34] The central government was virtually limited to taxation, investment, and preserving the economic unity of the country and the basics of socialism, plus the classic functions of federal governments, defense and foreign policy. Republic ministries of foreign relations consulted with the federal ministry.[35] The courts were made at least outwardly independent, with tenure for judges; and a constitutional court was established to decide the validity of laws.[36]

Marxism was treated as a general theory only, the party partially gave up its claim to monopoly of truth, science and culture were largely set free, and priority was placed in theory on individual freedom.[37] Universities acquired some autonomy, and the party lost control of the students.[38] From 1950 to the end of the 1960s there was an irregular tendency toward further relaxation. In 1966 the fall of Tito's lieutenant, police boss Alexander Rankovíc, further discredited centralism and coercion. By 1969 it seemed to many that Yugoslavia was evolving toward a new, more humane and democratic form of socialism.

There were strains, however. As a Slovene writer put it in 1966, "The wartime unity of partisans has broken down. There is no more solidarity. In the promised land, man is on his own."[39] Corruption pervaded all aspects of Yugoslav society. The pursuit of the dinar replaced the pursuit of equality, and those who once sought fulfillment in partisan or party work took their pleasure in elegant nightclubs.[40] So far as there remained any interest in ideology, Marxist scholarship increasingly ventured away from official interpretations. Worst of all, the republics began taking their nominal rights seriously. Workers' councils in the richer republics, especially Croatia and Slovenia, opposed transfer of funds to the poorer republics.[41] Tito and other leaders saw Yugoslavia losing its Communist ideals and in danger of disintegration, with "spontaneous democracy" undermining "true democracy," or party leadership. More centralized party management was advocated in order to protect self-management and prevent exploitation.[42]

In August 1969 Tito began calling for more discipline, but liberalization continued ascendant, and some began thinking of a multiparty system.[43] From 1968 to late 1971 there was something of a "Croatian Spring." Croatian demands became increasingly radical, and the republic party leadership felt obliged to go along with popular feelings. In late 1971 the students put forward proposals amounting to a call for independence, asking, for example, that Croatia have its own military units.[44] Alarmed, Tito purged the Croatian party with the support of the armed forces and closed numerous publications. Many offenders were imprisoned—all without a murmur of protest.

Nationalists, liberals, and revolutionary idealists were subsequently purged from other republic parties. In 1972 Tito issued a circular calling for purification of the party, setting forth the party's duty to control directly, and demanding that it impose its line, even if this meant "a reversal of decisions taken by bodies legally empowered to make decisions."[45] The party, which in 1952 gave itself the modest role of persuader, was in 1974 again called upon to exercise the "dictatorship of the proletariat."[46] Tito said in 1974, "A determined break has been made with all the remnants of so-called representative democracy, which suits the bourgeois class."[47]

There is no pre-censorship, but editors and writers are held responsible, and basic criticism is not allowed. Under laws outlawing criticism as starkly as the Soviet prohibition of "anti-Soviet propaganda," many persons have been prosecuted; and courts rule as desired by the party. Writers have been imprisoned for claiming there was no free speech in Yugoslavia. It became treasonous to call, even privately, for more rights for minorities. No organized opposition is permitted in "direct socialist democracy." The party is not to be preoccupied with short-range decisions, but the party determines what decisions it should make. Party secretaries, as in other Communist states, are superior to their governmental counterpart. The party assumes the duty of preventing "antisocial elements" from coming to the fore anywhere.

Workers' self-management is at best restricted by regulations, central control of investments, and the placing of approved persons in key positions.[48] Workers may participate in low-level decisions, but interest is not great because important questions are decided by others and because insiders have the expertise and determine the agenda. Members of workers' councils have short terms, while the director, who is proposed by a party-dominated commission, is permanent.[49] "Real freedom" for the workers requires party guidance. Deputies to assemblies at all levels above the commune are chosen indirectly through organizations and enterprises, which are subject to party domination.[50] The deputies, who hold regular jobs, are frequently rotated, and have little time, energy, or expertise to criticize the powers, and are expected to serve those who choose them, that is, the party.[51] Democracy is diluted by diffusion, as citizens are invited to participate more or less insignificantly in a host of agencies, while professionals manage at the top. The government is formally separated from the party, but the role of the party (or League) as governing force was explicitly stated in the 1974 constitution.

The party, as the sole organization holding the country and society together, is unchallengeable. Paradoxically, Yugoslav workers, who supposedly have the right of self-determination, have never opposed the party in the manner of Polish workers, who lack that right.[52] They go on strike with some frequency, but strikes lack the political significance they have where they are prohibited. The party itself is coherent and, having crushed nationalistic separatist movements, is united. Like other Communist parties, it prohibits factions; and Yugoslav Communists, like Soviet, are bound to carry out party decisions.[53]

The system is in principle opposed to pluralism; the vaunted autonomy of parts should imply only a means of better government. The leaders are probably much afraid of genuine pluralism.[54] The small band of onetime guerrillas who still rule the country were once thorough Stalinists, but they refused to give up their independence to Stalin—they were in fear of their lives from Stalin's police.[55] They set out to devise superior ways of ruling, but they never have really restricted their own power. They basically have similar problems of governing as Soviet and other Communist leaders. Hence they talk of the "crisis of capitalism"; and the masthead of *Borba* like *Pravda*, proclaims "Proletariat of all lands, unite!" while about a million Yugoslav workers employed by capitalists abroad sustain the socialist economy. Their foreign policy has looked toward the reduction of the influence of the United States, which contributes to their defense, and usually has supported the Soviet Union, which is dangerous to them. Some in the party even want to place their country in the Soviet orbit to safeguard Communist rule.

Titoist Yugoslavia desires to make a dictatorship more effective by covering it with a more impressive garb of democratic forms and practices than other Communist countries. By withdrawing from control of some areas, the party reduces its responsibilities and the danger of conflict over marginal issues.[56] It wants dialogue and participation of the masses—always under party guidance. The party should rule by consent and invisibly, so far as possible. The rights of the workers and of citizens are numerous and impressive, and they ordinarily are observed. A law of 1976 gave citizens new facilities for complaint against the bureaucracy at a time when sending an article to a foreign newspaper was cause for imprisonment. The autonomy of republics was increased on paper in 1974, shortly after separatist tendencies had been curbed. Under the mixture of concession and compulsion, minority separatism seems to have yielded ground to Yugoslavism. The courts may check abuse of power; one ruled that the practice of carting away improperly parked cars was illegal.[57] Those who wish to raise their voices about practical matters have freedom and channels to do so. The Yugoslav press sparkles by comparison with the Soviet. The forms of self-management and grass-roots democracy make for better relations, while leaving party rule untouched, perhaps strengthened.

This relatively open and relaxed Communism has given Yugoslavia a good reputation, and it made Tito a figure on the world stage far beyond the intrinsic importance of his country. The Yugoslavs have had the satisfaction of national and ideological independence. Workers like the idea of self-management, and most people seem to feel the system is the best they can expect. The economy has grown better over a long period than that of any country of the Soviet bloc, at least in terms of consumer goods. It has demonstrated that a Communist state can be governed in a rather relaxed manner without loss of power by the party. It raises the question why other countries do not deflate opposition by making similar psychological concessions.

Yugoslavia, however, has enjoyed special advantages. The sole leader of the party, Tito, has shown great capacity. He emerged from the victory over occupation forces with enormous prestige that to this day clings to his aged but vigorous figure. The crushing of competitive movements during the guerrilla struggle and the massacres at the end of war left no opposition. The decision to resist Stalin and Soviet domination in 1948 married the Communist party to the national cause. Under pressure to secure popular support, reforms were made that Communist parties leaning on the Soviet Union would find unnecessary and unacceptable.

Whether the Yugoslav way is permanently viable remains to be seen.

The complex political structure is a doubtful experiment. The self-managed economy is not very efficient and relies on the earnings of workers abroad and on small-scale private shops and artisans. Firms do not invest adequately, because workers prefer money in the pay packet. Economic growth recently has been below the world average. At the same time, the ideological foundations of party rule become weaker; many members do not consider themselves Marxists, and the party becomes a league of possessors.[58]

PROSPECTS OF LIBERALZATION

The capacity for substantial reform of the Communist system is slight and probably decreasing. Its special difficulties arise from monopolistic power, and reform violates the first axiom of the system. Hence, there may be no remedy available within the parameters of the system. For example, parties often berate careerism. But careerism could be checked only by a revival of revolutionary enthusiasm, which would require a new revolution removing the elite from power, or by a constitutional order, which would curtail the power of the rulership.

In Hungary in 1956, when the Communist system was relatively new, it was overthrown by a nationalistic libertarian uprising. In Yugoslavia, confrontation with Stalin loosened the system. In 1968 in Czechoslovakia, economic troubles led to demands for economic liberalization that implied political relaxation; Slovak resentments and reviving nationalism also contributed to the urge to democratize Communism. But it was naive for the party to hope to rule without coercion by truly serving the people.[59] It could have succeeded in implanting an effective constitutional order only by abolishing Marxism as the dominant ideology and ending the privileged position of the Communisty party.[60] Such measures were not on the agenda when the Soviets quashed the experiment. The liberals had accepted the legitimacy of independent groups but stopped short of proposing a legitimate contest for power, without which any concessions were revocable.[61] The experiment owed much to Czech traditions of democracy and freedom; its failure may have gone far toward killing them.

The problem of reform is complicated by the oligarch's lack of information and ideas. There is no one to propose changes costly to his position, as inputs come from servile lower echelons. Higher levels are relatively satisfied and opposed to ameliorative measures. They are not touched by shortages, and it is doubtless easy for functionaries to convince themselves that the country is as untroubled as their offices. Lifting of censorship would open a Pandora's box. As a Polish journalist put it, "We couldn't cope with the alternatives that would spring up if we allowed freedom of expression."[62] But censorship accustoms the authorities to the comfortable assumption that nothing needs to be done very differently.

The rulers may know, however, that the economy is not doing well, and they frequently move to invigorate it. But the superficial reforms that they can accept are at best temporarily helpful. Shortages are profitable for many, and the system of allocations and special access elevates the privileges of the elite. Low-level functionaries resist removal of controls. In various countries they have harassed peasant household production. Minor officials prey on whatever defenseless private business is allowed—and presumably also where it is illegal. Private farming in Poland is not very productive; it does not harmonize with the socialist state.

Partial economic reform is difficult and leads to imbalances. Administrative changes cause confusion and usually result at first in lowered production. Decontrolled enterprise probably does not work well; managers are habituated to dependence and bureaucratism. Most of them probably lack competence to survive in free-for-all competition. There is no evidence that anyone in the Soviet Union or other Communist states really wants economic freedom. Under the web of controls managers are less driven than they would be by the indefinite demands of the market economy, which is one reason why the controlled economy is less productive. Trade union bureaucrats also fear reform.

If an economic reform were continued, it would generate uncertainties, which the planners abhor. It would cause inflation, or release inflation currently repressed and manifested indirectly in change of products, lowered quality, under-the-counter payments, and so forth.[63] There is a large amount of redundant labor in the Soviet and other centrally planned economies; one of the first effects of removal of controls would be large-scale unemployment. The commitment to full employment, perhaps the best claim of the Communist state to superiority, practically precludes unleashing the economy and sacrificing security to efficiency. Freeing prices would give undeserved profits to many; even the United States has seen how difficult it is to unfreeze prices, like those of oil and gas, that have been fixed for a long time. Unmotivated workers dislike incentive wages; few want more differentials to reward skill and effort. Economic liberalization increases inequality among regions, enterprises, classes, and persons. Many would say the increase of goods is not worth the cost in social values.

Free enterprise, in any case, is not very efficient in the party-run economy. Producers cannot count on supplies, their prestige is low, credit is probably lacking, taxes and regulations are onerous and uncertain, and there is no protection from official molestations. The more successful an enterprise, the more it is vexed and bled;[64] and a semiparasitic class acquires a vested interest in the unfree system. Private money-making, always at the mercy of politics, is apt to be more a moonlighting operation than a career attractive to young talent. Indoctrination and propaganda associate private enterprise with speculation, greed, cheating, and corruption. "Of course, state capitalism in its breakdown gives rise to underground capitalism, but underground merchants evoke the scorn of Soviet people, and the most curious fact is that, as a rule, it is precisely the underground merchants who exhibit the worst servile Soviet qualities."[65]

The devolved centralized system is self-contradictory. The economic monopoly can hardly be ended unless political power is restrained, and the political monopoly can hardly be restrained while the economic monopoly continues. There is no checking of power unless the police power is checked. This requires an independent court system and freedom of speech. These cannot exist unless there are multiple institutional inputs to the political system, for which the sole accepted means is freely contested elections. Unless or until the governing party surrenders its status, it can retract any concessions or break any self-imposed restraints.

The Communist society is a whole, the parts of which are mutually supportive. Beliefs, institutions, and power structure are interdependent; and failure of any one threatens downfall of the others. The beneficiaries of the power structure can be counted on to resist loss in any dimension of their superiority, and they often seem paranoid about pinpricks. Many desire "socialism with a human face," a decent and respectable system of government; but they do not want freedom that allows people to be bad or to question the structure of power.

The system is well structured to prevent any change not desired by the rulers. Hence, deep change seems necessarily to entail a power struggle, uncertainty and disorder, probably violence, to break up and discredit the old and sanctify the new. Ordinarily change of social system has been propelled by war, as the historical record of Communist revolutions, the French and American revolutions, and Nazi and fascist accessions to power demonstrates. If Communist movements have not been able to conquer "bourgeois" societies without fighting, likewise Communist systems do not easily evolve into pluralistic systems by peaceful means.

NOTES

1. Vladimire V. Kusin, "An Overview of East European Reformism," *Soviet Studies* 28 (July 1976): 355.

2. Leonard Schapiro, *The Communist Party of the Soviet Union* (New York: Vintage Books, 1971), pp. 325–26.

3. Concerning economic reform in the Soviet Union, see Alec Nove, *The Soviet Economic System* (London: Allen and Unwin, 1977), chap. 11.

4. *Business Week*, July 9, 1979, p. 30.

5. R. V. Burks, "Technology and Political Change," in *Change in Communist Systems*, ed. Chalmers Johnson (Stanford: Stanford University Press, 1970), p. 294.

6. Joseph S. Berliner, *The Innovation Decision in Soviet Industry* (Cambridge: MIT Press, 1976), conclusion.

7. A theme of Moshe Lewin, *Political Undercurrents in Soviet Economic Debates* (Princeton: Princeton University Press, 1974).

8. Jan Marczewski, *Crisis in Socialist Planning: Eastern Europe and the USSR* (New York: Praeger, 1974), p. 240.

9. For example, according to *Ekonomicheskaya gazeta* 20 (May 1976): 18.

10. Stephen Osofsky, *Soviet Agricultural Policy: Toward the Abolition of the Collective Farm* (New York: Praeger, 1974), pp. 231–34. See also Dimitry Pospielovsky, "The Link System in Soviet Agriculture," *Soviet Studies* 21 (April 1970): 411–35.

11. *The Samizdat Bulletin* 31 (November 1975); Andrei Sakharov, *My Country and the World* (New York: Knopf, 1975), p. 46.

12. Maury Lisann, *Broadcasting to the Soviet Union: International Politics and Radio* (New York: Praeger, 1975), p. 120; Gayle D. Hannah, "Soviet Public Communications in the Post-Stalin Era," *Change and Adaption in Soviet and East European Politics*, ed. Jane P. Shapiro and Peter J. Potichnyj (New York: Praeger, 1976), p. 137.

13. Kusin, "An Overview of East European Reformism," p. 354.

14. Bogoslav Dobrin, *Bulgarian Economic Development* (New York: Praeger, 1973), p. 172.

15. Ibid., p. 158.

16. Michael Karen, "The Rise and Fall of the New Economic System," in *The German Democratic Republic: A Developed Socialist State*, ed. Lyman H. Legters (Boulder, Colo.: Westview Press, 1978), p. 75; idem, "The New Economic System in the GDR: An Obituary," *Soviet Studies* 24 (April 1973): 554–69.

17. Helmut Zimmermann, "The GDR in the 1970s," *Problems of Communism* 27 (March–April 1978): 24.

18. David Granick, *Enterprise Guidance in Eastern Europe* (Princeton: Princeton University Press, 1975), pp. 481–82.

19. Ray Taras, "The Process of Reform in Post-1970 Poland," in *Change and Adaption in Soviet and East European Politics*, p. 60.

20. Andrzej Korbonski, "Liberalization Processes," in *Comparative Socialist Systems: Essays in Politics and Economics*, ed. Carmelo Mesa-Lago and Carl Beck (Pittsburgh: University of Pittsburgh Center for International Studies, 1975), p. 209.

21. Alexander Matejko, "Structural Change under State Socialism: The Polish Case," in *Change and Adaption in Soviet and East European Politics*, pp. 50–53.

22. Taras, "The Process of Reform," p. 63.

23. Adam Bromke, "A New Juncture in Poland," *Problems of Communism* 25 (September–October 1976): 6–12.

24. Richard F. Staar, "Poland: The Price of Stability," *Current History* 70 (March 1976): 104.

25. *Christian Science Monitor*, February 13, 1980, p. 4.

26. *New York Times*, November 9, 1976, p. 6.

27. Richard F. Staar, *Communist Regimes in Eastern Europe*, 3d ed. (Stanford: Hoover Institution Press, 1977), p. 119.

28. Ivan Volgyes, "Hungary in the Seventies," *Current History* 64 (May 1973): 219.

29. Ivan Volgyes, "Limited Liberalization in Hungary," *Current History* 70 (January 1976): 109.

30. Ibid., pp. 108–9.

31. *New York Times*, June 17, 1975.

32. Dennison Rusinow, *The Yugoslav Experiment, 1948–1974* (Berkeley: University of California Press, 1976), pp. 50–51.

33. Alex N. Dragnich, "Yugoslavia: Titoism without Tito," *Current History* 70 (March 1976): 112.

34. Carl G. Ströhm, *Ohne Tito: Kann Jugoslawien überleben* (Vienna: Verlag Styria, 1976), p. 145.

35. Paul Shoup, "Yugoslav Nationalities," *Problems of Communism* 21 (January–February 1972): 18–29.

36. William M. Fisk, "The Constitutionalism Movement in Yugoslavia: A Preliminary Survey," in *Communist Systems in Comparative Perspective*, ed. Lenard J. Cohen and Jane P. Shapiro (Garden City, N.Y.: Anchor, 1974), p. 188.

·37. Kusin, "An Overview of East European Reformism," p. 352.

38. Paul Shoup, "The Limits of Party Control: The Yugoslav Case," in *Authoritarian Politics in Communist Europe: Uniformity and Diversity in One-Party States*, ed. Andrew C. Janos (Berkeley: Institute of International Studies, 1976), p. 190.

39. Francoise Fejtö, *A History of the People's Democracies: Eastern Europe Since Stalin* (New York: Praeger, 1974), p. 284.

40. Sharon Zukin, *Beyond Marx and Tito: Theory and Practice in Yugoslav Socialism* (New York: Cambridge University Press, 1975), pp. 206–17.

41. David McKenzie, "The Background: Yugoslavia since 1964," in *Nationalism in the USSR and Eastern Europe in the Era of Brezhnev and Kosygin*, ed. George W. Simmonds (Detroit: University of Detroit Press, 1977), p. 447.

42. Dennison J. Rusinow, "Yugoslavia: The Price of Pluralism Reassessed," *Common Ground* 2 (April 1976): 74–75.

43. William Zimmermann, "The Tito Legacy and Yugoslavia's Future," *Problems of Communism* 26 (May–June 1977): 42.

44. Ströhm, *Ohne Tito*, p. 198.

45. Cited by Andrew C. Janos, "Systematic Models," in *Authoritarian Politics in Communist Europe*, pp. 18–19.

46. Dragnich, "Yugoslavia," p. 112.

47. Cited by Edward F. Singleton, *Twentieth Century Yugoslavia* (New York: Columbia University Press, 1976), p. 274.

48. Rusinow, "Yugoslavia: The Price of Pluralism Reassessed," p. 70.

49. Staar, *Communist Regimes of Eastern Europe*, p. 185.

50. Ibid., pp. 195–96.

51. Gavriel Ra'anan, *Yugoslavia after Tito: Scenario and Implications* (Boulder, Color.: Westview Press, 1977), pp. 42–43.

52. Ströhm, *Ohne Tito*, p. 139.

53. Rusinow, *The Yugoslav Experiment*, p. 310.

54. Laurence Silberman, "Yugoslavia's Old Communism," *Foreign Policy* 26 (Spring 1977): 7.

55. Ströhm, *Ohne Tito*, pp. 11, 56.

56. Bogdan Denitch, "Succession and Stability in Yugoslavia," *Journal of International Affairs* 32 (Fall–Winter 1978): 231.

57. *New York Times*, July 21, 1978, p. A-5.

58. David A. Dykes, "Yugoslavia, Unity or Diversity," in *Political Culture and Political Change in Communist States*, ed. Archibald H. Brown and Jack Gray (New York: Holmes and Meier, 1977), p. 80.

59. H. Gordon Skilling, *Czechoslovakia's Interrupted Revolution* (Princeton: Princeton University Press, 1976), p. 219.

60. As observed by *L'Express*, February 28–March 6, 1977, p. 36.

61. Galia Golan, "Political Reform in Czechoslovakia," in *Change and Adaption in Soviet and East European Politics*, p. 85.

62. *New York Times*, December 28, 1976, p. 11.

63. George Feiwel, *Growth and Reform in Centrally Planned Economies: The Lesson of the Bulgarian Experiment* (New York: Praeger, 1977), p. 249.

64. As in "liberal" Slovenia. Ströhm, *Ohne Tito*, p. 238.

65. Vadim Belotserkovsky, "Outlines of a Synthesis," in *Demokraticheskie Alternativy*, ed. Vadim Belotserkovsky (Achberg: Achberg Verlaganstait, 1976), p. 89.

7

FIXITY

INSTITUTIONALIZATION

The leftist followers of President Allende of Chile (1970–1973) pressed him to use his powers to the hilt to destroy the private economy and the bases of the middle class in order, as they frankly stated it, to make their revolution irreversible. If independent organizations and forces could be eliminated, no constitutional processes or popular feeling could threaten their mastery. In Marxist terms, the party could create the objective conditions for its unrestricted rule as the political expression of the only important remaining class.

The Chilean Marxists failed because the middle classes and the military forces became alarmed at the attack on their independent existence, and the revolutionary regime was replaced by a rightist authorianism. But Communist states, almost by definition, are those in which competitive institutions and powers have been abolished.

The Leninists began immediately after their seizure of power to eliminate the bases of the traditional society and to reduce or dissolve non-Communist authority of all kinds. They immediately ended private property in land (although peasants retained private use for a few years), and restored censorship. In a few weeks they had a political police to make political opposition difficult and subsequently impossible. A barrage of decrees reshaped social institutions. The old army was dissolved and a new one was put together. Industry was progressively nationalized. The internal structure of the party was consolidated. The last non-Bolshevik political organizations were liquidated. The formal federal structure of the Soviet Union was set in place in 1922. At first Lenin saw little need for law, the courts being guided by "revolutionary conscience"; but civil, criminal, family, and other codes were introduced in 1922–23.

With a large, thoroughly controlled, indoctrinated party, police, and state apparatus, Stalin could carry much further the work begun by Lenin. He destroyed artisan industry, concentrated production in the hands of the state, built new industrial cities, and subjected the entire economy to centralized planning. He drove the peasants into party-controlled collective farms. He eliminated independent artistic and intellectual creativity. He attacked the remnants of organized religion. Whatever independence of mind had survived he crushed in the purges.

There has been little for Stalin's successors to do. The codes, administrative systems, police organizations, and economic controls have been patched and improved. Antiparasite laws formalized the obligation to work for the state. Education has been brought more strictly under centralized control. Even the organization of the Orthodox church has been brought virtually into the structure.

Soviet Communism was a pathbreaker and pioneer, and its institutionalization consequently was relatively slow. The Chinese Communists, coming to power in 1949, had only to copy from their Big Brother; and they did so with dispatch, collectivizing and inaugurating economic planning. Mao wanted not only to emulate but to outdo his Soviet teachers by fuller collectivization in the people's communes, greater mobilization in the Great Leap Forward of 1958, and more egalitarianism in the Cultural Revolution of 1966. In most of Eastern Europe, the full development of Communist societies was speeded not only by the Soviet model but also by the presence of Soviet force, although it was restrained in the first postwar years by Soviet concern for Western sensitivities. Communist-dominated coalitions were set up and then turned into one-party governments; elections progressed from semifree contests to demonstrations of solidarity; land reform led to collectivization; economic planning was instituted with priority for heavy industry; and a full range of police and cultural controls was inaugurated. In four to five years these tasks were virtually accomplished, and little Stalins ruled as satraps across Eastern Europe.

In many small ways, the solidification or enhancement of Communist structures continues for many years. For example, the Soviet paramilitary league, Dosaaf, founded in 1951, continues to expand, embracing a large fraction of the Soviet population and including 330,000 primary organizations by 1977.[1] Over a long period of time, Soviet workers have been more and more involved in party-directed activities.[2] The Soviet youth league, once a slightly autonomous body led by students and volunteers, has increasingly come under the supervision of regular professional party workers.[3] Not until 1977 was the Polish Scouts' Union brought into the Soviet mold and converted into a transmission belt of the party.[4] New programs also reach out to bring more of life within the party purview. In the mid-1970s East Germany was taking pride in its ever expanding and highly successful athletic program, a significant new political asset. Cuba likewise was developing sports education, with special schools and scientific training, as a credit to the system, a form of incentives, and an adjunct of indoctrination. In 1977 the Romanian government got around to closing private museums and seizing private art collections.[5]

The difficult process of completing the Communist order is illustrated by the management of agriculture, the least malleable sector of national life. It was incongruous for the young Soviet state that 80 percent of the population was engaged in private farming, so collectivization, previously a long-term goal, was made a proximate objective in 1929–30. Stalin encountered a storm of resistance and had to pull back early in 1930 to permit withdrawal from collectives and allow modest household plots. The campaign was soon resumed, however, and collectivization was virtually complete by 1934. Even so, consolidation has continued. In 1950 Khrushchev, then serving Stalin, began a program of merging collective farms; the number of which was reduced by nearly four-fifths by 1959 (254,000 to 54,000); the purpose was more effective party control. Much has been done to make the collectives more like state-run agricultural factories, thereby separating management further from workers. For example, chairmen of collectives are professionally trained and regularly rotated to prevent their forming local roots.[6] There are more and more intercollective links, including recently "Productive Associations" parallel to those in industry. Collective farm funds have been made subject to the state plan, and farms are increasingly to specialize. Mechanization, professionalization, bureaucratization, and centralization should crush any lingering idea of dividing the collective fields. For a long time it was party policy to work toward the extinction of the small household plots, and their area gradually diminished. It may be, however, that the need for food has brought this aspect of socialization to a halt, as Soviet citizens are exhorted to tend their gardens.

The institutionalization of Communism may at times halt or retreat in the face of economic needs, but the general goal is the subordination of all existence to the single authority. Everyone should work, in effect, for the party; there should be no livelihood (or only minor livelihoods in operations the party cannot conveniently manage) outside its sphere. The party, or party-guided activities, should be the channel or vehicle of ambitions, and those who rise on party ladders should have a vested interest in the system. People should be rewarded politically with status and power, not independence, and economically with revocable privileges, not private wealth. Many things are obtainable primarily as perquisites, such as preferred housing, vacations, and travel. Even such a material possession as an automobile is often a reward of service instead of an outright purchase (at an exorbitant price); and loyalty is the price of continued enjoyment.

The consolidation of Communism also implies overwhelming organization. "Socialism" means structuring society so that the individual is submerged and party guidance is unavoidable, if not indispensable. Vast farms engaging thousands of workers are linked into associations in the Soviet Union. Agro-Industrial complexes in Eastern Europe tie enterprises into a web of vertical and horizontal integration so that the human atoms are submerged, with no means for criticizing the policies even of the collective to which they belong. The larger the scale of operations, the better can it be kept under the oversight of the party apparatus and the less hope—perhaps the less desire—of individuals for autonomy. Self-will and defiance seem only irrational. The well-devised, tightly articulated framework of mutually reinforcing parts is a tour de force of modernity, possible only through modern technology of control and communications and the complexity of production that rewards bigness and specialization. It should be an impregnable fortress for those who rule it.

THE FORMATION OF MINDS

The complete triumph of Communism requires not only the elimination of non-Communist classes and structures, but the erasure of competing philosophies and the molding of character to the full acceptance of Communist ways and values, the extermination of religion, and the formation of the "New Man" envisaged by propaganda. In neither the eradication nor the formation is the regime fully successful; in neither does it fail entirely.

After competing political groups are crushed, the principal remaining philosophic rival is religion. Antichurch propaganda, the closure or destruction of many churches, penalties and discrimination against practitioners of religion, and severe reductions in the number of priests operated during the first half-century of Soviet rule to convert a population of believers to one mostly of nonbelievers. New churches are not built, so population shifts leave ever more people without places of worship. A large part of the people know churches only as architectural monuments. Few new priests are trained; unless this changes, there will be hardly any educated priests left in the Soviet Union in a decade. Less than two percent of the churches Georgia once had still function. One small seminary with a handful of students (who are subjected to "political education") serves the Catholics of Lithuania, and the Vatican has accepted that appointments are subject to the consent of Soviet authorities. In 1970 there was only one rabbi in Moscow, about a half dozen being permitted to study to serve the more than two million Soviet Jews. Hardly any new mullahs are prepared for tens of millions of Muslims. The upper hierarchy of the principal faiths is corrupted by the state, largely chosen by it, and infiltrated by the KGB. Practically no Bibles, Korans, or other religious texts are printed. Religious instruction of young people is prohibited.

Acknowledged religion is an almost total bar to a career. Overtly religious parents also sacrifice their children's chances of advancement, as parental religious affiliation is one of many disqualifications for higher education. All higher school graduates must qualify in an examination in atheism. A new generation knows little of the heritage of piety, which it sees largely in the poorer and less educated; young and old are taught to ridicule concepts of God, the soul, sin, and faith. Soviet police block young men from Easter services while permitting old women to enter. Leninism and Soviet ceremonials are given semireligious forms and made competitors of religious rituals of birth, marriage, and death.

Governments of other Communist states have succeeded in reducing organized religion to debility or insignificance. The exception is Poland, where the Catholic church seems morally and materially stronger than ever. In Albania and North Korea, organized religion is apparently obliterated. The most insidious and probably effective means of attack is infiltration of the hierarchy and subversion of the clergy through control of church finances. Everywhere in the Communist sphere religious affiliation is an impediement, if not a bar, to material success.

The result is not to exterminate religious feeling but to reduce the prestige of organized religion, leaving it to the weak, the poor, and those uninterested in ordinary careers, and hence usually uninfluential. Religion is atomized and left personal and individual, politically impotent, a means of withdrawal, not of opposition.

More important than the direct attack on old belief is the filling of minds with the new message. The Leninists have always laid great stress on propaganda, and its volume has increased enormously with modernization. For example, in the Soviet Union the number of radio receivers grew tenfold since Stalin. Even newspapers, the old standby of the Bolsheviks, more than tripled circulation in that period.[7] Television sets rose from zero to 34 million in 1970 and to 60 million in 1977. Television has the advantages, from the point of view of the propagandist, of absorbing attention and inducing passivity; moreover, it is easily managed from central broadcasting studios with taped and thoroughly censorable programming. Citizens of the Soviet Union and East European countries spend roughly as much time before television screens as do Americans. There is no reason to suppose that political messages are less effective than commercial ones.

Formal education is probably the most potent form of propaganda. It is assumed in the West that education is inherently liberalizing; however, Communist schools teach not independent but correct thinking. In the Soviet context, "rising educational level" means "rising indoctrinational level." Communist education is likely to be destabilizing only so far as persons may see themselves entitled to more than the system gives.

Marxist-Leninist education aims, while giving professional expertise, qualifying one for a slot in the political-economic structure, to fix patterns of thinking. It builds a special universe that relieves the student of the necessity of critical thought and excludes many unpleasant realities. It furnishes easy answers, simple enough for the uncritical, more sophisticated for those who would go deeper. Solzhenitsyn said, "To those brought up in Marxism it seems a terrifying step suddenly to start living without the familiar ideology."[8]

In the Soviet Union the party is confident of the power of indoctrination as extended through the university level. Higher education is virtually a prerequisite for a career in the apparatus.[9] Candidates for higher education are candidates for elite status, and they are politically screened; and they receive stipends and perquisities that obligate them to serve the party. They also undergo intensive ideological training, no matter how technical their field of concentration; and they are ideologically tested.[10] It is expected that everyone receiving a higher degree should have "mastery of Marxist-Leninist theory" plus "the convictions of an active builder of Communist society."[11] The greatest care is taken that university instructors, even in mathematics and physics, are wholly in tune with the regnant order. The idea that there can be autonomy in nonpolitical spheres is heretical. For a scientist, political work may be as important in securing promotion as scientific work. Selectees for elitehood have earned their status in large part because of mastery of ideology. The rulers are indoctrinated, and the indoctrinated are entitled to rule.

The profession naturally most prone to criticism is the literary, because writing interestingly about society is almost the same as writing critically. Yet the writers, too, are overwhelmingly conformist. Those who perform obediently are materially well rewarded; mavericks get nowhere. Young persons entering the profession must compromise in order to get published, and the habit of writing what the party wants becomes ingrained. Like editors and journalists, writers learn self-censorship; there is no point to producing what will not be accepted. The rules become part of the way of life, a condition of the profession.

Freedom is equated with anarchy, and fear of it is strong not only among the governors but also, apparently, among the governed. The hierarchy, the plan, and the rules represent security against chaos. Every effort is made to accustom people to seeing themselves not as individuals but as members of the collective in order to make it harder to conceive of independent action or to set oneself against society. Indeed, the concept of self seems to be devalued. People learn to think of rights not for themselves but for the masses for whom the party is spokesman. They cannot call themselves exploited; they have been taught that exploitation results from capitalism. If they go into opposition, they still think mostly in the collective mode, seeking not freedom but a better socialism, more equality, and a purer party without any idea how these may be secured. According to a dissident, "The mass of the people are materialistic slaves, not rarely idealizing their slavery and at the same time capable of being cruel tyrants."[12]

Communist education is not so important for the specifics, which may be rejected, as for developing habits of mind, including outward conformism and acceptance of authority, and the approval of violence toward the "class" enemy.[13] The workers probably feel themselves closer to the police than to the intelligentsia, and they have little sympathy with the dissident intellectuals who would like to liberate them.[14] Few know much of the misdeeds of the Stalinist era; some, perhaps a growing number, look back to that time as the good old days of order.

The idea of a real political alternative seems to have faded. There was no public pressure for de-Stalinization, which was begun and withdrawn entirely at the will of the leaders. It found echoes in Eastern Europe, where Sovietization in 1956 was only a decade old, but raised hardly a murmur in the Soviet Union, which had suffered most. Soviet youth may be critical of many shortcomings, but they remain committed to basics of the system.[15] Dissenters make modest specific demands, generally in terms given by the state, usually for concessions that would cost little. Workers emphasize that their complaints and aspirations are purely economic. The Soviet-trained mind has no room for ideas of individualism and freedom, and the contentions of Western-style pluralism. As a Soviet scientist said, "The only thing Communism has prepared us for is more Communist rule."[16] The state has preempted the vocabulary of freedom and democracy and perverted their concepts; it is difficult for rebels to express antidogmatic purposes without becoming dogmatic.[17] According to a Soviet writer in an international forum, "We define freedom as finding one's way in the historical process," while another said, "I think freedom is above all performance of one's duty to the people."[18] In the view of Solzhenitsyn, "Over the past half-century, Russia's readiness for democracy can only have diminished." He asked, "Should we not perhaps acknowledge that for Russia this path was either fake or premature, and that, for the foreseeable future, Russia is destined to an authoritarian order?"[19]

The passing of time has dampened boldness of thought in Eastern Europe. The Hungarians in 1956 rose up against the system as a whole; the Czechs in 1968 wanted to keep the system in changed form, even the party monopoly to which they had grown accustomed for 20 years. The Poles in 1970 demanded only remedies for grievances. The Czech writers of Charter 77 felt their group had to avow "no intention of initiating its own program for political or social change." Czech non-Communists and Communists agree that a new bath of liberalization like that of 1968 would be a catastrophe.[20] No party in Eastern Europe proposes a return to capitalism; the radical demand is simply "democratic socialism," understood as equality and benefits, state management without the abuses frequent in Communist governments.[21]

Most people accept the overwhelming reality of the state, which there is no point in judging, respect its power, and perceive no alternative. The fact that party-state rule has been unchallengeable so many years is sufficient reason to assume that it is permanent and that opposition is futile, if not insane, as the authorities declare. It is a fact of life, like the law of gravitation. Moreover, it has been successful in many ways; and it makes its successes conspicuous in its monuments and constructions. The Communist states have fulfilled missions of military strength, education, industrialization, and the restoration of national dignity. In nearly all Communist states, standards of living are much better than a generation ago. Countless peasants have left behind back-breaking, poorly paid toil in the fields to become city workers. Children of peasants and workers have acquired an education, to which they could hardly have aspired in the past, to become engineers, doctors, journalists, managers, or, best of all, officials. The success of the regime is their success. Criticisms of lack of freedom are meaningless for them.

Yet the intellectual price has been high. Traditional cultures have been to a large extent cast aside, less in Eastern Europe and more in Asia, and replaced by a skewed and partial vision of the modern world. Except for some politically innocuous learning and practical knowledge, the younger generation has been deprived of solid information not only about the outside world but also about their own society. They lack training in thinking for themselves, incentives to do so, and a factual basis from which to start. At one time during the Cultural Revolution in China hardly anything was put into print except thin daily papers and the works of Mao. Perhaps for lack of interesting reading material, illiteracy has increased in the past decade, in the admission of a spokesman for the Ministry of Education; and "the real standard of general knowledge and the student's ability in applying this knowledge" are lower than in the 1960s.[22] In the bitter opinion of a French writer, "If this regime persists, by the end of the century all Eastern Europe may have become a spiritual desert."[23]

In the Communist society in general there is little questioning and not much need for individual choices, while expectations are limited and concrete.[24] If indoctrination destroys independence, it also destroys creativity. Edward Crankshaw speaks of

> the almost total inability of Soviet officialdom, from the highest to the lowest, nurtured so long on lies and driven so long on fear, to distinguish right from wrong, to sustain a logical argument (even, perhaps, to perceive the desirability of logical thinking) or to understand what is meant by the rule of law.[25]

Officialdom is most afflicted, but very few are immune, as people cannot avoid being shaped by the system. There is no need for intellectual consistency; and educated people display their lack of it, for example, in blandly denying such obvious realities as the existence in the Soviet Union of intergenerational tensions or premarital sex.[26]

High priority for politics means low priority for knowledge, and less enlightened teachers prepare less enlightened students. Despite the thousands of higher schools, technicums, and universities, there is less liberal intellectualism in Russia today than there was before the revolution.[27] The background of the rulers narrows. Mao read Adam Smith, Rousseau, and many other thinkers; and a number of his followers had a fair education and some experience of the outside world. Mao's disciples have had the benefit of Mao Thought and little more, and very few have set foot outside China. It is unlikely that enlightened leadership can soon come to the fore in an Indochina that is deeply hostile to learning. The makers of the Communist revolution are brought up in a relatively open society with intellectual controversy and access to contending views; their state is carried on by persons brought up in a society blanketed by a single dogma.

VESTED INTERESTS

Under the Communist system, those in positions of power stand to lose from change, while those who might gain by change are deprived of means of influence. For this reason Communist states have an exceptional record of stability. Except where anticommunism has coincided with nationalism, as in Hungary in 1956, or where the chief figure has led an antiparty movement, as in China in 1966, no Communist government, once established, has ever seemed to be endangered.

A new Communist power moves first to assume control of the economy. New authorities are set up, as Communist managers take control of industry and trade and party bosses in the countryside inherit the influence of the landowners. Once their position has been established, it becomes unthinkable for them to surrender it. Every further step taken to improve their status means an increased stake in holding it. More and more persons become beneficiaries of the new order, and fewer careers remain outside the party framework. Every new control generates a vested interest of the controllers and to some extent, as people adjust, of the controlled as well.

The hierarchic party dominates society much as an officer corps dominates the army, by holding all strategic positions, denying organizational action to others, and making itself the sole exponent of the collective purpose. Persons at each level depend upon their superiors and look to them for directions. There is little pressure from below and little means for ideas to penetrate from outside. Those on the hierarchic ladder are more subservient and more resolved to retain their authority because there is nowhere else to go; to lose one's place in the apparatus is to lose everything. Even if the apparatus becomes parasitic and is irrelevant to national needs, apparatchiki are terrified of basic change, fearing not only loss of standing but also exposure of abuses of power. Marxists often reiterate that the possessing classes of capitalism will never voluntarily yield their privileged position. This is doubly true of the possessing-ruling class of Communism. Capitalists may envision the possibility of another mode of life; Communists can hardly do so.

The bureaucracy in Communist countries, like that of the Third World, functions as a provider of jobs and status for the educated. The bureaucrats and apparatchiki, having qualified for superior status, feel entitled to retain it. To advance on the party-state ladder requires total investment of the personality, and it would be folly to throw away this investment by deviance. At each level, those who defer to superiors have the satisfaction of lording over inferiors, down to the ordinary party members who comprise an elite over the mass of citizens; and all can aspire to an ascending level of power. For those who climb politically, the party must be practically a purpose in itself; without loyal feelings, it is difficult to display the requisite devotion. To prevent deviation among its servants, the party has only to destroy nonparty means of making a career.

Bosses on the lower levels are often more arbitrary than the higher elite, presumably because they feel less secure. Their resistance is a major impediment to the abolition of any established controls, and a prime obstacle to economic reforms. Freeing the economy would make the party redundant in its biggest role, overseeing production, and would imply a loss of power and wealth (or control over wealth) by a large part of the apparatus. Managers are necessarily political conformists, probably political activists whose training includes party schools; in a freer economy they probably would be replaced.[28] In particular, the hundreds of thousands of professional propagandists, whose qualifications are mastery of Marxism-Leninism and personal relations with higher personages, are totally committed to the status quo.

Auxiliary hierarchies, such as the trade union leadership, completely share the party interest; if unions were to become representative of the workers, the present bosses would go. Within the armed forces, likewise, those on top are there because they have best known how to play the game, and they stand to lose from any real change of the system. The political police are wholly committed. The force is very large because the rulers are suspicious and also because the political police make themselves necessary; it is the more difficult to restrain them because they can keep dossiers on not only dissenters outside the party but also personages within it. The Soviet

KGB is estimated to be at least five times larger than its counterparts in the United States and Western Europe combined.[29] In return for privileges, status, and power, its members are expected to show absolute loyalty. They have millions of informants, tentacles in the system of repression, for whom a change of system would be disastrous.

Those who have most reason to reject the regime, the peasants, are voiceless and isolated. The industrial workers might possibly, as in Poland, find means of making themselves heard; but they are flattered, relatively well treated, and divided. The party has been able to tame the intellectuals, who seem for the most part to have little idea of freedom, at least not for their inferiors. The scientific establishment is coopted into the elite and given privileges and consequently an interest in the system. The less gifted scientists, who have acquired their positions for political as well as scientific virtues, do not necessarily want more freedom. The controls that shelter them from competition with the West protect their incompetence, and they gain by expelling more brilliant nonconformists from their institutes.[30]

The press, relieved of competition and the necessity to write informatively, has a vested interest in censorship. Without it, the journalists would hardly know what to write, and all who have access to classified information would lose privilege. The bureaucracies that run the Artists' Union and Writers' Union, whose abilities are as much political as artistic or literary, similarly have an interest in the status quo, sheltered from competition. Most of the management of censorship can be placed in the hands of writers, who are among the materially most privileged of Soviet society.[31] They are probably better off than the majority of their Western counterparts, and certainly more secure and less hardworking. Of some 6,500 professional writers (members of the Writers Union), it was estimated that only about 100 (including many of the most talented), were active liberals.[32]

Like the hacks who run literary organizations, black marketeers would be injured by relaxation of controls. Salespeople would lose by an end to shortages, fixers by freedom to buy and sell. In Moscow, those who have acquired a list of telephone numbers of important people would lose if telephone directories became readily available. Those who allocate scarce housing possess a valuable property, as do auto repairmen who have means of getting spare parts.

In ordinary times most people have, or think they have, a stake in stability. The Communist society is exceptional only because it is engineered to limit influence to those whose welfare is bound up with the existent system. It holds all organizations closely bound, minimizes feedback, and prevents the competition and contest that might fuel demands for improvement. Thus it has the power to hold the system firmly in place even though efficiency is low, faults are evident, and change might seem very desirable.

INTERNATIONAL SUPPORT

Much of the stability of Communism, especially in smaller countries, derives from the world movement enabling Communist states to look to outside powers for moral, political, economic, and occasionally military support. Aid from the Soviet Union and China saw North Korea and Vietnam through difficult wars. Vietnam counts on the Soviet state for help in reconstruction and is flattered by fraternal visits by top-level Soviet leaders. Cuban Communism has rested on Soviet backing from the beginning. In 1961 Castro avowed his revolution to be "socialist" and invited himself into the Soviet fraternity in order to secure support against an expected renewal of the U.S.-sponsored Bay of Pigs attack. Khrushchev vaguely committed himself to the defense of Cuba and undertook to keep the Cuban economy afloat. The Soviet subsidy has totalled over the years 1960–78 some $13 billion, $2.9 billion in 1978,[33] far more foreign aid than received by any other Latin American nation. The Soviets bought sugar at above world prices, furnished petroleum at less than world prices, supplied arms, sent many technicians and advisers, and proffered much advice. East European countries did likewise, as did China for a time.

For a few years after 1962 Soviet-Cuban relations were troubled, but after 1968 relations again warmed. Castro undertook to model his state closely after the Soviet, joined the Soviet bloc economic organization (Comecon), began cooperating with Latin American Communist parties, and linked his foreign policy more closely to the USSR.[34] By the mid-1970s the Cuban police apparatus was working intimately with the KGB at home and abroad. Cuban-Soviet cooperation in Africa, wherein Cuba provided personnel and the Soviets furnished money and munitions, gave Castro glory and the Soviets an expanded sphere of influence. Cuban detachments in seven or eight African countries formed a praetorian guard for the respective dictatorships.

While the Soviet Union profits militarily and politically from overlordship in Eastern Europe, those regimes rest on Soviet influence and power. Having set up governments basically through its military presence, the Soviet Union has intervened whenever it thought the Communist system was imperiled. Its ultimate power is total, of course, where its forces are on the ground, as in East Germany, Poland, Czechoslovakia, and Hungary. The Soviet presence there, like the possibility of intervention in Romania, restricts freedom not only of action but also of thought. Large numbers of Soviet advisers guide the Bulgarian government, police, and army. Dissidents know that it is fruitless to attack the Soviet Union or criticize the alliance. Poles cannot call for freedom of the press because the Soviets would not allow it. It is similarly pointless to advocate workers' control in industry.

Rulers of East European countries can credit themselves with generously granting their peoples as much freedom as the Soviets permit. A somewhat Stalinist regime is more acceptable to Romanians because they know that they are required to have a Communist government and theirs at least upholds the national dignity.

Military power is the guarantor of the Soviet sphere through both Soviet occupation forces and defense cooperation. The Warsaw Treaty Organization (established in 1955 as a somewhat belated institutionalization of the relation) is an unbreakable alliance reinforced by many bilateral treaties, dominated by the Soviet Union within the framework of "proletarian internationalism."[35] Military integration and many organizational links make deviation almost inconceivable. East German Deputy Defense Minister Lt. Gen. Horst Stechbarth said: "There is not a single land unit of the National People's Army that does not have close contact with the corresponding unit of Soviet forces in Germany. Joint maneuvers and human contacts have become routine."[36]

The Soviets claim that their power alone saves the East European countries from American (or possibly German) imperialism; in a sense they are the protectors of Communism even in violently anti-Soviet Albania.[37] East European leaders assure their peoples that their nations depend upon Soviet protection. A Czech spokesman shrugged off a Dutch plea on behalf of dissidents with the comment that "certain people had lost the feel for what is the actual balance of power in Europe."[38]

Constitutions consecrate bonds with the Soviet Union in the basic law. The Soviet model is closely followed, even where smaller countries of different backgrounds might better develop their own patterns. Cooperative and consultative Soviet-East European organizations are legion. Foreign policy is coordinated, and there are conferences to organize propaganda lines. Soviet tactics against dissidents give cues to Czechs and Poles. When a ferment of protest broke out in East Germany late in 1976, planeloads of KGB men came to lend a hand.[39] According to an East German scholar, "there is not a sector of work or daily life that is not shaped in part by fraternal relations with the Soviet Union."[40]

Cultural relations are cultivated through a host of channels; it is typical that school children must study Russian in all members of the Warsaw Treaty Organization (WTO) except Romania. Proaganda exalts the great Soviet protector and identifies the nation with the invincible international movement. Ideology cloaks or rationalizes subordination to the Soviet Union; "proletarian internationalism" is most invoked by governments with the least legitimacy, the Czechoslovak and East German. It is the idealization of nonfreedom. The Czech leader, Gustav Husak, has earnestly urged the "right and obligation" of the Soviets to tell foreign parties what sort of leadership they should have.[41] In the words of Bulgaria's Todor Zhivkov, "Our patriotism is inseparable from our love and respect for the Soviet Union and its great Communist Party."[42] But it is not necessary for East Europeans to love the Soviet Union, only to respect and fear it.

East European economies depend on Soviet raw materials, especially oil, and on Soviet markets for goods not readily salable elsewhere; they are tied by their shortcomings. Five-year plans are coordinated, and specialization increases interdependence. Deals with the West, whereby East European countries often serve as conduits for the flow of technology to the Soviet Union, do not weaken the bonds. East European countries are called upon to invest in Soviet projects even though they may have to borrow at high interest in the West to do so.[43] They thereby increase dependence on the raw materials produced by their investments and acquire a stake in the Soviet economy. The Soviet Union helps stabilize East European economies; for example, it furnished large credits after the disorders in Poland in 1970 and 1976. There are many joint undertakings, including broadcasting and publishing enterprises; and Comecon, the economic organization that includes not only the Soviet bloc but also Cuba and Vietnam, has a huge bureaucracy.

Even Romania, which makes much of its nationalism and independence, goes its own way in foreign policy, and orients its trade to the West, cooperates rather closely with Comecon, WTO, and the Soviet Union and leans morally and politically on Soviet power. As soon as dissidents begin to make themselves heard, Romania stands firmly beside its allies. Most important, Romanians know that the Soviets would not permit a non-Communist regime.

Vassalage to the Soviet Union does not seem popular in Eastern Europe, except perhaps in Bulgaria. It is widely regarded as antinational, burdensome, and exploitative.[44] In the resurgence of Polish nationalism, many Poles believe all their troubles are caused by Moscow.[45] Even high Communists may have little enthusiasm for their junior status.[46] But the elites need the Soviet connection and cannot move away from it. There is a general distaste for things Soviet, but ambitious youths go to Moscow to study and make useful contacts. The leaders of Poland and East Germany seem to have been more worried by Czech liberalization in 1968 than were the Russians, and more eager to see "proletarian internationalism" prevail over democratized Communism.

The Soviet state, inversely, rests to some extent upon dominion in Eastern Europe. This represents a vindication of Marxism-Leninism and the Soviet messianic-imperial mission, and a satisfaction of power. Even if Eastern Europe has become economically burdensome, as is sometimes contended, it must be held.[47] With it, the Soviet Union is a superpower; without it, Russia would shrink to secondary status, and Marxism-Leninism might collapse.

The sharing of Communist patterns among a number of states thus contributes to stability in all. It contributes also to the extension of near-Communist ways, especially in Africa, where a big advantage of conversion to Marxism-Leninism is the moral and material assistance to be expected from advanced and powerful states. Soviet military strength is a major factor in convincing people anywhere of the rightness or acceptability of Soviet institutions. It also is satisfying to belong to a universal movement.

Communism has become the ideological basis for the mutual support of modernized autocracies in opposition to the pluralistic Western world. All dictatorships share an interest in the suppression of free institutions, which complicate their politics, provide an alternative model of society, and encourage dissidence. This shared interest is ordinarily not formulated, and in the case of most military dictatorships it has limited importance. However, rightist governments in Latin America have lent one another a helping hand, both in South and Central America. Brazil, for example, has backed military governments in Uruguay, Bolivia, and Chile. Prior to World War II fascist regimes in Germany and Italy bolstered each other, both on the world stage and intellectually by making fascism a broad-based, therefore respectable, political form. There was something of a fascist international in Eastern Europe, as parties in Hungary, Romania, Bulgaria, Yugoslavia, and Slovakia tried to imitate Nazi success and looked to Nazi power for backing. The Axis powers used their "international" to administer occupied territories in World War II.

Communism, however, is a far more effective, overtly internationalist authoritarianism, which upholds one-party rule and total control by a self-selected organized elite. It is the successful modern absolutism, and ambitious leaders or parties naturally take as their model (unless deterred by possible moral or religious repugnance) the absolutism that claims universal validity and has shown its strength and applicability. The states that have assumed Marxist-Leninist garb likewise feel more comfortable in company; hence they spend a good deal of their limited resources—as Cuba has in Africa—on the spread of their political species.

The extension of Communism has the secondary effect of making it more rigid. Change is inhibited by the desire not to get out of step, and mutual influence draws toward an inflexible common norm. Moreover, if Communist governments become less effective and leaderships grow more self-serving, they may become more dependent on foreign support and less responsive to their peoples and less adaptable.

In sum, the Communist state makes maximum use of its power in order to solidify its power. It destroys competitive organizations and grasps all bases from which an attack on it could be launched. It appropriates the existing means of production and builds up its own Communist economy. It represses contrary beliefs and educates people in its doctrines and thought patterns. It leads many people to identify their fortunes with it, from peasants made urban workers to newly educated professionals. Most of all, it places authority in the hands of people who owe everything to it. It also gathers strength from the support of like-minded, more or less dependent states, to form a broad international front.

If all this could be done with complete success, Communism would be irresistible and omnipotent. But in each area there is a darker side. The ideology of the revolution is falsified by the rule of the revolutionaries, and it inevitably decays. The destruction of competitive powers ultimately brings petrifaction of the rulership. There is no way to assure permanent economic expansion and concomitant satisfactions. Security for the apparatus ultimately confirms incompetence. Foreign relations erode the essentially isolationist Communist order. It must change.

NOTES

1. *Pravda*, January 23, 1977, p. 3.

2. Stephen White, "USSR: Autocracy and Industrialism," in *Political Culture and Political Change in Communist States*, ed. Archibald H. Brown and Jack Gray (New York: Holmes and Meier, 1977), p. 43.

3. Robert G. Kaiser, *Russia: The People and the Power* (New York: Atheneum, 1976), p. 34.

4. *RFE Research Situation Report*, Poland/lo, April 19, 1977, p. 3.

5. *New York Times*, December 15, 1977, p. A-9.

6. Stephen Osofsky, *Soviet Agricultural Policy: Toward the Abolition of Collective Farms* (New York: Praeger, 1974), p. 233. Osofsky gives a general picture of the bureaucratization of agriculture.

7. Gayle D. Hannah, "Soviet Public Communications in the Post-Stalin Period," in *Change and Adaption in Soviet and East European Politics*, ed. Jane P. Shapiro and Peter J. Potichynj (New York: Praeger, 1976), p. 135.

8. *Time*, March 11, 1974, p. 45.

9. Alec Nove, *World Today*, 32 (April 1976): 122.

10. V. Eliutin, "The Higher School at the Contemporary Stage," *Kommunist* 17 (November 1976): 49.

11. *Pravda*, January 18, 1976.

12. D. Donskoi, "For a Moral-Political Revival," *Arkhiv Samizdata*, vol. 23, doc. 1,175a, p. 2.

13. Alexander Vardy, "Die Erziehung zum Hass," in *24 Zeugen: Dokumente des Terrors*, ed. Hardmann Wippermann (Wurzburg: Neumann, 1977), p. 225.

14. As averred by a dissident, K. Volnyi, "The Intelligentsia and the Democratic Movement," *Arkhiv Samizdata*, vol. 23, doc. 1,175a.

15. Stephen White, "Political Socialization in the USSR: A Study in Failure?" *Studies in Comparative Communism* (Autumn 1977): 340–41.

16. Observer, *Message from Moscow* (New York: Vintage Books, 1971), p. 347.

17. John B. Dunlop, *The New Revolutionaries* (Belmont, Mass.: Nordland, 1976), p. 166.

18. *Literaturnaya gazeta*, May 10, 1978, p. 15; *Current Digest of the Soviet Press* 30 (June 7, 1978): 6.

19. *Time*, March 11, 1974, p. 44.

20. *New York Times*, January 28, 1977, p. 6.

21. Vladimir V. Kusin, "An Overview of East European Reformism," *Soviet Studies* 28 (July 1976): 361.

22. *New York Times*, February 12, 1980, p. C-4.

23. Pierre Emmanuel, cited by Abraham Rothbey, *The Heirs of Stalin: Dissidence and the Soviet Regime, 1953–1970* (Ithaca: Cornell University Press, 1972), p. 287.

24. Paul Hollander, "Soviet Society Today," *Current History* 71 (October 1976): 138.

25. Edward Crankshaw, "Introduction," in Peter G. Grigorenko, *The Grigorenko Papers* (Boulder, Colo.: Westview Press, 1976), p. 3.

26. Kaiser, *Russia*, p. 143.

27. As is true in Romania and elsewhere. Trond Gilberg, *Modernization in Romania since World War II* (New York: Praeger, 1975), p. 246.

28. Jeremy R. Azrael, *Managerial Power and Soviet Politics* (Cambridge: Harvard University Press, 1966), p. 166.

29. Harry Rositzke, "America's Secret Operations," *Foreign Affairs* 53 (January 1975): 341.

30. Mark Popovsky, "Three Letters on Soviet Science," *Survey* 23 (Spring 1978): 143.

31. Kaiser, *Russia*, p. 362; Arkady Belinkov, in *Soviet Censorship*, ed. Martin Dewhirst and Robert Farrell (Metuchen, N.J.: Scarecrow Press, 1973), pp. 12–13.

32. Peter Reddaway, "Introduction," in *Uncensored Russia: Protest and Dissent in the Soviet Union*, ed. Peter Reddaway (New York: American Heritage Press, 1972), p. 29.

33. *Economist*, November 3, 1979, p. 6.

34. Archibald R. M. Ritter, "The Cuban Revolution: A New Orientation," *Current History* 74 (February 1978): 54–84.

35. Walter C. Clemens, Jr., "The European Alliance System," in *The International Politics of Eastern Europe*, ed. Charles Gati (New York: Praeger, 1976), pp. 220–23.

36. *Christian Science Monitor*, November 23, 1976, p. 4.

37. Adam B. Ulam, "The Destiny of Eastern Europe," *Problems of Communism* 23 (January–February 1974): 2.

38. *Christian Science Monitor*, March 28, 1977, p. 14.

39. *Time*, December 20, 1976, p. 35.

40. Henry Krisch, "The German Democratic Republic in the Mid-1970s," *Current History* 70 (March 1976): 122.

41. *New York Times*, May 1, 1976, p. 3.

42. Cited by Peter Rained, "Intellectuals and the Party in Bulgaria," in *Change and Adaption in Soviet and East European Politics*, p. 193.

43. For the Polish example, see Arthur R. Rachwald, "Poland between the Superpowers: Three Decades of Foreign Policy," *Orbis* 20 (Winter 1977): 1081.

44. For Hungary, see Peter A. Toma and Ivan Volgyes, *Politics in Hungary* (San Francisco: W. H. Freeman, 1977), p. 151.

45. Vincent Chryponski, "Recent Polish Nationalism: A Commentary," in *Nationalism in the USSR and Eastern Europe in the Era of Brezhnev and Kosygin*, ed. George W. Simmonds (Detroit: University of Detroit Press, 1977), p. 376.

46. Alexander Matejko, *Social Change and Stratification in Eastern Europe: An Interpretive Analysis of Poland and her Neighbors* (New York: Praeger, 1974), p. 217.

47. Adam B. Ulam, *Expansion and Coexistence* (New York: Praeger, 1974), p. 747; Charles Marer, "A Soviet Liability: Economic Issues," in *The International Politics of Eastern Europe*, p. 79.

8

AUTHORITARIAN INERTIA

The prevalent form of government in most of the world today is oligarchic or dictatorial; only countries that have undergone a rather special evolution have come to the democratic pluralist forms characteristic of the Western industrial states. Within the Western sphere itself, representative government has been the general rule only since the victory of the antifascist side in World War II. Outside it, Japan is the only very strong and stably democratic power; it was made so by defeat and occupation. India and Sri Lanka (Ceylon) owe what they have of democratic structures to the British heritage and their social systems. Otherwise Asia is authoritarian, as is Africa. In Latin America there have been many moves toward democratic government for 150 years, in large part because of the influence of the successful republic to the north. However, one can hardly find a firmly functioning democracy aside from diminutive Costa Rica and the most modern countries of South America, Argentina, Chile, and Uruguay, which not long ago seemed to be on the liberal road, have been sidetracked to military rule. In this situation, it is unrealistic to suppose that Communist states, whose societies have been purposefully restructured for authoritarianism, can move in any foreseeable time by any imaginable path to democratic or liberal government.

It is not even necessary that a government pretend to speak for the majority. South Africa, whose government represents only one-sixth of its population, would seem to demonstrate that a minority determined to hold power can do so indefinitely even without ideological legitimation in the eyes of the ruled. Positions of command in the economy, government, and the armed forces are kept in the hands of persons who have a vested interest in the maintenance of the system, in much the same fashion as in a Communist state. This domination by a self-aware minority can be shaken only by very strong external pressures.

The durability of one-party rule in Mexico is also discouraging for ideas of change toward a representative or democratic evolution of Communist states. Prior to the revolution of 1910 Mexico had a constitution patterned after that of the United States and some traditions of aspiration to republican government. Nonetheless, Porfirio Diaz seized power by force and reelected himself president eight times. The revolution was launched in the name of free elections and no-reelection, but the first part of the slogan never became effective. The rulership by the revolutionary clique was strengthened in the 1920s by the formation of a governing party, the position of which became somewhat like that of a ruling Communist party although much weaker.

For over 50 years Mexico has been governed by the same party, the monopoly of which is outwardly more complete today than when it began. Elections are held regularly and are easily managed. The press is nominally free, citizens have extensive rights, courts are far more independent than in any Communist country, oppositionists can organize and propagandize, yet the monopoly of power remains unblemished. Continuous and massive cultural and intellectual influences from the United States, the existence of a strong free-enterprise economy, urbanization, and the shift from an agricultural to a largely industrial economy have not touched the dominion of the ruling party. This manages so comfortably that it recently allotted 100 of 400 seats in the lower house of the congress to opposition parties, even though they may win no seats in the elections.

Practically by definition, an authoritarian regime can be overthrown only by revolution. If a dictatorship becomes too odious, it ordinarily is removed not by the people but by the military. There is an enormous gap between widespread disaffection and willingness to fight for freedom. The desire for freedom is a learned one, a part of a social order, not a datum of human nature; at best, if some aspire to be free, others aspire to rule, while the majority are probably willing or resigned to be governed.[1]

The desire for change or freedom must be channeled in order to become effective, but a powerful dictatorship eliminates alternatives and makes itself the sole focus of society. Only thus can the persistence of Nazism be understood. After the beginning of 1943 German armies were in continual retreat, and German cities were ever more pulverized. Eventually allied troops were pushing near the German heartland. The army was exhausted, the airforce was smashed, rubble was piling up in the cities, and the people were hungry. Hitler himself was sick and secluded. Yet after the plot of July 20, 1944, was crushed, there was no organized opposition. Hitler's government was the sole German authority until German armed forces were virtually destroyed and Hitler killed himself.

Even if an authoritarian state permits ostensible freedom of organization and expression (like the Mexican), there are many ways to keep a firm grip on the levers of rule. The governing apparatus is the dispenser of benefits; it is always more advantageous for people to cooperate than to oppose. The official apparatus provides jobs and careers. As soon as there is evidence of strong popular discontent the state makes at least gestures toward alleviating it. Persons who show talent as independent leaders are bought off or coopted into the system. Those who prove disruptive and cannot be neutralized are harassed or repressed. If there is a strike, workers' demands may be met but leaders are punished. Idealists are given opportunities to do good in cooperation with the rulership. In sum, the well-managed dictatorship makes it seem foolish to go against the state; and the hierarchic system of patrons and clients, whereby everyone has a stake in the system except the powerless people at the bottom, can be quite firm. The Communist hierarchies are the most strongly organized in history.

An authoritarian regime can be imposed by force channeled by organization; a military leader can establish and rule an empire. But a highly structured pluralistic system with counterbalancing parts can evolve only from a long tradition. Terror, which need not be massive if it is an ever present possibility, legitimizes authority and at the same time promises unity and wholeness; it atomizes and insulates, and it overrules truth.[2] It is often said that Communist rulers, the Soviets in particular, can no longer use gross terror, exposed as they are to world communications. The only evidence is that they have not done so since Stalin. The obvious reason to refrain is the conservatism of the apparatus and the fact that apparatchiks want security for themselves, which implies some security for all. However, arbitrary actions are acceptable. It is not likely that in case of need the General Secretary would shrink from bloodletting. It is a frequent assumption that the political system must correspond more or less closely to the needs of the society, with the implication that the Communist system must change if it proves unable to carry on the tasks of economic growth and modernization. But countless states through history and in recent years have regressed economically under bad government; incompetence does not make ruling classes open to change. Foreign pressures help to moderate tyranny and encourage some respect for human rights, which amount to human decency. But they do very little to democratize or transfer power to the people.

Technological development favors democratization through increased self-awareness and the need of governments for modern legitimation, but it also places instruments of persuasion and coercion in the hands of the elite and raises needs for security and protection. There is no close correlation between economic and political systems; modernization and rule of law are not covariant. At present, the advanced industrial states may be called generally democratic; but there have been powerful despotisms at all levels, from the Incas, without the use of the wheel or well-developed writing, to Nazi Germany and advanced Marxist-Leninist states. Where the government controls the means of information and communication, it is probable that modernization serves, at least if external influences can be discounted, to increase inequality and strengthen political power. Russian tyrants have not promoted education and industrialization for centuries in order to weaken themselves.[3]

Economic development is assisted by freeing the economy from bureaucratic meddling and official exploitation, but this does not require democratization. Such countries as Taiwan, Singapore, South Korea, and Brazil have enjoyed growth rates among the world's highest under authoritarian but probusiness regimes. Much less does Communist industrialization build up independent power and horizontal bonds among the people.

Communist governments have ruled regardless of unpopularity in industrialized states (such as East Germany and Czechoslovakia), as well as in economically backward states (such as Albania and Cambodia). Communist parties keep order, get people to cheer them, make the economy function and even grow, and build military power in countries of the most varied economic levels and political traditions. East Germany after the building of the Wall in 1961, Hungary after the crushing of the revolt in 1956, and Czechoslovakia after the occupation of 1968, have all been tolerably prosperous under unpopular rule. The Baltic republics have been the most productive area of the Soviet Union, although very few Balts welcomed the Soviet army that crushed their independence. It seems sufficient that the government is regarded as unalterable, or that people remember (as in Hungary) that an effort to shake off Communist domination was drowned in blood.[4]

The highly organized, ostensibly egalitarian, and partially open ruling elite, supported by an elaborate modern ideology, is the Leninist contribution to the ancient art of rulership. It is much more sophisticated than its best precursor, the Chinese imperial bureaucracy. Hatred of the rulers is reduced by the fact that there are no too obviously idle rich and privilege comes supposedly through earned status instead of accumulated wealth.[5] Individuals have no way of getting together effectively, and there is no defense against the all-penetrating power. The force the party might exercise is limited only by the desire of its own apparatus for security and some considerations of foreign reactions. It becomes sanity to conform. Most Communist states probably use far more force than necessary. To minimize dissent it should suffice to apply only quiet repression, manufactured social pressure, surveillance, and exclusion from good jobs, higher education, and travel.

The masses cherish simplicity and serenity and regard politics as the responsibility of the elite. Hating the petty tyrants, they humanly hope that those high above are well intentioned. They are likely to be stirred only by sudden economic deprivations, and they understand little of the quarrels of principle of intellectual dissenters. A Czech office worker commented bitterly concerning the civil liberties advocates:

> Remember, the people whom the police are hounding right now are nearly all former party stalwarts, political, cultural, or whatever. Whatever the party is doing to them now, they should remember that communism is their religion. It isn't mine, and this whole fuss is no business of mine, either.[6]

The Soviet people have long become accustomed to political non-thinking, to letting the party leaders decide.[7] According to dissidents, they are uninformed and uninspired, incapable of social action, generally capable only of seeking material betterment.[8] Decades of harsh rule have made personalities uncongenial to the democratic spirit of relativism and compromise. Those who have broken out of Marxism retain Bolshevik habits of dogmatism, intolerance, and manipulation of history.[9] Customs of obedience or at least deference to superiors, political apathy, reliance on manipulation, retreat to private concerns, acceptance of hypocrisy, loss of initiative, poor work habits, and distrust of everyone outside the intimate circle disqualify people for self-government. The intellectual dissidents, too, think in terms of status and are regarded—and regard themselves—as members of the upper class, above the commoners with whose help they might dream of changing the system.[10] Intellectuals must look to the Communist leadership to democratize voluntarily; there is no other force to which to look.

Concessions may be made, but they are mostly of form. They do not necessarily lead to more demands as long as the propaganda machine is operative to satisfy some and disarm others. The Soviet regime corresponds to popular prejudices and expectations, to the traditional respect for authority, the fear of invasion, the abhorrence of anarchy, the limited value of the individual, and the lack of social mobility.[11] There is fear in principle of moving against the established leadership lest chaos result; hence arbitrariness and purges are to be accepted. For a person in Soviet or Chinese society, and increasingly in Eastern Europe, the presumed rewards of the loose, pluralistic society are distant and obscure, whereas the dangers of dissolution are plain and fearsome. To try to throw off Communist rule would bring danger of war. Free elections might only lead to a contest rending the state or to the victory of unknown "dark forces."

The decadent authoritarian state suffers corruption and the willfulness of petty bosses, but the ready answer to corruption and disorder is to strengthen the controls instead of making them unnecessary. If little bosses are willful, the solution is a big boss who can rein them in, more authority rather than less, as in the Russian tradition.[12] If some people begin to escape control of the state, they enrich themselves, raise jealousies, and arouse calls for restraint of profiteering. The growth of lawbreaking makes the society not more but less equipped for legal government. Salvation can visibly come only from the firm hand that promises a return of justice, stability, and glory. Thus, an oppositionist like Solzhenitsyn hopes for a new moral order imposed by a good emperor, although a new strong man might be an unvarnished despot, lacking even the inspiration that gave some meaning to Stalinism.

Exalting the common man in propaganda, the Communist order gives a place to everyone prepared to fit into the system. People are put to work, albeit often uneconomically, instead of being wasted by unemployment and told they are unneeded. The system of controls is able to save the state from some of the amorality that afflicts the free-swinging West, or at least to drive it out of sight. The Communists then congratulate their people for manifold moral superiority, from absence of pornography to freedom from the mercantilism and greed of capitalist societies. Something called socialism should be able to check the vices, perversions, and ailments of modern technological society. This fond hope is persuasive; the idea of private ownership of industry has become incomprehensible to Soviet youth.[13]

The real firmness of the Communist structure, however, lies in its utility for the organized, self-selected, and self-promoted elite, with its strong we-group feeling based partly on shared philosophy and more on shared status. No enlightenment can convince the Communist aristocracy that it stands to gain from change that involves loss of material, psychological, and social superiority. So long as the elite holds together in its determination to keep all important positions in the social order, there is no means short of war for its displacement. Instead of giving diverse groups and organizations a share of power, the Communist system puts its committed servants into positions of power, while coopting a few persons who may acquire influence outside the control framework, such as sports champions, artists and scientists. Elitehood is much more important than ideology; so long as one belongs, it does not matter much whether one believes, provided disbelief is not openly flaunted.

In this condition, there is no politics outside the party; even those who would change the system must convince themselves (except for a desperate minority) of the need to compromise and work within it. Only as a loyal Communist can one hope to become influential for good or ill. The Communist kind of politics by secret management is the only kind anyone knows, perhaps the only kind anyone understands. Political institutions have value only as related to the needs of the party. The idea that civil rights, independent courts, a representative legislature, or other institutions have intrinsic value is a sophisticated one acquired through long education. It is also an idea for which a Marxist-Leninist education unfits the mind.

The ideological set is frozen. The mature Communist society no longer needs militancy. Fervor is an encumbrance when the party has settled down to enjoy monopoly of power. Not only the enthusiasms but the rancors are left behind. Marxism-Leninism, moreover, becomes ill suited for the immobile status-conscious society. Marxism is above all a critique of the establishment order, and intellectuals in Eastern Europe have applied it against the party hacks. It is unmodern in temper and counterproductive as a principle of management. But it has been deformed into an intellectual support for authority; its revolutionism is made antirevolutionary just as pseudodemocracy is made antidemocratic. To set it aside would amount not only to admitting that a generation of sacrifices was folly; it also would mean giving up the only developed antidemocratic myth extant, the only rationale for the position in society for hundreds of thousands of big and little bosses.

There is no ideological basis for an alternative society except nebulous ideas of a few most receptive to Western influences. Western society may be admired, but it is not understood; exiles from the Soviet Union seem to have difficulty comprehending its strengths even after prolonged alienation from Marxism-Leninism and exposure to Western ways. Accustomed to the pressures and guidance of the absolutist society, they find the looser society disconcerting even though they may like it. They find it hardest to divest themselves of the paternalistic mentality and the idea of responsibility of the state guided by an elite. The building of a constitutional democratic society requires not the easily assimilated idea of equality, but a sophisticated sense of legality and restriction of authority. The overwhelming majority of the Soviet people hope only for an improvement of the kind of society they have.[14] Even a radical, militant, Christian, anti-Soviet, revolutionary group wanted, according to its blueprint of the future, to keep collective ownership of property, a socialized economy (dedicated to the general welfare), and elections without competing political parties; their head of state would be a monarch confirmed by a plebiscite.[15] They were like the nineteenth-century revolutionaries hoping to solve Russia's troubles by getting a good tsar.

The West, in any case, reduces its own attractiveness. It also faces problems of alienation, crime, demoralization, and economic mismanagement. Depression or recession in Europe and the United States helps Communism today just as it served Stalinist radicalism in the 1930s. The self-denigration of the West, especially the United States, provides a chief source of materials for Communist propagandists who lack the imagination to invent what is furnished ready-made by the antagonist-victim. The influence of West German television on East Germany is reduced by the fact that programs are often almost as critical of Western society as if they had been produced in East Germany, and are more interesting and intelligently critical. The vices of the pluralistic world are very visible; its virtues are often less conspicuous. Democracy promises no quick solution to anyone's problems.

This makes it easier for the Communists—Soviet, Chinese, or other—to claim moral, political, and ideological superiority, the special claim that stands in the way of fundamental change. Both the USSR and China are too big and proud to take lessons cheerfully from the West. The problem is most severe for the Russians; there is no way to reconcile a pluralistic society (or any visibly available alternative form) with the dominion of Russia in its sphere. Soviet leaders can easily convince themselves that democratization would be dangerous not only for themselves but also for the state.

For such reasons the Communist system is stable and has shown itself to be self-restorative when strained. Throughout many changes in leadership, collective or single, and under quite diverse personalities, it has continued much the same for decades. The Soviet state returned to fullest absolutism after the semiliberal interlude of the 1920s. It came through the purges bloodied but entire, despite the immensity of losses, the destruction of layers of the elite, and the grip of fear. In World War II ideology yielded to realism; it returned in full force afterward, when rulership again became more important than material performance. In his latter years, Stalin tended to set the party aside, but after his death it reasserted itself. Malenkov's apparent supposition that the mobilizing party would yield primacy to the administrative state in the normalization of the system proved false. The overlordship of the party apparatus remains as strong today as ever. Mao came near dismantling the party in his Cultural Revolution, and the army had to be called upon to restore order, but the party came back as the chief agency of government.

The Communist system thus has seemed to vary without altering its political essence. Modernization does not mean liberalization, and those who decades ago saw solidification leading to rationality and technocracy were too functionalist.[16] There has been some pluralistic segregation in the maturing society, but it remains true that in the Soviet and other Communist states specific interests may be better promoted by *not* being articulated.[17] Outwardly there has been no mellowing of the Leninist spirit. Mensheviks and non-Leninist socialists are as damned as ever. Only a small part of the Stalinist heritage has been jettisoned; many coworkers of Lenin are still traitors. The party continues to speak of evil capitalists, good workers, and inevitable class struggle. A sign of opening the system might be to allow a little more life in pseudodemocratic institutions, but this has not occurred. Elections have become even more unanimous.[18] Neither the Supreme Soviet nor the party congress has moved toward open discussion of any issues.

In 1962 a rise in the price of meat and dairy products provoked riots in Novocherkassk and some other Soviet cities. Since then the authorities have kept the lid tight except for minor disorders here and there. A little later Garder viewed the ouster of Khrushchev as the beginning of the end of the Stalinist state and foresaw a power struggle necessarily leading to revolution.[19] But so long as the elite associate their well-being with the power of the party, the party remains fixed.

Many writers see the Communist system as compressing the vital forces of dynamic, inherently progressive societies; but the system may devitalize society. Stalin was able to attack the majority of the Soviet population (in collectivization), cut the average standard of living nearly in half, and kill a tenth of the people. Although there was no improvement in the Chinese standard of living for 20 years (1957–77), political problems rose from elite conflicts, not popular pressures. The Communist states may not be able to solve social and economic problems, but this does not mean that they lack the means to stay in power. Their degenerative diseases of closure, degradation and aging of the rulership, corruption, and demoralization, are probably incurable; and as they progress, nonparty forces acquire some strength. But the state, if necessary, could retreat (in appearances, as in Yugoslavia) without surrendering more than tokens of power. Even if there were some sort of collapse or disorderly breakdown, the system that emerged from anarchy would very likely be much like the Marxist-Leninist state. Really to change it would require rebuilding from the ground up. Communism has above all demonstrated that the political system can be decisive.

THE MILITARY-CONSERVATIVE MODE

The revolution, once a glorious aspiration, becomes a remembered glory. As the party uses up its stock of ideas, there is less and less to look forward to, finally nothing but a hope indefinitely postponed, like the early Christians' expectation of the Second Coming. Legitimation of party rule shifts from the promise of the receding utopia to past victories; the party's gaze turns backward to memories of struggle and heroism. Change being no longer desired, order becomes the supreme virtue; and the past becomes sanctified—not only the party's past, but the past of the whole society. The canon, the works of Lenin or Mao, is fixed; today's policies are allegedly right because they are in accordance with ideas set forth by Lenin 60 or so years ago, or by Mao 30 to 50 years ago.

The rundown Communist state is fundamentally less like a Western pluralistic state than was tsarist Russia (at least in its last decade of semiconstitutional government), and is more conservative. The Communist state has fewer means of bringing younger persons to the top. The network of controls is far denser, hence there are far more positions of interlocking privilege; each position in the apparatus is a little peg helping to hold the entirety in place. The lesser officials, all concerned with their own small sphere, form the most inflexible sector, primarily concerned with stabilizing their position.[20]

To be conservative is practically to be nationalistic. The traditions and destiny of the nation fill the void left by the shrinking of the proletarian cause. The big subject is the revolution and the wars—the Russian civil war, the Great Patriotic War of the Soviet Union, the Chinese guerrilla war against

Nationalists and Japanese, or the battles of Tito's partisans. World War II renewed the decaying Stalinist system, healed wounds, and brought together discordant elements of Soviet society. Its memory and emotions are hence kept aflame so far as the state can do so. It is not hard to keep them bright; tales of battles and spies, of narrow escapes, courage, and sacrifice are as popular as Marxism-Leninism is dull.

In the revival of nonproletarian, and nonsocialist values, the nationalistic side of the Soviet mentality has been growing ever since the revolution, overtly since Stalin's "Socialism in One Country" (1924). Stalin openly revived the tsarist past and conservative values, such as the family, in the early 1930s; this was carried much further in the war, which was fought not for the proletariat but for Mother Russia. Whereas Lenin berated "Great Russian chauvinism" and made concessions to minorities, his present-day successors condemn all manifestations of nationalism except Russian. Russian neo-Slavophile nationalist dissenters, who are antimodern, antiforeign, and antiminority and see Russia disadvantaged in the empire built and governed by themselves, have grown in strength since the latter 1960s.[21] Some of them speak of the sufferings of Russia under Communism, but they have been practically immune to arrest and even on good terms with the KGB.[22] Anti-Semitism sometimes has seemed to replace anticapitalism.

Love for Russia is very strong. Lenin was an antipatriot, but modern Russians who take his name are "perhaps the world's most passionate patriots." With neither God nor socialist revolution to inspire them, the people have patriotism left, and the party makes the most of it. The large majority of Soviet people were in favor of using force against the Czechs in 1968, and they take great pride in military strength.[23] There is a species of nationalistic xenophobia, a primitive clannishness, a feeling that Russia is different and beyond the comprehension of outsiders.[24] There has been an enormous revival of antiquarian interest, encouraged by the party, a fondness for icons, antiques, and old churches.[25] Russianists advocate restoration of the rule of Orthodoxy and return to village life and the patriarchal family.[26] Much of the religious revival is nationalistic and neo-Slavophile.[27] Soviet literature has turned, with party blessing, toward traditional, even peasant themes along with military heroics. In the emptiness of Soviet culture, the past glows alluringly.[28] There is a hunger for roots, for belonging to a tradition deeper than the Soviet and stronger than love of socialism. Even the Communist Youth League has turned to Russianism to fill the void.[29]

In Eastern Europe old ethnic antagonisms have resurfaced; traditional anti-Semitism, following the Soviet lead, has come back after years of inhibition. Marxism everywhere has been mixed with nationalism, or overlaid by it; Communist parties preempt patriotic symbols with perfect ease. In Bulgaria old tsars have been restored to glory.[30] To discipline the young, the Bulgarian party looks to patriotic education plus military training.[31] The Czechoslovak government has increased spending on historical restorations.[32] The strongest force in Hungary is nationalism; Communism is acceptable chiefly as defender of the nation.[33] In Hungary and Poland the nouveaux riches hunt for pedigrees to legitimize status in traditional terms.

Romania has reversed the Soviet motto and has made a state socialist in form and nationalist in content.[34] The Romanian party was originally dominated by persons of non-Romanian background, principally Jews, Hungarians, and Germans;[35] as late as 1965 about half of the top leadership was non-Romanian. Recently, however, it has been essential to be Romanian to hope for advancement. The party is representative not so much of the proletariat as of the nation, and Marxism-Leninism is a means of idealizing patriotism. Modernization and industrializatin are the vindication of nationhood.

Children become "Falcons of the Fatherland" at age four. Historical studies and historical fiction are immensely popular.[36] Medieval princes, whom the Communists denigrated a few years ago with some justice as feudal exploiters, have been reglorified as heroes of the Romanian people. Even the sadistic Vlad the Impaler, prototype of Dracula, was exalted in 1977 as a noble patriot.[37] Ceausescu in 1970 became "Conducator," a title equivalent to Duce, Fuhrer, or Vozhd; the same honorific was used by the fascist dictator Antonescu (1940–44), who has been partly rehabilitated.

Conservatism, nationalism, and militarism go together, but Soviet Communism was militaristic in tone nearly from its genesis. After the civil war, an attempt was made to reconstruct by military command, and four "labor armies" began operations in February 1920.[38] This proved impractical, but Stalinism often has been compared to a war economy. "Patriotism is the supreme law of life," *Pravda* was saying in 1934.[39] These many decades after the end of hostilities, the Soviet economy is still managed essentially like that of a country at war. Soviet science is largely military oriented. The military helps where the civilian economy has trouble, especially in the harvest and large construction. Troops worked on the Baikal-Amur railroad as in a battle.[40]

The Soviet Union maintains and continues to expand armed forces quantitatively superior to the American in most categories, such as numbers of soldiers, armored divisions, aircraft, and nuclear megatonnage, despite a GNP approximately half that of the United States. The Soviet Union is a lesser economic power on the world scene; its status as a superpower rests on the world's numerically largest navy, the world's biggest land army, the ability to arm its friends anywhere, and powerful strategic nuclear forces. It is difficult to suggest whether it is the purpose of the military to defend the civilian economy or of the latter to support the military.[41]

There is an immense program of military-patriotic indoctrination, ranging from the collection of trophies to lessons in nuclear defense for school children, war games, and prizes for inspirational writing, all going forward with little reference to the international situation or possible threats to the fatherland. There are at least 123 military academies and institutes, and each secondary school has a military supervisor.[42] Children are taught the virtues of the Soviet army before they learn to read. Conscription is for two or three years, and there is no provision for conscientious objectors. The Communist party and the Soviet Army are closely linked. Soldiers are mostly Komsomol (Communist Youth League) members, and officers belong to the party (junior officers to the Komsomol) and are subject to party and military discipline. "Ours is an army," said Marshal Grechko, "in which the officer as well as every soldier is called upon to be a political warrior, an active propagandist and agitator."[43] The Soviet military makes much of the trust and cooperative relations resulting from the supposed absence of property instincts in Soviet society.[44]

In peacetime, civilians are called upon to administer; but if the party should become less capable of management and less secure in authority, it would be logical to expect the state to take on an increasingly military character. The military has a more secure base of authority than the party, and its appeal is deeper. Power may one day go to those who best incorporate the strength and glory of the nation—the soldiers, who have less need of myth to sanctify their guns. The party stands for a fading utopia; the army represents undeniable force.

The Soviet party, historically much afraid of Bonapartism, has developed elaborate mechanisms for multiple party penetration and control of the armed forces, and has kept strictly military men away from the center of power. Marshal Zhukov was briefly a full member of the Presidium (Politburo) but was expelled in 1956, allegedly for attempting to remove the army from party supervision. In April 1973, Marshal Andrei Grechko, Minister of Defense, became a full Politburo member and remained until his death; he was replaced by Dmitry Ustinov, whose entire career was in the munitions industry. In April–May 1975, General Secretary Brezhnev, who has made much of his war record and has close associates in the military and security forces, became General of the Army, and then Marshal. The prominence of the military has increased; but there seems little political-military conflict because the two vocations are, as in medieval Europe, close together. It might represent no immense change if Marshal Brezhnev were replaced by a genuine marshal.

The Chinese party, as rebuilt after the Cultural Revolution, became representative mostly of the military. In 1969 nearly half of the Central Committee and over half the Politburo wore a military uniform. According to Mao, "The Chinese Red Army is an armed body for carrying out the political tasks of the revolution."[45] Beginning in 1971 there was an effort to return to civilian rule, but in subsequent years the military was still prominent in administration and the economy.[46] The party and military bureaucracies merged both at top and bottom, and control was exercised through the party-military hierarchy as well as through the party chain of command.[47] The army was the only group held up as a general model for the people.[48] There was a military tone in propaganda, with stress on loyalty, determination, dedication, abstinence, and self-sacrifice. "Nothing is hard if you dare scale the heights."[49]

The basic support for the poorly known Hua Guofeng's elevation to the premiership and chairmanship was military.[50] Hua himself was associated with the security forces. The army played the key role in the quick defeat of the radicals (Gang of Four),[51] and military commanders were reported to have replaced the civilian administration in some provinces.[52] After the August 1977 party congress, all four members of the standing committee of the Politburo were military figures, including two powerful vice-chairmen of the party, 78-year-old Marshal and Minister of Defense Ye Jianying and the likewise aged Wang Dongxing, chief of the security guard.

Various other Communist states are not far from military rule. In Cuba, soldiers comprise a large majority of the upper echelons in the party. The East German army and police forces—proportionately several times larger than the West German—are the mainstay of the regime. Detente made no difference; compulsory military training was introduced in secondary schools in September 1978. In North Korea, not only does the high leadership have a guerrilla or army background, but the whole society has been entirely militarized, with every factory made a battlefield.[53] In the Vietnamese revolution, as in the Chinese and the Yugoslav, to be a Communist was to be a soldier. Tito is not often seen without his marshal's uniform. He is said to regard the military, not the party, as the guarantor of order and unity. The Yugoslav army has its own party structure, representation in local party organizations, and delegates in Chambers of Associated Labor. Generals hold several important ministries and virtually dominate the party just below the top.[54] The army is expected to be the chief source of unity after Tito.

Yet the military organization can only supplement, not wholly replace, the party, which is indispensable for the housekeeping tasks of government and management of the economy. Conservative moralism and militarism mix poorly with Marxism-Leninism, but the latter is too valuable for the total state to be dropped. There are no military coups in Communist states (unlike Third World states) because the armed forces are too penetrated by the party. But in the evolution of Communism from revolutionism to the keeping of order, the intrinsically elitist soldiers, exercising power as they are called upon to help the party, are more likely to increase their influence than are liberal politicians, intellectuals, or technocrats.[55] The generals may come to see themselves as more capable than an overaged and decreasingly competent party oligarchy because they are more objectively selected and more patriotic. In that case, and especially if in a lagging economy civilian authorities could no longer fill their wants, they might well assume control of the state, partially or completely, as their counterparts have done in scores of countries of the Third World.

CONVERGENCE WITH THE THIRD WORLD

Excepting those in Europe converted by external force, Communist states previously belonged to the non-Western world. As the revolutionary tidal wave of egalitarianism, radicalism, and utopianism recedes, the Communist state may be expected to look less like an innovative political form and more like many non-Western states that have not undergone a deep revolution. Without its special ideology the Communist system would be just one variety of dictatorship. As Talcott Parsons foresaw this many years ago,

> I do indeed predict that [Communist society] will prove to be unstable and will either make adjustments in the general direction of electoral democracy and a plural party system or "regress" into generally less advanced and politically less effective forms of organization, failing to advance as rapidly or as far as otherwise may be expected.[56]

Marxism began as a product of the Western world, but it always had a potential appeal to less developed countries because its passions were turned against the economic system of the rich countries. Lenin, before the Russian revolution, gave poor and dependent countries somewhat the role of the proletariat; the exploited masses were to make a revolution not only against the exploiting class, but also against the imperialist-capitalist industrial nations. It was an old idea that various Marxists, from Rudolf Hilferding and Rosa Luxemburg to Trotsky and Parvus had toyed with. Generations earlier, Russian Slavophiles had seen poverty as a virtue and looked to a contest of poor nations led by Russia against the rich.

Although Marxist theory promised that the proletariat of advanced countries would continue the revolution begun by the Russians, the Bolsheviks very soon began to identify their cause with that of the peoples of Asia. Within two weeks of the seizure of power, *Pravda* was seeing China, India, and Persia as reserve armies of Bolshevism.[57] As revolutionary flickers in the West died out after 1919, Lenin and his fellows increasingly hoped that preindustrial Asians would give the world revolutionary cause the needed shove. Lenin considered the Soviet form of government suited the Asians; it was applied in Central Asia and Mongolia with some succes. Stalin even more than Lenin identified with Asia, which was seen as virtuous in primitiveness and poverty.[58] Communism first became a real political force outside the Soviet Union in China, where the Kiangsi Soviet Republic was set up in 1930. All of Communism's triumphs since 1920 (except for those directly due to the Soviet army) have been in poorer countries.

Third World Communist countries, moreover, have been more thoroughly Communist than European ones. The mobilization of the masses in China and the emphatic equalitarianism and xenophobia of Maoism were beyond the capacity of the postwar Soviet Union. Kampuchea under the Pol

Pot regime was an extreme, one might say a caricature, of Marxism-Leninism: there were no books, practically no press, no postal service, no temples, no money, no exports, and almost no foreign contacts. Everyone worked in the fields under the guidance of the party and its shrouded leaders. Communism characteristically overrides the individual, and it does so more completely in more backward societies; it is more effectively revolutionary in Albania and Romania than in Poland and Hungary.

Khrushchev stressed the kinship of the Soviet bloc with the nonaligned Third World states, which he wanted to draw into his "Camp of Peace" to swamp the West by force of numbers. Soviet expansionism under Brezhnev has been directed entirely toward the Third World. Romania formally joined the third World bloc (Group of '77); it advocates the "New World Economic Order," under which Romania can claim reparations for past exploitation, and claims for itself the tariff preferences granted by the European Economic Community to less developed countries.[59] Yugoslavia has long acted as part of the Third World; Tito was a principal organizer of the nonaligned bloc. Post-Maoist China frankly acknowledges poverty and backwardness and considers itself champion of the poor nations against the superpowers (chiefly in practice against the "tsarist revisionists"). Cuba sees itself as a leading part of the Third World. Latter-day Marxism expects little of the working class of industrial nations but much of the peasantry of the less developed countries.

Third World nations, for their part, generally feel a kinship with the Communist states, sympathizing more or less with the Soviet Union and East European countries and still more with the Asian Communist states, as fellow sufferers from the cultural, economic, and formerly political assaults of the more powerful Western states.[60] There is little inclination to condemn Communist states for lack of freedom or economic failures, any more than Third World countries censure themselves. The Soviet Union seems to be exempt from blame for its dominion over Central Asians. Imperialism is equated with the power of the West; and there is less fear of the Communist states, whose existence is welcomed to counterbalance the power of the West. In conclaves of Third World countries, scores of countries speak in virtually the same accents as Cuba and Vietnam.

The Communist states share with the Third World their relative backwardness and a preoccupation with relations with the West. Marxism-Leninism, while losing its force in the Communist sphere, spreads in the Third World as a weapon in the intense and often strident confrontation with the richer countries. Foreign-owned corporations take the place of the capitalist class for the intellectuals of the Third World, and the economic gap between the prosperous and the poor guarantees a long life for the doctrine that supports claims for reparations from the advanced industrial (that is "capitalist") world. The less developed countries are inevitably resentful, even though they have to cooperate (as Communist countries increasingly have) for practical purposes. Freedom of the press is seen as a Western intrusion. Subject to comparisons and criticisms by world or Western standards, their leaders are driven to deprecate Western success, which must be the result of bad character or at best luck, certainly not work and a better social order. The West, or "capitalism," is to be blamed for their troubles, through its economic, political, and cultural penetration.

For the Third World nations, Communism serves to prevent Westernization or bourgeoisification, which implies loss of identity and the moral basis of life. It harmonizes with the basically elitist structures prevalent in the non-Western world. The political reality of the Communist sphere and nearly all the Third World is stark inequality, oligarchic if not dictatorial rule, and an economy controlled by the political elite. The Leninists carry further and implement more thoroughly the general imperative of maximizing political power, reversing the secular progress of the West from status to contract.

Much of the Third World inclines toward something called "socialism," usually understood to mean a state-controlled economy, rejection of Western ways, and perhaps recovery of native virtues. Nearly all African states favor nationalized industry, economic planning, and theoretical income leveling.[61] The interests of the ruling classes are served by the political approach to economic problems. The elite is set off by education, which qualifies one for bureaucratic and political positions in the Third World as in Communist states, confers status, and gives a right of tutelage over the less enlightened. Capitalism is both alien and more antiegalitarian than in the West; it works less well in the unfavorable political and social climate. Thus it becomes the task of the Third World state to promote industrialization, although the statist economy—overstaffed, politicized, probably poorly planned, perhaps designed as much for nationalist display as utility—is even less efficient than in the Communist sphere. In most Third World countries a political opposition is hardly more acceptable than in Poland or China. Control of the state (the chief employment of the educated) is too valuable to be surrendered merely because of the wishes of the unenlightened. Unity is too fragile (the large majority of countries of Africa and Asia are, like the Soviet Union, an ethnic patchwork) and society is much too divided to permit meaningful elections.

The party or leadership assumes the responsibility of ruling on behalf of the people.[62] It uses the rhetoric of egalitarianism and brotherhood, partly to broaden support and win acquiescence as a modern government, partly to facilitate reform. It undertakes improvements to legitimate its claims, and it may evoke a better future to compensate for present shortcomings.[63] Here again, however, the Third World moves in the same direction as the Second; egalitarianism and real concern for the masses decline in the postrevolutionary generation, hopes of a radiant tomorrow fade, and an aging leadership increasingly bases its legitimacy on the fact of possession, in Africa or in the Soviet bloc. Class lines in Communist states have been growing more marked, and class differences have tended to grow ever since the revolution. The peasants are bound to the soil in the Soviet Union like medieval serfs, while the rulers of the giant farms acquire the power of medieval lords.

Like Communist states, military governments and dictatorships of all degrees seek legitimacy and respectability as representatives of the people; but no such government cares to be voted out of office.[64] Consequently, regimes permit more or less democratic rights and institutions with the understanding that these must not seriously menace the incumbents; if they threaten to do so, the concessions are withdrawn. Elections thus may lead to stricter dictatorship. African parliaments serve basically the same purposes of show as Communist parliaments.[65] In the Communist pattern, Third World elites usually seek to mobilize the masses to support the government and its purposes without allowing them to make demands upon it.[66] Singapore, for example, is a rubber-stamp democracy in which the Peoples' Action Party controls not only the government but also trade unions and media.[67]

A considerable number of Third World countries, especially in Africa, stand on the margins of the Marxist-Leninist group of states, having adopted some of their ideology and institutions, rhetoric, and vocabulary. From South Yemen to Mozambique, these are among the most economically and culturally backward countries of the world. None of the relatively prosperous Third World countries, such as Thailand, Singapore, Brazil, or Mexico, designates itself officially as socialist or adheres to Marxist Leninist patterns. In most African semi-Communist states, however, ideology is much behind reality. For example, the Congo and Benin use the language of Marxism-Leninism mostly as a means of self-identity while the economies depend on foreign assistance and investment.

The oldest and perhaps most thorough African imitator of the Leninist model is Guinea, of which Sékou Touré is "Guide."[68] There is a single political party dedicated to the making of the "New Man" free of colonialism and capitalist exploitation, and to revolution, social justice, African culture, and the promise of future happiness. The economy is controlled, and private enterprise (beyond family business) is practically outlawed except for the big foreign-managed and partly or mostly foreign-owned mining companies. The rights promised by the constitution are meaningless, and elections show 99.99 percent for the official candidates. The political police are active, and there have been purges of intellectuals, teachers, merchants, and others; plots are regularly blamed on "imperialists." "Democratic Centralism," mass mobilizatons, use of unions to control workers, people's military formations, and egalitarian rhetoric are also reminiscent of Marxist-Leninist states.

However, early enthusiasm for construction, road building, and the like, wore out in a few years as they bogged down in poor planning.[69] Agricultural collectives failed, public funds have been squandered or embezzled, and the socialist economy relies on foreign-managed capitalist enterprises for nearly all its exports. State-managed industrialization has been a failure. Since 1964, the economy has stagnated, with agriculture sinking back to subsistence. Despite rich natural resources and much foreign aid, the income of the masses has been pushed downward. The result of over twenty years of mobilization has been to fix in place a new parasitic official-bureaucratic class. The experience of other countries that have attempted similar semi-totalitarian mobilization, such as Ghana or Mali, has been hardly more encouraging. In Burma, state management of manufacturing and commerce and the effort to control agriculture have led to a radical decline in production, dependence on smuggling and black markets, and virtual demodernization of the country.

The obvious difference between Third World countries whose leaders have tried to copy Communist ways and the Communist countries themselves (aside from the economic and cultural advantages of the Soviet Union and Eastern Europe) is that the former have had little revolutionary inspiration and generally have not carried out so thorough a renewal of elites. But if the fundamental difference arises from an unrepeatable receding event, it seems unavoidable that Communist countries, as their ideological enthusiasm recedes, will look increasingly like Third World states that share their basic problems and aspirations. The results of state-managed economics in the Third World are a poor omen for the long-term future of Communist systems.

The smaller Asian Communist countries have the least hope of lifting themselves from poverty. The new governments of Indochina, for example, cannot possibly approach the economic level of Singapore or Taiwan in several decades. The banning of nightclubs, bribery, modern songs, and Western dress is unlikely to remain effective much longer than the emotions of the war remain. There is no reason to expect state-managed economic development to be more successful in Laos or Vietnam than it has been in Burma.

The situation of China is slightly more promising. Although China has shown rather modest economic results in its first and doubtless best generation under Marxist-Leninist-Maoist rule, it has demonstrated some ability to handle major problems burdening most non-Western countries. It has exerted strong pressure against large families, and care of the aged in communes renders numerous offspring unnecessary to assure sustenance in later years.[70] The control of residence and the shipping of millions to the countryside have their positive side; Chinese cities, unlike those of most poorer countries, have no huge shantytowns filled with peasants streaming in to urban life. Chinese education does not create a stratum of unemployable semi-intellectuals.[71] The Chinese spread simple technology and sundry improvements; they do not develop new rice varieties, but they quickly generalize the varieties that they find satisfactory. Small factories in communes, "intermediate technology," and industrial decentralization are doubtless sound policies.

The assets, however, are less basic than the weaknesses. Maoism has been compared to the establishment of a new dynasty. In the timeless Chinese cycle, decadence and collapse of central power were followed by a period of disorders until a new ruling group selected by competition for power could take the helm. The new rulers would reunite China, clean out the legacy of corruption, set austere standards, and construct grand public works. But the new authorities in turn lost ambition and vigor, lapsed into the old vices, and eventually decayed to impotence. China may expect to suffer, and to some extent has been suffering, classic difficulties of imperial rule. These include, as in ages past: intrigue by intimates of the ruler, tension between the inner court and the governing apparatus, the difficulty of separating loyal and disloyal opposition, competition for power among various agencies and councils, identification of bureaucrats with diverse constituencies, greed of the officials, inability to obtain reliable information, and lack of means to regulate the succession.[72]

While he lived, Mao tilted power toward those who made the most of ideology, the fundamentalists who believed passionately in equality for everyone but themselves and hoped that the peasant masses could overcome anything by indoctrination and organization if evil foreign influences were kept out and the leaders remained close to the people. After Mao, power shifted to the other end of the political spectrum, to those who stress the city over the peasantry, expertise over ideology, rule by the party-state apparatus, technological borrowing, and trade with the West even at some cost in independence. The new policies are like those of most Third World countries.[73] Post-Maoist China's problems are apparently to be managed more pragmatically than in a special Chinese way based on the Chinese revolution.

The Chinese frankly regard their country as underdeveloped and themselves as members of the community of the poor. The Russians, however, wish to be treated as Europeans, which they are racially and in medieval cultural roots. The Soviet Union is consequently more ambivalent, with high-energy particle accelerators in a countryside virtually isolated by the spring thaw. Like Soviet medicine, which uses modern computers and radiation devices as well as herbal concoctions and leeches, Soviet society has one foot in modern Europe and one in traditional Asia. When the United States urges the Soviet Union to share in aiding the poorer nations, Soviet diplomats assert that theirs is a socialist state with no responsibility; privately they confess, "Look at our Moscow shops and compare them with London and Paris—you'll see we can't afford it. We too are a developing nation in a sense; there is all of Siberia."[74] Like Third World nations, the Soviet Union exports raw materials to the West in exchange for industrial equipment;

increasingly, too, it seeks technology and capital from abroad.[75]

The distinctiveness of the Soviet and East European part of the Communist world is its relatively high level of productivity and technological sophistication. But a higher technological level ultimately requires better government. Communisn does not represent political development but rather a substitute, probably of limited useful duration, for institutions for the better management of society. Communism must be accounted antimodern as it increasingly favors ascriptive over achievement rights, making origins and affiliations the means of success. If it contributes to economic progress during a time of inspiration, this gain is probably outweighed in the long run by overcontrol, which perpetuates the political domination indefinitely.

The lack of any orderly means of checking power and relating it to general needs inevitably must detract from technological capacity. It is difficult enough for the best organized Western societies to handle the technological civilization they have created. Where the interests of the rulership can be largely divorced from those of society, it must be far more difficult. A modern economy ultimately requires that the rights of governors and governed be defined and that authority be derived from recognized rules. But the elaborate system of controls that constitutes the essence of Communism serves to protect the rulership from the need to regularize and limit power.

It may be, as suggested by Alec Nove, that Russia can be governed only as a shut-in autocracy.[76] If this is so, its destiny probably will run parallel to that of the majority of mankind. With little special mission, it would come to look more like the many dictatorships of the Third World whose absolutism is based on force, the need for an authority to hold the country together, and the fact that the government in place holds the levers of power. It is significant that in recent years the Soviet Union increasingly has identified itself with the Third World and supported miscellaneous dictatorships on the basis of their anti-Westernism.

It seems unlikely that there will be any patent danger to national security to prod the somnolent state. The effect of intellectual deprivation is more spiritual debility than popular anger. So far as the masses are de-Westernized by decades of Communist education, they are less likely to become rebellious than to become apathetic, like the masses of Peru or Bangladesh. No one expects them to rise in wrath at their misery. The technology lag will probably continue to grow. Increased influence of the military would imply a slightly looser society, because the military is less concerned about improper thoughts and more secure in its possession of force than the party is in its possession of ideology. A major step away from Communist idiosyncrasy would be a shift of power from the party to the government, which is a more natural locus of decision making; such a development is presaged in the fusing of party and governmental structures in Romania. It may become increasingly difficult to maintain the common purpose of the bureaucratic-military elite, as it was in tsarist Russia. If such changes occur, the wheel set moving by Lenin's revolution will have turned full circle, and an episode of Russian history will have passed.

In Eastern Europe there is more of a contest between the effort of the state to de-Westernize and the dissolvent effects of Western influences. A traveler from the Soviet Union to Eastern Europe (Romania and Bulgaria more or less excepted) is struck by the relative absence of political slogans, more Cola signs than pictures of Lenin, the greater variety and imaginativeness of buildings, the better and more varied consumer goods, the relatively free art, and the usually somewhat more interesting and informative news media. The East European governments are under far more pressure to open to foreign trade and travel, to allow freer discussion, to seek legitimacy by heeding popular desires, and so ultimately to permit change away from Communism. At the same time, however, one should not underestimate the narrowing effects of official education and the difficulty of maintaining any agitation that most people view as hopeless. East Europeans know their fate is mostly to be decided by the relative strength and health of the Soviet state on the one side and the Western powers on the other.

For the Communist states, no outcome can be logically excluded, and none can be called inevitable. The Third World is diverse, with a multiplicity of patterns, and it diverges as some countries modernize while others stand still or perhaps demodernize. But it increasingly appears that the problem of Communism is basically akin to that of the Third World dictatorships, whose ability to make good use of modern technology is hindered by political backwardness and ineffective social structures.

A look into the future of the Third World would tell a great deal about the future of Communist societies. In the past, observers failed to perceive the close relations between and probable convergence of Communist and "developing" nations because of assumptions that the former were permanently oriented toward utopian change and the latter were inevitably growing toward open, pluralistic systems through industrialization and modernization. These assumptions have been falsified by the last fifteen years. Communist and most Third World governments are in many ways similar and face the same basic problems. Communism is, or was, an effort to hammer out an immediate solution by moral, political, and physical violence; but the will and ability to wrench society into modernization have ebbed away.

In some respects, moveover, Communist states even at a relatively high level of industrialization are further from the political patterns of the West than most Third World dictatorships. They have gained ideological strength at the price of political demodernization and hence are left handicapped as inspiration turns to cynicism. They have no regular means of promotion of leaders; the anomalous authority of the ruling club (the party) wholly dominates the state; lines of control are confused; and there is no civil service in the ordinary sense with regularized entry, advancement, and tenure. There is no idea of impartiality in any political sphere, there is little responsibility to the people or the nation, centralization is excessive, and overregulation is stifling. The political culture of Communist states has been thoroughly compressed by authoritarianism, as people have learned to look to the authorities for decisions and concessions and take for granted the right of the powers to watch over and direct them. Unless Communist states somehow regularize their institutions of rule, they will enter the latter part of this century politically less well equipped to function in the modern industrial universe than such countries as Mexico and Brazil.

TRENDS

Three sets of forces are evident in the evolution of Communist states: the capacity for system maintenance and restoration of engineered authoritarianism, the disintegrative forces of decadence, and solvent influences from without. At almost any moment, the first of these seems strongest. The individual is unimportant, opposition is loose as sand, there are no economic grounds from which to exert pressure on the state, there is no free means of communication, and there are no independent power centers. The legitimacy of revolutionary or social vocation is replaced by the legitimacy of habit and inevitability. The democratic apparatus serves to confuse. If there is trouble, the answer is more or better regulation; the Communist state stands out for serenity, certainty, and security in a world of philosophical chaos. Some Communist states, such as the Soviet or Chinese, obviously have enormous reserves of authority; Poland, Hungary, and Yugoslavia show that a regime can concede a great deal and remain firmly Communist.

Yet, while Communist states keep structures and authority ostensibly unaltered, their meaning changes. The capacity and morale of the leadership cannot remain constant. The generation nurtured under Communism are strangers to those formed in the revolution, and there must be deeper changes when personalities untempered by violence eventually come to the fore. The leaders of the revolution have more in common psychologically with the old intelligentsia than with those born in a settled Communist society. Institutionalization and socialization are opposed by disaggregation and decadence, the former tendency being inherently limited, the latter of indefinite moment.

Modernization grinds down. The economy outgrows the capacity of control, and the quality of management declines. It is possible that the scorn for manual labor prevalent in most Communist countries will ripen into scorn for technology. Economic growth ceases to be a major legitimation of the party; economic difficulties cause uncertainty, demoralization, and divisions. With a stagnant or shrinking national product, there will be more quarreling over distribution and fewer means of assuaging discontent. At first, ruthlessness is effective in overriding particular interests for the common benefit, but it becomes unscrupulousness and license for self-seeking.

If the close-knit Communist state deteriorates in one aspect, it may expect to deteriorate in others. So far as the quality of leadership declines, so in all probability do the ability to advance the economy, respect for law, quality of education, cultural level, and general morale. With mutually reinforcing institutions, Communist states are designed for self-maintenance rather than for problem solving; and these values become contradictory. They have done well at problem solving only when their motivation was high, but ultimately system maintenance depends upon problem solving.

The major menace to the Communist system is not purposeful action by its usually rather confused opponents, but private interests undermining its integrity. Often historically a new dynasty has raised up new elites to serve it, and they serve well because they are wholly dependent upon the favor of the ruler. Yet in time they become a possessing class with their own status. Power becomes a form of property and convertible into wealth; Soviet elites may already be seeking security by accumulation of property.[77] Communist elites cannot be expected forever to deny themselves the satisfactions of conspicuous consumption. Marxist-Leninist states are no more able to cope with this phenomenon than were Chinese emperors—perhaps rather less so. When leadership becomes oligarchic-bureaucratic, initiative falls away from the center; people learn to use the system that initially set out to use them, and the supremely political order becomes partially depoliticized.[78] Groups achieve reality, although perhaps not legality. There is little to prevent the regime from becoming increasingly a congeries of parasites.

Degradation might hypothetically proceed very far if the Communist society were cut off from the outside world. But the modern would-be absolutist state can isolate itself even less completely than the tsarist empire could. The elite cannot rule totally for their own pleasure because of objective needs of defense and security, economic and political competition, and the desire for world prestige. So far as the system is or becomes disadvantageous in the interaction of states, the rulership inevitably feels pressure toward reform and rationality, perhaps even toward basic change so far as the system is poorly adapted to competition in the technological world.

Foreign ideas become more effective as ideological commitment wanes. This opens a gap between the state and the best-informed and intellectually most active sector, such as plagued the tsarist state and to a lesser degree the latter-day imperial Chinese. If the incapacity of the Communist state becomes more blatant, there must be some search for new ideas and ideologies, which the apparatus in need of technological borrowing is increasingly unable to screen out or neutralize. It is difficult even to take refuge in militarism, which is singularly inappropriate to modern needs. It is conceivable that some of the political elite will move away from indifference to the truth of ideology and toward self-doubt and guilt feelings like those that troubled many of the nineteenth-century Russian upper classes. If they seek to keep ruling in the old way at home, yet measure themselves by world standards, they must at best suffer dissonance and come to doubt their special mission. Real change may come if Communist leaders become ashamed of the results of their political system, in the manner of educated Russians or Chinese in the first years of this century. This is more likely if access to power becomes hereditary. Those who inherit status are more likely to doubt than those who achieve it. On the other hand, so far as the West loses self-confidence its message loses force; and if rapid economic growth ceases in the outside world, pressures on the Communist elite will diminish.

Communism is most secure in the Soviet Union. Its hugeness makes it a universe unto itself. Outside the centers of contact with foreign diplomats, newsmen, and businessmen—chiefly in Moscow and Leningrad—the outside world seems far away. Russia historically has been better able than any other imperial society to combine autocracy with the importation of Western ideas. The Soviet oligarchy has been remarkably successful in maintaining unity; if there were serious policy differences at the top, they would surely become known. The messianism that runs deep in the Russian character also makes it easier to reject alien philosophy. Marxism-Leninism coincides with Russian power interests; it is the only means at hand, perhaps the only possible means, to sustain the predominance of about 125 million Russians in a sphere of about 360 million. Marxism-Leninism is a Russian invention, designed for Russia by a great Russian hero figure. In Russia, the essence of Communist ideology is We versus They. Against this outlook, rational argument is difficult.

Long ago George Kennan foresaw that, in the lack of independent organization, debility of the party might well lead to pitiable weakness.[79] Dominion over minority peoples in the Soviet Union and vassal states abroad represents an increasing problem. Just as cultural, political, and above all economic problems caused an upsurge of minority feeling in Yugoslavia in the latter 1960s, so any serious economic weakening of the Soviet state must make the management of lesser peoples more difficult, and costs of retaining dominion over Eastern Europe can hardly fail to rise. On the one hand, Russian superiority in the multinational conglomerate impedes change; on the other, multinationality compounds the tasks of rulership.

The ex-Soviet historian Andrei Amalrik said in Paris, "What you consider signs of liberalization are only symptoms of decrepitude."[80] Change is likely to come much less from learning than from loss of capacity. It is predictable that the uncontrolled sector of the economy will grow, and that censorship and border controls will become leakier. It is hard for the Soviet leadership to play the world role it desires and maintain the domestic controls it cherishes.[81] The mental emancipation of a fraction of the intelligentsia may be irreversible.[82] It is not impossible that in a few years Soviet jailers will cease to kick political prisoners and will sympathize with them as tsarist jailers did. Possibly the KGB will patronize dissident movements for its own importance, as the Okhrana did. Yet the party may relax tensions and undercut opposition by concessions of form, while keeping its tight hold on the substance of power. It seems clear that the Soviet Union cannot be democratized without a revolution, as foreseen by Amalrik, according to whom, "To save my country, a crisis would be necessary."[83] Yet the Soviet Union probably cannot be democratized by a revolution either. If the present regime should somehow fall, there would follow a struggle not to give power to the people but to gain control of the state and make it better and stronger.

The outlook for Chinese Communism is cloudier. It is odd for a notably proud and ethnocentric people to revere German scholars such as Marx and Engels; it is even more contrary to nature that they bow to Lenin and Stalin, leaders of the state that is their particular hate. The favored theme of self-reliance, if not simple patriotism, would seem to indicate emancipation from deference to Lenin and Stalin, whose work could not have been perfect if it turned so bad in the hands of successors brought up by them. To reject Lenin would be injurious for Russians; for Chinese, it would be a lift for pride.

Communism also fits the international situation of China less than that of Russia. For Russia it is an affirmation of superpower status and leadership in the world movement of socialism against capitalism. But China's most disliked and feared antagonist is "socialist" Russia, against which the Chinese, as the weaker party, desire U.S. and European support. Marxism-Leninism and "proletarian internationalism" are not needed as a bond for China's peoples, who are overwhelmingly of a single cultural tradition. Moreover, the authoritarian set of Chinese culture may make legitimation of party rule by Marxism-Leninism more or less superfluous.

China has never been quite Leninist, since the party has never been regarded as the sole exponent of right. Chinese Communism in its relatively brief life has had violent swings and discontinuities. Not only has it undergone such turmoil as the Great Leap Forward and the Cultural Revolution; there have been new constitutions in 1954, 1969, 1975, and 1978. The power of Mao, unlike that of Stalin (after gaining supremacy), fluctuated widely, and the Soviet Union has never seen such an abrupt swing of political climate as China did in a few months after the death of Mao. Before the death of Mao, it appeared that the ruling elite had lost its consensus to a degree never observed in Soviet history: part of the leadership had come to regard Mao's ideas as obsolete, dysfunctional, and an impediment to modernization.[84] There were criticisms of Mao while he was on the stage and capable of reacting. Without Mao, Maoism seems at best symbolic. The Great Helmsman was unsuccessful in most of his important policies of the last twenty years of his life, and he offended many important persons. Unlike Stalin, he left alive nearly all of those whom he injured.

The period since Mao's demise has seen a veritable cascade of changes, all toward pragmatism and away from revolutionism. All of Mao's policies of his last decade have been turned around except for opposition to the Soviet "Polar Bear." Tens of thousands of those victimized by the radicals were released, and "rightists" were removed from the list of enemy classes.[85] Science is no longer suspect but regarded as the hope of China. Priority was placed on economic development, and wages were raised as an incentive to production. The number of foreign tourists multiplied many times over. The idea of self-reliance was set aside, as China energetically sought Western technology, imported thousands of technicians, and sent thousands to study abroad. Examinations and grades were restored, and egalitarianism in education was forgotten. Special schools were established for better students; and these were preferred for entrance to the universities, that is, to elitehood. Some concessions were made to freedom of speech, and there sprang up a small civil rights movement. The courts and legal system were regularized, and the political system was slightly opened up and liberalized. Voters were offfered a choice of candidates in local elections.[86] Leaders discussed faults and shortcomings with a frankness unprecedented in the Communist world.

Needs of security and modernization drove China more powerfully than the USSR toward accommodation with the modern industrial world. The Chinese leaders know that their country is poor and in many ways weak, and they seem determined to reach out to learn and modernize. The people are proud, but hardly antiforeign; they snap up with great avidity Western books newly placed on sale. Japan is the principal channel through which external influences flow into China. The racial and cultural distance is not great, propinquity favors intercourse, and the economies are complementary. Several times as many Japanese travel to China as Europeans and Americans combined. Japan, with its modern economic and political system, is, of course, a promising model.

In Eastern Europe, Westernization is a powerful current, propelled not only by extensive and growing intercourse with Western neighbors and a desire to modernize in the successful Western image, but also by dislike for Soviet domination. For most East European countries, Communism is an affront to nationhood. It comes less naturally; they suffered little of the old Russian ambivalence of Westernizers versus Slavophiles. The Soviets can claim that the revolution lifted Russia from backwardness and darkness to modernity, but such a claim is less plausible in East European vassal states, except perhaps Romania and Bulgaria. So far as Communism comes to be associated with subservience to an unappreciated foreign power, economic difficulties, and cultural sterility, its appeal will be narrow, and its greatest strength will be the Soviet military presence.

In Romania Communism coincides with nationalism as the price of a qualified independence of the Soviet Union. It is probable, as suggested by Gilberg, that Romania will continue to swing, as it has in the past, between the admittance of a little pluralistic development and its repression.[87] For Yugoslavia Communism has some of the value it has for the Soviet Union as a cement for the minority nationalities. But genuine federalism is much more feasible for Yugoslavia than for the Soviet Union, and genuine federalism would contradict Marxism-Leninism. The personality of Tito held Yugoslavia on course, but pluralistic forces are much stronger here than in any other Communist country. In 1977 the party was annoyed that state enterprises patched U.S. flags on shirts, jeans, and bathing suits.[88] Yugoslavia may be on the way to becoming a semiauthoritarian state run by an oligarchy of contending elites.[89]

Albania has clung to Stalinism. This can hardly be permanently practical. The country is too small, too incapable of cultural and economic self-sufficiency, and too much alone. The Albanians wrote into their constitution a prohibition against obtaining foreign credits.[90] But continued isolation can only mean backwardness, a price perhaps too high to pay when the leadership of revolutionary vintage has left the scene. There has been a slow but steady broadening of foreign diplomatic, cultural, and commercial relations since the early 1970s.

The future of Castroism is also problematic. For Cuba, too, Lenin can hardly be a popular figure. The chief ideological nourishment has been anti-Yankeeism, and normalized relations with the United States would change the environment. The Soviet Union is distant, alien, and not well suited as a trade partner; intimacy with it is dictated only by hostility for the big neighbor. If the United States should become again the dominant economic and cultural influence for the island, the character of the regime could easily revert to something like traditional Latin American military caudillismo. Castro, a man without Marxist-Leninist education, has long tried to relate his revolution to native themes. In 1975, for example, he portrayed it as a continuation of the work of the nineteenth-century Cuban hero, José Martí.

Communism has a powerful appeal to idealists and power bosses. It is difficult to discredit; parties here and there still regard one of history's harshest despots, Joseph Stalin, as a great guide and hero. Communism responds to basic realities of the modern world. A system for structuring inequality by calling it equality, it was generated and is nourished by the inequality of classes and nations. It has been especially propelled by the superiority of the educated, Westernized few over the masses of non-Western countries, of the leaders in the struggle against the West over their troops, and of dominant peoples over weaker ones. Communism, with its essentially primitive utopia, is also a refuge from the social and political effects of Western industrial civilization. Hence, barring unpredictable violence, it is not likely to disappear soon from the modern universe. It may come to an end only in the triumph of the ultimate convergence theory.

But the capacity of the ruling parties declines, while erosive currents, both internal and external, swirl around the foundations of their state.

Normalization, which is loss of special revolutionary virtues, has been under way in some form since the inception of the Marxist-Leninist state. It probably can be reversed only with great violence. It proceeds at different rates in different countries and under varying international conditions, but it seems certain that the next decade or so will see major evolution away from what has been known as Marxism-Leninism in most or all Communist states.

These states will not, however, evolve directly into open or pluralistic societies. The trend is to the contrary. In twenty years the intellectuals who owed a liberal education to the old regime will have disappeared in Eastern Europe; only a tiny fraction of the new generation has been able to preserve intellectual independence, and they disqualify themselves for positions of influence. Demoralized peoples forget how an open society operates, and traditional values are lost in the struggle to survive, maintain a modicum of comfort, and to avoid conflict with the authorities. The representatives of authority, meanwhile, become fixed in their prerogatives.

Thus the Second, or Communist, World may be expected gradually to merge into the Third, or broadly non-Western, World. Already there is a blurred group of states between these two and it probably will become ever less important with which world a nation is identified. At some distant future it may be that the entire earth will be brought together politically as well as culturally by the omnipotence of modern technology, or that all together will sink toward general poverty in the failure of civilization. But by that time the dichotomy of Communist versus democratic probably will have been submerged.

NOTES

1. As observed by Donald G. McRae, "The Future of East-West Relations," *Survey* 22 (Summer-Autumn 1976): 107.

2. Frederick J. Hacker, *Crusaders, Criminals, Crazies* (New York: W. W. Norton, 1976), pp. 281–85.

3. Peter Wiles, "Leninism and Weltinnenpolitik," *Survey* 22 (Summer–Autumn 1976): 157.

4. Peter A. Toma and Ivan Volgyes, *Politics in Hungary* (San Francisco: W. H. Freeman, 1977), p. 146.

5. Jeremy R. Azrael, *Managerial Power and Soviet Politics* (Cambridge: Harvard University Press, 1966), p. 173.

6. *New York Times*, January 28, 1977, p. 6.

7. Leonid Pluisch, "Interview," in *Demokratischeskie Alternativy*, ed. Vadim Belotserkovsky (Achberg: Achberg Verlaganstalt, 1976), pp. 17, 21.

8. Efim Etkind, "Politics and Truth," in *Demokratischeskie Alternativy*, pp. 255–56.

9. German Andreev, "Christianity, Tolstoy, etc.," in *Demokraticheskie Alternativy*, p. 137.

10. George A. Breslauer, *Five Images of the Soviet Future: A Critical Review and Synthesis* (Berkeley: Institute of International Studies, 1978), p. 45.

11. As observed by Robert G. Kaiser, *Russia: The People and the Power* (New York: Atheneum, 1976), pp. 21–22.

12. Alexander Yanov, *Detente after Brezhnev: The Domestic Roots of Soviet Foreign Policy* (Berkeley: Institute of International Studies, 1977), p. 13.

13. Anatolii Levitin-Krasin, "Letters on Russian," in *Demokraticheskie Alternativy*, p. 236.

14. Roy A. Medvedev, *Political Essays* (Nottingham: Spokesman Books, 1976), p. 101.

15. John B. Dunlop, *The New Revolutionaries* (Belmont, Mass.: Nordland, 1976), pp. 186–90.

16. Such as Barrington Moore, Jr., *Terror and Progress, USSR: Some Sources of Change and Stability in the Soviet Dictatorship* (Cambridge: Harvard University Press, 1954), p. 189.

17. T. H. Rigby, "Politics in the Mono-Organizational Society," in *Authoritarian Politics in Communist Europe: Uniformity and Diversity in One-Party States*, ed. Andrew C. Janos (Berkeley: Institute of International Studies, 1976), p. 37.

18. Theodore H. Friegut, *Political Participation in the USSR* (Princeton: Princeton University Press, 1979), p. 120.

19. Michel Garder, *L'agonie du regime en Russie sovietique* (Paris: La Table Ronde, 1965), pp. 10, 196.

20. Hedrick Smith, *The Russians* (New York: Quadrangle/New York Times, 1976), p. 304.

21. Alexander Yanov, *The Russian New Right: Right Wing Ideologies in the Contemporary USSR* (Berkeley: Institute of International Studies, 1978).

22. Peter Reddaway, "The Development of Dissent and Opposition," in *The Soviet Union Since the Fall of Khrushchev*, ed. Archie Brown and Michael Kaser (London: Macmillan, 1975), pp. 124, 144.

23. Smith, *The Russians*, chap. 12, esp. pp. 303, 314.

24. Donald G. McRae, "The Future of East-West Relations," *Survey* 22 (Summer–Autumn 1976): 107.

25. Kaiser, *Russia*, p. 53; Jack V. Haney, "The Revival of Interest in the Russian Past in the Soviet Union," *Review* 32 (March 1973): 1–16.

26. *New York Times*, November 12, 1978, p. 14.

27. Yanov, *Detente after Brezhnev*, p. 68.

28. Anatole Shub, *An Empire Loses Hope: The Return of Stalin's Ghost* (New York: W. W. Norton, 1970), p. 138.

29. George L. Kline, "Religion, National Character, and the Rediscovery of Russian Roots," *Slavic Review* 32 (March 1973): 33.

30. Marin Pudeff, "Bulgaria under Zhukov," in *The Changing Face of Communism in Eastern Europe*, ed. Peter Toma (Tucson: University of Arizona Press, 1970), p. 113.

31. Peter Raina, "Intellectuals and the Party in Bulgaria," in *Change and Adaption in Soviet and East European Politics*, ed. Jane P. Shapiro and Peter J. Potichnyj (New York: Praeger, 1976), p. 191.

32. *New York Times*, January 22, 1977, p. 2.

33. Toma and Volgyes, *Politics in Hungary*, p. 152.

34. Trond Gilberg, *Modernization in Romania Since World War II* (New York: Praeger, 1975), p. 232.

35. Richard F. Staar, *Communist Regimes in Eastern Europe*, 3d ed. (Stanford: Hoover Institution Press, 1977), p. 153.

36. *New York Times*, December 2, 1976, p. 6.

37. *Time*, May 23, 1977, p. 60.

38. James Mavor, *The Russian Revolution*, (New York: Macmillan, 1928), pp. 217–21.

39. Cited by Max Eastman, *Stalin's Russia and the Crisis in Socialism* (New York: W. W. Norton, 1940), p. 83.

40. *Krasnaia zvezda*, October 24, 1974.

41. William E. Odom, "Who Controls Whom in Moscow," *Foreign Policy* 19 (Summer 1975): 113.

42. William E. Odom, "The Militarization of Soviet Society," *Problems of Communism* 25 (September–October 1976): 37, 42.

43. *Krasnaia zvezda*, November 27, 1969.

44. As in A. V. Barabanshchikov et al., *Psikhologiia voinskogo kollektiva* (Moscow, 1967), passim.

45. *Quotations from Chairman Mao Tse-tung* (Peking, 1967), p. 100.

46. A. Doak Barnett, *Uncertain Passage: China's Transition to the Post-Mao Era* (Washington: Brookings Institution, 1974), p. 85.

47. Harry W. Nelson, "Military Bureaucracy in the Cultural Revolution," *Asian Survey* 14 (April 1974): 373. See also Ellis Jaffe, "The PLA in Internal Politics," *Problems of Communism* 24 (November-December 1975): 1–12.

48. Alan P. L. Liu, *Political Culture and Group Conflict in Communist China* (Santa Barbara, Calif.: Clio Press, 1976), p. 31.

49. *Peking Review*, headline, January 2, 1976, p. 8.

50. O. Edmund Clubb, "China after Mao," *Current History* 73 (September 1977): 50.

51. Harry Harding, Jr., "China after Mao," *Problems of Communism* 26 (March–April 1977): 10.

52. *New York Times*, December 13, 1976, p. 3.

53. Ilpyong J. Kim, *Communist Politics in Korea* (New York: Praeger, 1975), p. 30.

54. Edward F. Singleton, *Twentieth-Century Yugoslavia* (New York: Columbia University Press, 1976), p. 277.

55. Cf. Eric Nordlinger, *Soldiers in Politics: Military Coups and Governments* (Englewood Cliffs, N.J.: Prentice-Hall, 1977), pp. 15–17.

56. Talcott Parsons, "Evolutionary Universals in Society," *American Sociological Review* 29 (June 1964): 356.

57. *Pravda*, November 7, 1917, cited by David Shub, *Lenin* (Garden City, N.Y.: Doubleday, 1948), p. 258.

58. Francis B. Randall, *Stalin's Russia: An Historical Reconsideration* (New York: Free Press, 1965), pp. 18–19.

59. *Scinteia*, June 3, 1976.

60. Intellectual independence by nonruling Communist parties has been confined to Europe and Japan; Third World parties have shown no disposition to break away from Soviet leadership and Leninism. See Peter Wiles, "Leninism and Weltinnenpolitik," *Survey* 22 (Summer–Autumn 1976): 161.

61. Peter C. W. Gutkind and Immanuel Wallerstein, *The Political Economy of Africa* (Beverly Hills: Sage Publications, 1976).

62. As, for example, the Baath party in Syria. See George Lenczowski, "Socialism in Syria," in *Socialism in the Third World*, ed. Helen Desfosses and Jacques Levesque (New York: Praeger, 1975), p. 67.

63. Pye, "Identity and the Political Culture," in *Crises and Sequences in Political Development*, ed. Leonard Binder et al. (Princeton: Princeton University Press, 1971), p. 122.

64. Nordlinger, *Soldiers in Politics*, pp. 133–35.

65. Newel M. Stultz, "Parliaments in Former British Black Africa," in *Politics in Transitional Societies*, ed. Harvey G. Kebschull (New York: Appleton-Century-Crofts, 1973), pp. 262–77.

66. Myron Weiner, "Political Participation: Crisis of the Political Process,' in *Crises and Sequences in Political Development*, ed. Leonard Binder et al. (Princeton: Princeton University Press, 1971), p. 197.

67. Stanley S. Bedlington, *Malaysia and Singapore: The Building of New States* (Ithaca: Cornell University Press, 1978), pp. 227–29.

68. Cf. Claude Rivère, *Guinea: The Mobilization of a People* (Ithaca: Cornell University Press, 1977).

69. Ibid., p. 114.

70. Sterling Wortman, "Agriculture in China," *Scientific American* 232 (June 1975): 21.

71. Jan S. Prybyla, "The Chinese Economic Model," *Current History* 69 (September 1975): 80–84.

72. Michael Oksenberg, "Peking, Making out under Mao, 1949–1968," in *China: Management of a Revolutionary Society*, ed. John M. H. Lindbeck (Seattle: University of Washington Press, 1971), p. 111.

73. Michael Oksenberg and Steven Goldstein, "The Chinese Political Spectrum," *Problems of Communism* 23 (March–April 1974): 1, 13.

74. *New York Times*, June 1, 1976, p. A-6.

75. A French critic sees the Soviet Union becoming part of the Third World, Emmanuel Todd, *La chute finale* (Paris: Robert Laffont, 1977), pp. 273–74.

76. Alec Nove, *Stalinism and After* (London: George Allen and Unwin, 1975), p. 182.

77. Yanov, *Detente after Brezhnev*, p. 3.

78. Such points are made by Samuel P. Huntington, "Social and Institutional Dynamics of One Party Systems," in *Authoritarian Politics in Modern Society*, ed. Samuel P. Huntington and Clement H. Moore (New York: Basic Books, 1970), pp. 40–41.

79. George F. Kennan ("X"), "The Source of Soviet Conduct," *Foreign Affairs* 25 (July 1947): 480.

80. *L'Express*, February 28–March 6, 1977, p. 36.

81. Gayle D. Hannah, "Soviet Public Communication in the Post-Stalin Era," in *Change and Adaption in Soviet and East European Politics*, p. 154.

82. As supposed by Valery Chalidze, "How Important is Soviet Dissent?" *Commentary* 63 (June 1977): 58.

83. *L'Express*, February 28 March 6, 1977, p. 36.

84. Parris Chang, "Mao's Last Stand," *Problems of Communism* 25 (July–August 1976): 16–17.

85. *Newsweek*, June 18, 1978, p. 52.

86. *Beijing Review*, July 13, 1979, p. 9.

87. Gilberg, *Modernization in Romania*.

88. *New York Times*, August 16, 1977, p. A-6.

89. As foreseen by Dennison Rusinow, *The Yugoslav Experiment, 1948–1974* (Berkeley: University of California Press, 1977), pp. 346–47.

90. Staar, *Communist Regimes of Eastern Europe*, p. 16.

POSTSCRIPT

In the last days of 1979, after this book had gone to the publisher, the Soviet Union sent its armed forces into Afghanistan. The action confirms the decay of ideology, the decreased ability of the Communist state to work its will, and the reliance on force and the military—the last excellence of the Soviet state.

After the May 1978 pro-Soviet military coup in Kabul, it was assumed that the Communist or near-Communist government, employing well-tested and ruthless methods of control and enjoying ample Soviet support, would have no trouble in subduing a poor and backward population. However, discontent turned into seething rebellion. Two murdered heads of state later, the Soviets found it necessary to send a sizable army of their own to counter the popular movement. Never before has such massive external force been necessary to protect a Communist regime from its own citizens. It appears that Communists no longer have much advantage over less sophisticated and less thoroughly organized dictatorships in imposing their rule.

The explanation or excuse for the move, that Soviet intervention was invited by the leader who was killed upon arrival of the Soviet forces if not by them, did little for the Soviet reputation for honesty. Meanwhile, Soviet troops were told they had to go to Afghanistan to repel invading Chinese and Americans.[1] The Kremlin, which may be becoming increasingly isolated, seems to have been genuinely surprised at the angry reaction not only in Washington and other Western capitals but also in the Third World, especially Moslem nations. A minor miscalculation was to employ forces from Soviet Central Asia because they would be able to communicate with the Afghan people, to whom they are religiously, racially, and in some cases linguistically close. They were soon withdrawn, supposedly because fraternization had the wrong results. There were many reports of black marketeering and looting by Soviet soldiers, and of atrocities committed by the Soviets or under their supervision. Accounts of use of poison gas were too numerous and detailed to be disregarded.

The spectacle of Soviet gunships blowing up Asian villages has been an even greater blow to the image of Leninist beneficence than the nearly bloodless invasion of Czechoslovakia in 1968 and the Soviet reconquest of Hungary, which lasted only a few days in 1956. The Soviet image as patron of the Third World cannot be restored, and the international Communist movement has lost much of the stature it has rebuilt since 1968. In Western Europe, Eurocommunism has had its coup de grâce and the parties' bid for influence has been set back sharply. Several East European governments were notably unenthusiastic in declaring the support demanded of them by the Soviet overlord. Inside the Soviet Union, the already low credibility of the government sank when news about the fighting and losses spread by grapevine—Soviet soldiers being forbidden to communicate with their families. Already pessimism had become the prevalent mood of the Soviet middle class because of the perceived decline of the standard of living over the past several years.[2]

The extent of demoralization will depend to a large extent on the success, or lack of it, in pacifying Afghanistan. But even if the military operation should be fairly successful soon, the action can only aggravate the insoluble problem of how the Russian-dominated Soviet state can handle its rapidly growing, alien, unassimilable, and predominantly hostile Muslim peoples.[3] The situation would seem manageable only if the state had very large amounts of capital to invest, but its resources are shrinking in relation to the needs of the military for arms and of the economy for modernization.

The invasion of Afghanistan is more a continuation of the Russian empire's centuries-old march into areas of weakness in Asia than an outgrowth of the Leninist revolution. It signifies another step backward toward the military-bureaucratic tsarist state. The Politburo had to call upon the military to save their position where the civilians had failed, and to be needed is to be politically powerful. The generals can certainly expect compensation in increased influence; they may well regard the superannuated Politburo as incompetent and act accordingly. Khrushchev lost stature from the fiasco of the Cuban missile crisis, which contributed to his subsequent ouster. Afghanistan is much more serious for the Soviets than Cuba was, and Brezhnev, in dilapidated health, is less capable of reacting than Khrushchev was. In any case the state faces a succession crisis, which Brezhnev seems to have contrived to make as difficult as possible by eliminating potential heirs.

For many years, the Soviet system has held back change while presenting a facade of solidity and confidence. But war crashes through pretenses and thrusts change on the unwilling. Even a little war in Afghanistan will hasten inevitable change in the Soviet scheme of things, as war has repeatedly brought change to Russia.

NOTES

1. *New York Times*, February 2, 1980, p. 5.
2. John Bushnell, "The New Soviet Man Turns Pessimistic," *Survey* 24 (Spring 1979): 1-18.
3. Steven L. Burg, "Soviet Policy and the Central Asian Question," *Survey* 24 (Summer 1979): 65-82.

ABOUT THE AUTHOR

ROBERT WESSON is professor of political science at the University of California, Santa Barbara, and senior research fellow of the Hoover Institution, Stanford University.

Dr. Wesson has published 14 books, a majority of which concern the Soviet Union, and scores of articles in a wide variety of journals and papers.

He received a B.A. from the University of Arizona, an M.A. from the Fletcher School of Law and Diplomacy, and a Ph.D. from Columbia University.